GARN YEM

Haydn Watson

The Memoir Club

© *Haydn H. Watson 2021*
First published in 2022
The Memoir Club
34 Lynwood Way
South Shields
NE34 8BD
0755 2086888
memoirclub@msn.com

All rights reserved.
Unauthorised duplication
contravenes existing laws.
British Library Cataloguing in
Publication Data.
A catalogue record for this book
is available from the
British Library

Printed by plb print. Phoenix House. Angel Park.
Chester le Street. County Durham. DH2 1AQ.

To friendship, being there all the time and still making each other laugh.

To Melvin Paterson.

CONTENTS
Chronological order

Acknowledgements ix
Author's note xi
The Nine xiii
1. Piles and Piccolos – Aug 1970 1
2. Pick a Window – Dec 1970 3
3. The Young Generation – Dec 1970 9
4. Communication Breakdown – Jan 1971 16
5. A Gathering of Souls – March 1971 23
6. It's Alive and Looking at Me – May 1971 31
7. Rituals and Recompense – Aug 1971 34
8. The Converted – Sept 1971 40
9. The Horse – Sept 1971 47
10. Biscuits to Bolivia – Sept 1971 55
11. Money – Oct 1971 61
12. Love and War – Nov 1971 68
13. The Shape of Things to Come – Dec 1971 75
14. The Eyes Have It – Dec 1971 79
15. Family Values – Dec 1971 85
16. A Meeting of Minds – Jan 1972 96
17. Dare to Dream – Jan 1972 102
18. Food for Thought – Feb 1972 109
19. Make Fast and Avoid the Beer Goggles – March 1972 ... 118
20. Everyone a Winner – Apr 1972 126
21. Beer, Birds and Bedouins – Apr 1972 140
22. It Will Never Happen to Me – May 1972 148
23. The Stag Night – July 1972 153
24. Life – Sept 1972 172
25. An Empty Chair – Nov 1972 178
26. Beside Still Waters – Nov 1972 185
27. In Search of Love – Dec 1972 192
28. Gone to the Dogs – Jan 1973 203
29. The Future Beckons – Jan 1973 215
30. The Letter – Feb 1973 220
31. Laughter is the Best Medicine – March 1973 227
Bibliography 233

ACKNOWLEDGEMENTS

I would like to give my thanks to those who have helped in this venture. To Christine, for her guidance, encouragement and influence. To my family, for their constant support and to my friends, who have been a particular feature of this narrative. In addition, I would like to give my grateful thanks and appreciation to Lynn Davidson and memoirclub@msn.com for their hard work in bringing this book to fruition.

My sincere thanks to Kris Makuch for his innovative jacket design.

AUTHOR'S NOTE

We all look back on our formative years as young people with memories of laughter, love, sadness, desire, aspiration and friendship. If we could somehow turn the clock back and in doing so, change some elements of our past; would we be any better for it? Life throws things at us and we make decisions that will have a huge bearing on our future.

This book is a short history of a group of young men embarking on their odyssey as teenagers. The narrative is set in the early 1970s, in and around South Shields. I have used fictional characters to portray individuals and I have created settings and locales to embellish the storyline. There are some true events portrayed within the book and I have changed names and places to avoid any contradictions.

The narrative conjures up a picture of young people grasping life with both hands. It is about friendship; and with that affinity, comes sadness, humour, love and tragedy. This was the 70s, a brave new world of free-thinking young people. I was grateful to be one of the nine young men who challenged the norm and lived their lives with a smile on their face. I hope you can identify with the characters in this book and how they handle the experiences they encounter.

Finally, I do hope you enjoy *Garn Yem* and in order to maintain a sense of progression within the book; I would encourage you to read the individual short stories in chronological order beginning with *Piles and Piccolos* and ending with *Laughter is the Best Medicine*.

I make no apologies for the content of the book; this was a period in time when political correctness was a vision for the future. Any aspects of this narrative that appear to be factually incorrect, then that is my error and mine alone. I dedicate this book to friendship and I hope in reading it, you reflect upon your own friends past and present.

THE NINE

A pen picture of the main characters in the book

Harry Wainwright: The narrator; an apprentice sheet metalworker. Living in Simonside, South Shields. Height 5 ft 7 in, slim with dark brown hair, brown eyes. Educated at Westoe Secondary Boys School. Born June 1954.

Keith Harper: Height 5 ft 10 in, with light brown hair and blue eyes. Employed as an apprentice joiner with a local firm. Educated at Stanhope Road Secondary School, South Shields. Lives in Mortimer Road, South Shields. Born February 1954.

Andy Smith: A fisherman working for his father on the fishing boat *Lady of The Sea* out of the River Tyne. Educated at Ocean Road Secondary School. Andy lives in Roman Road, South Shields. Born November 1953. Height 5 ft 8 in, with long fair hair and blue eyes.

John Telford: An employee of the South Shields Parks and Gardens Dept. Living in H.S. Edwards Street. Educated at Dean Road Secondary School. Height 5 ft 6 in, slim with ginger hair and blue eyes. Born July 1953.

Norman Kennedy: Height 5 ft 10 in, slim with short light brown hair and brown eyes. Educated at South Shields Grammar School for Boys. Born May 1954. A student at South Shields Marine & Technical College. Lives in Tynedale Road, South Shields.

Tom McBain: Height 6 ft 1 in, slim with black hair and brown eyes. An apprentice electrician with the local council. Lives in Westoe Road, South Shields. Educated at the South Shields Grammar School for Boys. Born April 1954.

Geordie Stevens: Height 5 ft 9 in, slim with short cropped fair hair and blue eyes. Employed as an apprentice plumber at a local firm in South Shields. Educated at Dean Road Secondary School, South Shields. Born August 1954 and lives in Brockley Whins, South Shields.

THE NINE

Malla (Malcolm) Carpenter: Height 5 ft 7 in, with brown hair and brown eyes. Employed as an apprentice plater at Middle Docks in South Shields. Educated at Mortimer Secondary School and lives in Clifton Terrace. Born December 1954.

Stan Wainwright: (Cousin of Harry). An apprentice welder, living in Simonside, South Shields. Height 5 ft 11 in, slim with dark brown hair and brown eyes. Educated at Westoe Secondary Boys School. Born January 1954.

PILES AND PICCOLOS

It has been said that the summers were longer then, and at times the reality of life passed us by. Summer holidays were usually spent at home and this year was no different. My parents could not often afford a holiday away, the last one was three years ago, camping in the Cotswolds. Never mind, who knows what the day would bring.

I had arranged to meet up with my pals Andy, Geordie and Malla to spend a day at Simonside Cricket Club. There we would play tennis, footy and generally see what transpired as the day progressed. We all duly met at around 11 am and sat on what was loosely termed the pavilion and related the happenings of the recent days. It was a warm day and there was a slight wind blowing south-easterly that brought forth the smell of the Bonty Hills. The term bonty relates to the word bonfire and the place where we would collect any timber for November 5. This was not an area of outstanding beauty, but the local landfill site, that had a healthy population of brown rats.

Some days we would try and inflict genocide on the *genus rattus* and attempt to reduce their numbers by hurling large stones or half bricks at them. Needless to say, we did not make an impact and often failed in our mission.

Back to our conversation, Andy was trying to come to terms with the goings on of his older sister. He related to a number of expressions provided by her boyfriend that bemused him. An example of which was the boyfriend's insistence that Andy's sister was very musical. Andy had never seen his sister sing or play any musical instrument. But the boyfriend was adamant that she was brilliant at playing the 'one-eyed piccolo.'

Some days later, Andy raised the issue at the table during dinner; in the presence of his sister, his mam, dad and younger sister. We were intrigued by this and asked what it meant? Andy gave us his rendition of what happened next.

'Well, when I suggested she was lush at playing the one-eyed piccolo my dad launched across the table and cracked me over the head with the bastard soup ladle and sent me to bed, do you know why? Because my sister was trying to blow her boyfriend's nuts up.'

We all laughed, but not really knowing why. Andy showed us the egg on his cranium where his dad had lamped him with the soup ladle and Malla suggested; 'It could have been worse Andy; she might have tried to blow your nuts up instead.'

Then Geordie asked; 'Does the boyfriend possess small bollocks Andy?'

'How the hell would I know, you idiot,' replied Andy. There ended that particular conversation.

Geordie then related to us an instance involving his dad the previous night. His dad liked his beer and he was always the last one out of the club at weekends. But on Saturday night, having been on the drink all day, his inner workings sought revenge for the assault that had been inflicted upon them.

He went on; 'My dad returned home about 11 pm rolling drunk and stood on the cat as he fell through the front door.

My mother was not amused; 'You are a bloody disgrace, go to bed. I don't know what the neighbours must think.'

As it was a Saturday, I was still up watching a *Dracula* film and I heard my mother say as she followed him up the stairs. 'I'll put a stake through your heart you bastard if you have spent all that money.'

Geordie's mother was not one to cross, but she did have a sense of humour. Geordie continued with his story.

'My dad fell on the bed and my mother just screamed; You dirty pig. My dad had farted, followed through and shit had travelled up his back to his shirt collar and my mother shouted; Your piles have burst and your arse will be like a Japanese flag.'

Once Geordie had explained what piles were, we were helpless with laughter. As a result of the 'follow through' Geordie's dad kept a low profile around the house and never made the club that Sunday.

PICK A WINDOW

It was a cold Friday evening in early December 1970. The temperature was hovering around 2 degrees centigrade and the friendly people of South Shields were wrapped up against the elements. My pals Stan, Geordie, John, Tom, Norman and me, had agreed to meet up at The Holborn Rose and Crown pub at 6.30 pm.

I arrived ten minutes early to find Norman sitting at the bar with his head in a book. 'Well then Norman, what's the script?' I asked.

'Welcome young Harry, you are a sight for sore eyes. What are you having to drink?

'I will join you in a brown ale, if it is cool enough? I replied.

'Oh yes it sure is, but it's hot soup we should be having in this weather.'

'Damn right, it's bloody freezing out there. I have just seen a brass monkey looking for its bollocks.'

'What is the book Norman?'

'It's *Hard Times* by Charles Dickens and it is one of the books I have to read as part of my English Literature O-level,' he answered as he placed his bookmark and closed the book.

'What other books do you have to read then?'

'After this I need to bone up on *The Tempest* by Shakespeare and *To Kill a Mockingbird* by Harper Lee.'

'Why didn't you sit the O-level last year then?'

'Well, it's a long story but it was all down to my teacher at school suggesting I was not cut out for the literary world, based on the coursework I had produced. He suggested I would be better off doing a CSE. However, he failed to tell me that I would need the O-level in order to progress to the A-level. So, I am now doing the O-level in English literature and an O-level in history.'

As he finished his explanation in walked John, Stan and Geordie. Stan was quick to make comment on our presence; 'You buggers are quick off the mark, it's just turned 6.30 pm. How long have you been sitting here then?'

'Oh, about an hour; I was beginning to think you lot had cried off,' I answered.

'That's bullshit, they don't open till 6 pm,' added Geordie.

'Never mind that, your turn for the beers Geordie, what you having then Stan?'

'Brown ale for me Geordie thanks,' he replied.

'And the same for me Geordie bonny lad, now be quick about it, if you value your teeth,' joked John.

'Where is Tom then Harry?' asked John.

'He is on his way; I think his old man is dropping him off. He went to the dentist after work and he is running late. He rang and left a message with my mother, just before I returned home from work,' I answered.

'I have been looking forward to this all week, a few beers with like-minded fellows and some cheerful banter,' added Stan.

The pub was starting to fill up with workers from Redheads and the Middle Dock arriving for a swift pint, before setting off for home. We decided to find a table away from the bar and settled down for a recap of the last week. Norman felt the need to enhance the atmosphere with a little monologue and went on; 'As we sit and discuss the events of the last week, I should remind you all that as a student I do not have the financial clout that would enable me to absorb the cost of copious amounts of the golden nectar.'

'Right then Norman, what you are saying is that you are skint. Is that correct?' asked Stan.

'To quote Captain Kirk, that is affirmative,' he replied.

'No need to worry, you are in auspicious company here and we will be very accommodating in that regard. It means you will be drinking halves when we secure the round of drinks,' added John.

Norman laughed and said; 'I plan to acquire a part time job soon, which will provide me with some much-needed funds.'

Five minutes later Tom arrived, bought a pint and joined the group. He informed us of his visit to the dentist saying; 'It has been a bad day fellas, listen to this. I was pulling cable out of a wall with my heavy pliers, when they slipped and I whacked myself in the mouth breaking a bloody tooth. I had to have it pulled out at Scrafton dentist practice in Chichester Road. He told me it was beyond repair so he yanked it out.'

He revealed the gap in his upper set of tombstones and Geordie joked; 'That gap is big enough to hold a puncture repair kit.'

'Now that is very original, if not a little over-exaggerated Geordie,' stated Norman.

'Well, what the hell, I am here for copious amounts of beer and some convivial discussion boys,' joked Tom.

Stan then gave us a joke to lighten up the proceedings; 'A bloke was walking home when a tramp stopped him and asked him for money. What do you want the money for? Is it for booze? asked the man. No, said the tramp. Is it for cigarettes? No. Then do you want it to gamble with? No, none of those things. Well, said the man, you're coming home with me. I'll show my wife what a man looks like when he doesn't drink, smoke or gamble.'

Laughter erupted around the table and Norman added; 'The moral of that joke is of course; marriage should be given serious consideration before you take the plunge. One should savour the *joie de vivre* in readiness for that *coup de foudre*.'

'Alright forgive our ignorance Norman, explain the French please you arse,' I uttered.

'It means be content with the 'joy of living' before that sudden amazing event Harry.'

'We didn't do French at Westoe School Norman,' I stated.

'Ah well, that's were Tom and I have the advantage, correct Tom?'

'Wouldn't know, I hated fucking French,' added Tom.

'Actually, it speaks volumes about our education Stan when you consider. Westoe School was a boys only school and we didn't do foreign languages. In fact, I can't remember doing science at exam level,' I declared.

A general debate continued about our schooling and where it had taken us. Stan and I left Westoe to embark on a career in engineering. Norman and Tom were educated at the Grammar School for Boys and John Telford and Geordie Stevens went to Dean Road. John worked for the Parks and Gardens Department and Geordie was a plumber for a local domestic heating firm. Tom sought employment as an apprentice electrician with the local council. He was not too impressed with his day job; 'I don't fancy doing this for the rest of my life, the money is not wonderful and it does not interest me to be honest.'

'Just bide your time Tom, once you have completed your apprenticeship you can work anywhere. You could even start your own business and make more money,' suggested John.

'Norman is doing what he really wants to do and I envy him for that,' added Tom.

'Yes, I am but it is a gamble and I don't gain a penny for it; but it is

PICK A WINDOW

something I want to do. I love the written word and theatre. The prospect of writing, acting or working in the theatre excites me. This will take time and I will need A-levels and probably a degree, so college will be my environment for the next few years boys.'

John thought of an idea; 'I have been thinking……'

'Now careful John, your doctor has warned you against this activity,' joked Norman.

'Go and boil your nuts Norman,' said John and he continued; 'Why don't we make this gathering a regular thing, we could get a few more mates along. We can select a pub and meet every other Friday or Saturday, what do you think?'

'That sounds like a fine plan, we could ask Andy Smith, Malcolm Carpenter and Keith Harper to join us, that would make nine,' suggested Stan.

As we discussed the proposal, two guys stumbled into the pub. They were well-oiled and it was only 7.30 pm. The manager gave them a disparaging look as they stood at the bar counter; 'I think you fellas have had quite enough by the look of it.'

The taller of the two answered; 'It's fine mate, we have been to a funeral and we are a bit downcast.'

The manager seemed to accept this explanation and asked what they wanted to drink? They opted for two pints of lager and having paid for their drinks they found two seats opposite our little conclave. They sat and talked of their departed relative, their discourse was loud enough for all the pub to hear and the manager asked them to lower their voices as the language became offensive. They seemed a little put out by this, but they did lower the volume. Then the shorter of the two looked across at our table and shouted across; 'I know that bastard, it's Tom McBain. He works for the council as a sparky.'

Tom looked up; 'Don't think I know you mate and anyway there is no need for the insult.'

'Yes you do, you were poking my sister.'

Tom now knew who he was and quietly announced to us that he had met him once when he was seeing his sister; that was over a year ago.

'Yes you know who I am don't you? I am Bob and my sister is Gloria.'

Tom just smiled at him and raised his thumb in agreement.

However, Bob was not to be humoured and he rose to his feet. The manager was keeping a watchful eye; 'I think you fellas need to leave; I want no trouble in here.'

'Oh, don't worry it's no trouble at all,' and he shouted across to Tom saying; 'Pick a window McBain you are leaving.'

What Bob was blissfully unaware of, was that Tom was one of the two hard hitters in our little group, along with Stan.

Tom tried to diffuse the situation; 'Look pal, you are very drunk and I am sure you will regret this tomorrow. So, if I were you; I would leave now before this gets any worse.'

Stan had heard enough; 'Ok Bob, why don't you and I go outside and have a chat about this, what do you say?'

Bob was somewhat surprised at Stan's suggestion and his mate said; 'Come on Bob, let's go home.'

Bob was having none of it; 'Right then, so Tom's boyfriend wants to talk; come on then, let's go outside.'

Both Bob and his mate followed Stan outside. Tom just sat back down; 'It won't take long; Stan will be back soon.'

Once outside, Bob swung a punch Stan's way. Stan easily dodged the strike and landed a right hook onto Bob's chin. This sent Bob flying into the road. Bob was lifted onto his feet by his mate and the pair of them staggered away as a light covering of snow fell.

Stan walked back into The Holborn Rose and Crown and sat down; 'It's snowing fellas and Tom, when a bird gives you the elbow; leave on friendly terms with the brother.'

'Time for a joke I think,' suggested John and continued; 'A man went to the doctor one day and said, 'I've just been playing rugby and when I arrived home; I found that when I touched my legs, my arms, my head and everywhere else it really hurt. The doctor considered his problem; 'You have broken your finger you idiot.'

A further round of drinks was ordered. Norman was given special dispensation and the rest of us chipped in for his beer. The manager thanked Stan for his intervention with Bob the firebrand.

Geordie revisited the idea of a regular gathering; 'So, where and when are we going to have another session then?'

'How about the Stanhope Hotel, they have a jukebox in the back room?' I asked.

'Sounds like a plan, let's make it Friday December 16 at 6.30 pm.

We can then jump on a bus to go into Shields if we want to extend the night,' replied Tom.

'I will tell Keith all about it; Tom will you see Andy and Malla before that?'

'Yes, I see Malla every morning on the bus and Andy lives not far from me,' he suggested.

We discussed all sorts of issues related to our lives and what the future had in store for us. 1971 was just around the corner and we were energised with a desire to cement our friendship and face the challenges as young men we would have to navigate. We left the Rose and Crown at 9.30 pm and bid each other goodnight. As we walked off Geordie slipped in the snow and fell on his arse in the middle of the road, much to our amusement. 'You have had too many sherbets Geordie,' declared John.

As he gingerly rose to his feet he answered; 'I have drunk more yacht varnish.'

THE YOUNG GENERATION

Nine young men of South Shields descended on the Stanhope Hotel on December 16, 1970, at 6.30 pm. This would be the start of a journey of camaraderie and attachment that would create lasting friendships. There were light flurries of snow descending as I jumped off the bus and walked into the lounge of the Stanhope Hotel. I was early but Stan and Norman had beat me to it. *All Or Nothing* by the Small Faces was playing on the jukebox and Norman greeted me with; 'Here is the second Wainwright to grace us with his presence, what you having your cousin Stan is in the chair?

Stan stood up and walked to the bar; 'I am on the brown ale, it's off the cooler, it's fine.'

'That will do me Stan,' I answered.

'Well, it's 6.30 pm and this is a poor show,' added Norman.

'Have faith Norman, they will all be here,' said Stan.

He had just finished his comment as the lounge door swung open and in trooped Keith, Andy, Tom, Geordie and John.

'Where the hell is Malla, I hope he knows Tom?' I asked.

'Don't panic he is on his way; he has gone for a haircut,' added Tom.

'Champion, fuggy cracks all around. His head will be buzzing,' added John.

They all collected their drinks and joined us and Keith said; 'Still skint then Norman?'

'It just so happens that I have acquired employment young Harper. So, I will be able to continue to attend these gatherings and not be concerned as to my financial situation,' he answered.

'Let me guess what the job is; it's a job in Green Lane fish shop, am I correct?' announced Tom.

'Nope, incorrect.'

'You've acquired a job cleaning windows,' I said.

'Nope, wrong again.'

'Now then, let me think; you are delivering milk,' added Stan.

'Nope, incorrect.'

'Come on then you tosser, what is it?' asked John.

'I am surprised you have not guessed, but then again you are all retarded. So, I will avail you of my employment. I have gained a position as a member of the library staff part-time in South Shields.'

'Where will you be working then?' asked Tom.

'I will be based at South Shields, but I might be asked to go to the local libraries in Cleadon, Boldon Lane or Jarrow.'

'Well, that serves a purpose then Norman, you will get access to books. Now that's preferential treatment is it not?' said Geordie.

'Oh yes, the world looks after literary genius my good man,' added Norman.

'What are the hours then Norman?' asked Andy.

'I work three nights a week and Saturday morning.'

'Come on then, how much are you getting paid then? said John.

'It's £1 an hour at 10 hours per week.'

'That's £10 a week,' stated Andy.

'God you are quick Andy, I wish I was good at mathematics like you,' I added.

'Piss off Harry, sarcastic git.'

'That's not bad for doing sweet fanny adams,' suggested Keith.

'I will have you know Harper; that my role is a very important one within the organisation. It takes intelligence, charisma, an attention to detail and immense patience to carry out my duties.'

'What a load of bollocks, you put books on shelves, stamp customers books and collect fines,' declared Geordie.

'I will tell you this; it sounds better than freezing your nuts off in the fabrication shed in Brigham's, for another £5,' said Stan.

Keith changed the subject and brought up his old man's car, which he had just recently purchased saying. 'My old man has this Volkswagen Variant; it is like a Sherman Tank. It has an air-cooled engine, which is in the back and it is bastard freezing cold when you're in it. The heater is next to useless.'

'Where did he get it then?' asked Tom.

'He bought it from a bloke in Brockley Whins called Herman Hitler,' said Keith.

'Is he any relation to Adolf?' said Andy.

'Yes, it's his brother. He escaped just before the Nuremberg Trials and jumped on a ship to Blyth,' added Keith.

'Alright, enough of this shite, Hitler's brother my arse,' said John.

As the discussion meandered into lunacy; in walked Malla, smarting a close to the swede haircut.

'Now then, here is the all-American marine with a crew cut close to the wood. Let me be the first to give you a slap Malla,' suggested Geordie.

'I wouldn't if I were you Geordie, I will bounce one off your chin if you try. That goes for all of you, I hate getting whacked on the back of my head.'

'I am with you on that one Malla,' I added.

'Come and join the party Malla, what you having to drink?' asked Keith.

'A pint of lager thanks Keith.'

Malla grabbed a seat and joined the rest of us; 'I like this idea of meeting up and having a few beers, I am looking forward to a catch up with some of you lot.'

'Yes, our plan is to meet every other week if possible. The idea is to choose different watering holes around the town on a Friday or Saturday. Times can vary from lunchtime or early evening,' added Norman.

The banter concentrated on the various working environments we were all involved in and Malla was not looking forward to a spell of nightshift; 'I have to do two weeks nightshift from next Monday. The firm have a rush job and it's all hands to the pumps, around the clock graft. The benefits are that I only work four nights Monday to Thursday and the money is better.'

'I have worked nightshift at Brigham's, I hated it. It's only for burglars and club committee men. It screws up you're sleeping and your mealtimes,' added Stan.

I related to some extension work being carried out at my place of work in Simonside; 'The company is extending the floor space and building an extension to the rear of the factory. This means the back wall has disappeared. Because the factory is not far from the river and the landfill site at Tyne Dock, the place is overrun by rats. I arrived at work on Wednesday to find a few workmates surrounding a big plastic bin. When I looked into the bin, I saw a big rat running in the bottom. Discussion centred around how to kill the bastard. So, I had a brilliant idea and I managed to find a bloody big boulder from the building site. This will fettle it I said, and I dropped the boulder into the bin. Sadly, I missed the rat and the swine jumped on the boulder, then jumped out of the bin to freedom, as we all leapt back in horror.'

'Daft sod Harry, remind me not to have you in my darts team,' joked Keith.

'Never mind that, what about them Russians? They just landed a spacecraft on the planet Venus,' said Tom.

'Hang on a minute, how the hell can they do that. Them spacemen would die of starvation; it will take them ages to get there and back,' suggested Andy.

'Who said they would be coming back? You know what those Russians are like,' added Geordie.

'Listen you idiots, it's a spacecraft not a spaceship. There are no crew members on board you mindless cretins,' said Norman.

'I reckon they have put a monkey on board,' suggested John.

So, Andy which member of your family volunteered then,' joked Stan.

'Shite off Stan,' shouted Andy.

Norman was in a reflective mood and continued with this topic; 'Let's just take a few minutes to consider this space adventure. Why does anyone want information about distant planets, are we searching for extra-terrestrial life forms?'

'Norman, you are sitting next to one, it's Geordie remember,' added Malla.

Laughter ensued at Geordie's expense, but Norman pressed on with his monologue; 'It is a strange conundrum that preoccupies us. The search for other life within our galaxy seems to fascinate our curiosity and yet the human race can't even look after its population. Half the world is in poverty and there are wars in Asia and Africa.'

'I blame the Common Market, decimalisation and Peter Glaze,' said John.

'Who the hell is Peter Glaze?' asked Keith.

'Come on Keith, it's Friday, it's five o'clock and it's *Crackerjack*,' joked Tom.

'You're not right in the head Tom,' Keith added.

'Look knucklehead, Peter Glaze is that annoying little tick, that plays Leslie Crowther's sidekick,' replied Tom.

'Oh yes, he gets on my tripe,' said Keith.

'How the hell did the conversation go from missions to Venus to *Crackerjack*, that is beyond me, added Andy.

'It's time for some humour I think, listen to this,' said John.

'What do you call a man with a spade in his head?'

No response from those gathered.

'Doug.'

'Is that the best you can do, it's not even as funny as Malla's haircut,' joked Stan.

'Stan, go and play with the traffic on Stanhope Road,' replied Malla.

'Tell you what though, this little snippet is a lot funnier,' suggested Andy and continued; 'John can you remember a lad called Terry English he was at Dean Road School?'

'Yes, he was a bit strange, why?'

'His brother was telling me that his mother had to ring the fire brigade last week. Would you believe that the stupid swine managed to get his todger stuck in the bath tap?'

'Was it the hot or the cold tap? asked Geordie.

All eyes were now on Geordie and I said; 'What difference does it make, you pisspot?

'Well, he might have tried to stop the flow of water, if the tap was knackered.'

'Geordie, I am somewhat confused and worried that you would consider such a conclusion. It begs the question that somewhere within your subconscious, you may have given this procedure some thought,' added Norman.

Andy continued with the tale saying; 'The fire brigade arrived prepared to fight a fire and were surprised to be escorted to the bathroom to find Terry with his love stick jammed in the tap. His member had swollen and a fireman had to apply some lubricant to remove his knob from the tap.'

Raucous laughter was now in evidence and the barman looked over at our gathering, wondering what the joke was.

'Why didn't his old man pull it out?' I said.

'Very funny that Harry, his old man pulled out his old man,' joked Keith.

'Time for more drinky poos I think,' suggested Tom.

We furnished ourselves with more libations and the conversation moved onto a sporting theme with the local football scene getting prominence as Stan announced; 'Have any of you lot signed up for any teams for Saturday or Sunday?'

'I am signed on for Boldon, but I have only played twice. I can't be arsed to go to training,' replied Malla.

'I still play five-a-side at Mortimer on a Thursday night for Trinity House,' I said.

Then Tom announced; 'Well, I was asked to sign for Bishop Auckland. I trained for two weeks and they asked me to join them. However, I do not have any transport and my old man can't get me to the matches, so I reckon it's a non-starter.'

'Sadly, it seems that England will never see Tom play at Wembley Stadium, it is indeed a loss to the footballing world. But do not be despondent young Tom McBain; time is on your side. The twin towers of Wembley may still afford you a platform in which to entertain thousands, with your ability and talent,' added Norman.

John fed the jukebox and selected songs by the Kinks, Led Zeppelin and Bob Dylan. Stan touched on the subject of our generation and how as young men, we differ so much from our parents; 'You know what, our parents are so predictable in their outlook to life. They go to work, come home, have tea, watch the news and go to the club. And that's just my old man, that's no life at all.'

Norman had a more pragmatic outlook when he added; 'To look at the big picture you need to accept where your parents started Tom. They too would have enjoyed days like this before they were married. When you start a family, your responsibilities increase immeasurably. There will be many aspects of their life that have been a challenge and perhaps many difficult situations had to be endured; to get where they are now.'

'Christ, you sound like my mother,' said Andy.

'Yes, I agree with Norman for once. Our parents have had to make sacrifices for us, so that we are cared for, clothed and fed,' said Malla.

'My old man makes a sacrifice on Thursday, Friday, Saturday and Sunday. Instead of being home with my mother, he goes to the Unionist Club and gets pissed,' joked Geordie.

'Listen, this is the new generation, the world is a different place. Men are on the moon, some of us have central heating, telephones, colour television and cars,' added Keith.

'Hang on, we haven't got BBC 2 on our telly yet,' quipped John.

'Alright, that's enough of that mind-numbing subject; I think it's time for a joke,' announced Andy; 'What happens to a frog's car when it breaks down? It gets toad away.'

'I can better that,' declared Stan; 'My mate at work thinks he is clever and he told me that an onion is the only food that makes him cry. So, I threw a coconut in his face.'

Geordie changed the conversation to romance when he asked; 'Anyone managed to acquire a girlfriend then?'

'Yip, I have a second date with a lass from Mortimer Road next Thursday. She works in the office at Newman's in Commercial Road.

'What's her name then Malla? I asked.

'Debra and she plays badminton and tennis,' added Malla.

'She must be fit then, what's her measurements?' asked Andy.

'No bloody idea, but just to keep you informed; I will take a tape measure with me on Thursday Andy,' joked Malla.

'Trust you Andy, the resident pervert. What about her other interests or her hobbies, perhaps she enjoys music and film. You will have to smarten up your chat-up lines if you are to attract a female companion,' added Norman.

'I have a fantastic chat-up line for you fellas listen to this,' said John.

'If you spot a lass that floats your boat, tell her this: I would swim across a crocodile infested River Nile, just to throw bricks at your shite.'

'Well, romance is not dead. John, we are in your debt for that eloquent and incisive example of how to get a girl interested. This august body should all take this as a sign, that John has the charm and charisma to woo the most sceptical of the fairer sex,' added Norman with just a hint of sarcasm.

After more humorous banter and at 10.30 pm a discussion ensued relating to our next get-together.

Keith suggested the Marsden Grotto, but this was quickly abandoned due to the distance involved. Stan suggested The Chichester Arms and general agreement was reached. Assembly was agreed for 6.30 pm in the lounge in three weeks time to welcome the new year of 1971. We then said our goodbyes and left for our respective buses home.

COMMUNICATION BREAKDOWN

1971 was upon us, and as agreed, our band of brothers assembled at The Chichester Arms for 6.30 pm on a cold Friday, January 8. At the appointed time all were present except Stan who arrived five minutes later to a crescendo of cheers, jeers and general abuse. In order to avoid congestion at the bar, we decided to stay in groups of three to buy the rounds of drinks. I was in a threesome with Keith and Tom. Stan, Andy and Norman formed a trio, with Geordie, Malla and John making up the final team.

There were a few punters in the lounge and two bar flies, in the form of bus drivers; who one would assume had completed their shift. The local bus depot was just across the road. Drinks were ordered and we found two tables close to the bar with enough seating to accommodate our conclave. Malla was quickly subjected to interrogation in relation to his new girlfriend and Andy said; 'Well, did you take your tape measure and acquire Debra's numbers then Malla?'

'I bet that is all that you have thought about for the last three weeks, am I correct Andy?' quipped Norman.

'All I will say is this my reliable friends; she is very attractive and far too classy for the likes of you lot. She has long black hair and hazel eyes and I am sorry to say this Andy, but she is way out of your league my son, she can read and write,' replied Malla.

'Cheeky bastard,' grunted Andy.

Two more bus drivers joined their colleagues at the bar and one of the new arrivals spoke to one of the drivers present saying; 'You finished your shift then Bob?

To our surprise he answered; 'No, I start in half an hour. I am on the Simonside to Pier Head route. I work through my shift better if I have a couple of beers first.'

This raised a few eyebrows in our group and I quietly said to Tom; 'Is he for real, drinking before he takes charge of a bus?'

'If he has had more than two pints, he is breaking the law the minute he turns the ignition on,' stated Tom.

After some ten minutes the two original bar flies left to start their shift. Tom's concern stirred him into action and he went to the bar and he said to one of the drivers: 'Excuse me mate, should that driver be driving a bus after drinking in here?'

'Well, it's not my problem and to be honest it's not yours either, is it?' he answered.

Tom was far from happy at this response; 'It's reassuring to know that we are all in safe hands when we travel on public transport,' and he returned to our table. Tom was more than a little upset with the situation and made sure our resident bus drivers heard, when he added; 'You know what fellas; every time this council elects a mayor it always seems to be a bus driver. That's worrying really, bearing in mind they drive under the influence of alcohol.'

The driver who had provided the terse reply turned; 'I think you have said enough pal, I would just keep your gob shut if I were you.'

Tom was not having that, and stood up; 'If you want me to rearrange your facial features, just step outside and I would be more than happy to carry out just such a procedure.'

The driver could see that Tom was not bluffing and turned ignoring Tom's invitation, without replying.

We carried on with our conversation, although the atmosphere was still a tad strained. Norman returned to the topic of Malla's new squeeze; 'So, can you see any mileage in this relationship Malla?'

'You never know Norman; we will just have to wait and see,' he replied.

The two bus drivers finished their drinks and made a sharp exit. As they were leaving Tom could not resist a parting comment; 'Take care now gentlemen, there are a lot of drunken bus drivers out there.'

The pub landlord gave Tom a concerned stare; 'I hope you are not going to cause any bother in here tonight.'

'No, just a communication breakdown, but it does concern me that these guys are drinking before they start their shift,' added Tom.

'Yes, I appreciate that, but I cannot refuse to sell them alcohol, under current legislation,' he replied.

'Fair enough, but I will be checking who the driver is, when I next board a bus in this town,' said Tom.

John decided to lighten the mood with a joke; 'What did the elephant say to the naked man?

'Alright let's have it,' I said.

'How do you breathe with something so small?'

'Here's a better one than that,' added Geordie; 'A Camel and an elephant are talking and the elephant says why do you have tits on your

COMMUNICATION BREAKDOWN

back? The camel replies, that's rich coming from an animal with a knob on his face.'

Norman returned to the subject of romance; 'It is fascinating when you consider that men and women have been on this planet for thousands of years and yet there is often a reluctance to engage one another. How many times do we find ourselves on a bus or a train, sitting opposite a woman and yet even making eye contact is avoided? Take Harry and Stan, you both went to Westoe, a boys school. This would not give you the opportunity to converse with the fairer sex. How do you both feel about that fellas?'

'Never thought about it Norman, life is too short,' replied Stan.

'Well, you have touched a nerve there Norman, I have never told anybody about this, so, pin back your lugholes,' I said.

'Last year I was in Newcastle getting tickets for The Who, they were coming to *The* Mayfair.'

'Oh yes, and we were drunk in the Adelaide before we went in and we missed Black Sabbath,' added Geordie.

I carried on, 'Correct Geordie, but what I didn't tell you, was what happened after I bought the tickets and made my way home. I decided to opt for the train instead of the bus, I would leave the train at Brockley Whins and just walk home to Simonside from there. So, normally you can pay on the train and I noticed one was waiting at platform 3. I asked a porter if that was the train for South Shields and he replied it was, and I boarded.

I found a seat and after a couple of minutes it set off. Sitting opposite me was a woman, I would say she looked about thirty years old and she was very attractive. She smiled and I returned the gesture. As the train crossed the Tyne it picked up speed and it passed two stations without stopping. The conductor was coming down the carriage collecting fares and I noticed that the woman sitting opposite had a ticket in her hand. She smiled again and I returned the gesture thinking, she fancies me. We continued to travel at speed passing stations and a realisation began to form in my head that maybe I was on the wrong train. As the train hurtled on, it became bloody obvious that I was on the wrong train. Now I realised why the woman sitting opposite was smiling, she knew that I was on the wrong bastard train.

I had to think fast, I didn't have a ticket and I didn't know where the train was going. So, as the conductor approached my seat I stood up and went to the toilet. I waited in the bog until I thought it was safe to return to my seat. The train was still travelling and as yet had not stopped. I returned to my seat just as the train was slowing down, we arrived in Durham. I was on the train to Kings Cross, London.

I somehow avoided the ticket collector on the platform and made my way to the bus station in Durham. I got the bus back to Shields. I arrived home at 9.15 pm after an hour on the bus. I boarded the train at 6 pm.'

'When I arrived home my mother said; Where have you been Harry, your tea is in the dog?'

'I just looked at our cocker spaniel, who seemed to be grinning at me,' and I replied, 'I missed the bus mam.'

'I will do you some beans on toast,' she said.

'That is another perfect example of communication breakdown young Wainwright. The moral of the story, don't trust British Rail porters,' joked Norman.

Keith then provided a little humour; 'A lorry has just overturned on the M6, it was loaded with Vicks Vapour Rub. The police said there would be no congestion for eight hours.'

Not to be outdone John gave us another joke; 'A bloke went into a bar and saw a fat girl dancing on a table. He walked over and said, wow, nice legs, she is flattered and replies, do you think so? The bloke said, oh yes, most tables would have collapsed by now.'

Another round of drinks was ordered and the pub was beginning to fill up. It had started to snow and we made a collective decision to stay in The Chichester Arms for another hour before moving onto a different hostelry. Tom asked Andy if he had been out in his old man's boat that week and Andy replied; 'We had a heavy catch on Wednesday, we were off St Mary's Island and we hauled in two-ton of cod, it was amazing. It's the biggest catch I have ever seen and we also caught a dozen lobster. With that many fish, the boat slowly chugged back to North Shields, it took an hour to arrive at the Fish Quay.'

'It must have been bloody cold out there Andy,' added Stan.

'It was, but we are always wrapped up in thermals and waterproofs,' replied Andy.

Norman chose the moment to add his own commendation for Andy's efforts; 'I would just like to express my thanks to Andy and his father for their courage and fortitude in the face of mother nature's extreme weather in maintaining a vital service. The bravery of fishermen is legendary and I salute them for their resolve and determination. Many souls have been lost in the tempest that is the North Sea and we are eternally grateful. As the messiah said:

Follow me and I will make you fishers of men.

'Here, Andy Smith, we salute you,' added Malla raising his pint.

'Do you know what Norman, when you prattle on like that; you could send a glass eye to sleep,' joked John.

It was now approaching 8.30 pm and the snow had relented. We then jumped on a bus for town and Tom could not resist a quip to the conductor; 'Is it safe to travel? I do hope your driver is not heavily intoxicated.'

The conductor was a little perplexed; 'I would seriously doubt that he has been on shift for four hours mate.'

'Oh well, just thought I would enquire that's all,' said Tom.

The conductor gave him a quizzical look and continued to collect our fares. We arrived in the Market Square and made our way to the City of Durham public house for further refreshment, just as more snow began to descend. The pub was reasonably well-populated but we managed to cobble together some chairs around a couple of tables. A few of us stood and 'chewed the cud' as Tom, John, Keith and Stan took the seats. We were all drinking brown ale apart from Tom who opted for a Guinness. At 9.30 pm in walked Sergeant Jack Brown, an officer of the South Shields police department. He was accompanied by a constable, they looked around at the punters and then went to talk to the manager.

Two blokes at the end of the bar were chatting and the one facing the door must have said to his mate that Jack had walked in. Unfortunately, the other bloke had not bothered to check the proximity of our esteemed law enforcement officer and chose to laugh and say; 'That bastard Jack Brown, he wanders around this town as if he fucking owns it. He will be hospitalised one of these days and I hope I am there to see it.' The bar fell silent and Jack slowly walked along to where the orator of that statement stood. His mate just looked at him with trepidation and the guy who voiced his vitriol, turned to see Jack towering over him.

His first reaction was to urinate where he stood. Jack looked down and watched as the piss flowed out over his shoes onto the floor. It was like a scene from a John Wayne western. Jack stepped back to allow the onrushing piss to be diverted; 'I am now in the process of deciding if you have broken the law. I could certainly charge you with urinating in a public place and that will cost £50. I could also charge you with threatening behaviour in relation to a police officer.'

The bloke was speechless and his mate began to speak, then Jack raised his hand. This suggested that what ever he was about to say, would not be a wise policy and the other bloke just stopped in mid-sentence.

Jack then said; 'We seem to have a communication breakdown here, have you anything to say in your defence?'

'I looked at Norman and whispered; 'That's twice I have heard that today.'

Norman just smiled; 'Shush, hold your tongue Harry.'

Having syphoned off the contents of his bladder, the defendant said; 'Sorry, I didn't know you were in the pub.'

'That was bleeding obvious. Are you always so offensive to police officers or have you just singled me out for this abuse?'

Again, the bloke was struggling to come to terms with his catastrophic error; 'I have had too much to drink, I was just mouthing off.'

'Ah, another charge of drunk and disorderly. That tots the fine up even further. Now listen very carefully, you pathetic little man. You will report to Kepple Street police station tomorrow morning at 9 am. I will decide what charge to impose upon you, if you do not appear. You will be arrested and charged accordingly; do you understand?'

'Yes,' he answered.

Jack looked at him; 'Yes what.'

'Yes sir,' he added.

'Very well, now leave this establishment and do not visit any other boozers in the town tonight, is that clear?'

The two protagonists then quickly left the scene. Jack looked at the manager; 'You should be more careful who you allow to drink in this establishment landlord. Respect for law and order is the cornerstone of our society. I would also suggest you clean up this unfortunate spillage on this side of the bar.'

Jack and his colleague, then left the pub. The City of Durham was still silent until the landlord said, 'Now there is a lesson for all of you.'

Stan was first to comment; 'It could have been worse landlord; he could have followed through and shit himself.'

Laughter was generated around the pub and conversations were reactivated among those present. We ordered another round of drinks and at 10.30 pm we all decided it was time to *Garn Yem*. We all boarded our respective buses home and me and Stan jumped on the 32 back to Simonside. As we sat and gazed out of the bus window at another fall of snow Stan said; 'I wonder if Tom has that driver from The Chichester Arms taking him home?'

'I bloody hope not, he is also likely to be appearing at Kepple Street at 9 am in the morning,' I replied.

A GATHERING OF SOULS

It had been a few weeks since our last assemblage at the City of Durham; the pressure of work and financial constraints had resulted in a temporary suspension of our reunion. Through the miracle of the telephone and word of mouth we agreed to muster at The Old Ship in Harton Village on Saturday, March 6, at 7 pm.

Stan, Geordie and I arrived to find Norman, Andy and Keith already seated in the bar, having just acquired their drinks. As we stood at the bar contemplating what to have, Tom walked in; 'John and Malla are outside having a spliff, I will buy their beers; what we drinking in here then Harry?'

'Got to be Newcastle Brown Ale Tom,' I replied.

'That's what those two dunderheads outside want, but I reckon I will start with a Guinness.'

We bought our drinks and managed to find a corner table and a window seat, along with enough chairs to accommodate our nine souls. Malla and John appeared suitably invigorated and John announced; 'I am choking for a drink; I could shift a pint of lukewarm badger's piss.'

'We don't sell that in here and watch your language please,' exclaimed the barman.

'Sorry chief, will do and if you have any bother in here tonight; Tom will deal with it, is that not the case Tom?'

Tom just looked at John; 'Just sit your carcase down or I will give you a good slap.'

'I wonder if our highly respected Sergeant Jack Brown will make an appearance tonight,' quipped Keith.

'He won't venture to these parts; this is an out-of-town boozer in a much more affluent area. There is never any bother in this place I reckon,' added Stan.

'It seems ages since we were in the City of Durham boys, and that arse stood and pissed on the floor; that was hilarious that was,' said Andy.

'I bet he got some grief the next day when he turned up at the big house in Kepple Street,' added Geordie.

'It must have been a month since that night; I am just glad to get out, I have been working all sorts of shifts. I have done Saturday mornings, half-shifts twice a week and the odd Sunday,' declared Malla.

'Yip, me too, it was a case of, get your bait, don't tell your mate, you're working late. I even did some night shifts. The extra money is good, but it screws up your social life,' added Stan.

John felt the need to lighten the atmosphere with a joke; 'I was sitting in the Eldon Arms last week with a mate from work and suddenly I noticed two old drunks sitting across the bar from us. So, I pointed them out and said to my mate; That's us in ten years time. My mate said; That's a mirror you stupid bastard.'

Laughter commenced and Norman felt the need to discuss the news of the day; 'Well, the postal strike is over thank God and that new film *Get Carter* has just been released.'

'Is that it, is that all you have got to tell us Norman?' replied Andy.

'There is a lot more, but you would soon become bored Andy; the reason being is that you have the mental capability of a soup ladle and any form of coherent dialogue will be totally lost in translation.'

'I think that means that you are a complete idiot Andy,' joked John.

'Norman, have you ever tried eating without the benefit of teeth? You may have to get used to it, if you continue to cast aspersions on my intellect,' replied Andy.

'My word, that was impressive Andy, have you been reading the dictionary again. I thought you were a *Beano* and *Fiesta* devotee,' joked Tom.

More laughter at Andy's expense and the conversation moved onto the topic of music and which bands were creating the greatest interest. Stan enlightened us on the American band Grand Funk Railroad; 'I hope I get the chance to see them, they are something else. They played Hyde Park in London recently along with Humble Pie. They are massive in the States and play in front of thousands at stadiums.'

'I have just bought *Nantucket Sleighride* by Mountain and Chicago 3; I will also be getting *Harmony Row* by Jack Bruce when it comes out in July,' I said.

'Listen to this you bunch of halfwits; there is a new band in America called ZZ Top. I heard them on *John Peel*, they sound great. They have their first album out soon, get with the programme and buy into these guy's,' added John.

'That comes from our resident musical director and dog molester, his holiness the Right Reverend John Telford, the acclaimed dodge pot and peeping tom of Corstorphine Town,' joked Keith.

'Thank you Keith, for that eloquent pen picture of our drinking chum John. However, the world must be awakened to this exuberant, astute, legendary and zealous aggregation of individuals. We nine souls have so much to offer modern civilisation and we should cry out from the highest peaks, seize the moment and say; hear our voice, we have come to free you from the bondage of mediocrity. We nine have been sent here on a mission to glorify and cultivate an aura of divinity that will empower mankind.'

'Bloody hell Norman, you're not sleeping with Edward Heath are you?' asked Malla.

'Does that mean we have to go to Penshaw Monument and start shouting and balling to any daft sod that walks past?' queried Geordie.

Norman gave Geordie a look of exasperation; 'You have failed to see the significance of all this Geordie. Why are we here?'

'Because we are not across the road in The Vigilant,' he replied.

Raucous laughter now filled the bar and Tom said; 'Norman, all this verbal diarrhoea is lost in this company, remember we went to the grammar school; these idiots all failed their eleven plus.'

'Alright if you two are so much cleverer than us answer this,' said Stan and went on; 'What is the difference between a stoat and a weasel then?'

'They are spelt differently,' quipped Andy.

We all looked at Andy in despair and Tom said; 'I rest my case.'

'Let's have it then Stan, what is the difference?' I asked.

'Well, a weasel is weaselly recognised and a stoat is stoatally different,' he replied.

More laughter and Andy added; 'See, I told you they were spelt differently.'

More drinks were ordered at the bar and the pub was beginning to fill up. Andy and Malla decided to have a game of darts while the rest of us discussed where we might venture to as the night wore on. The consensus of opinion was that we should head into Shields to enjoy a few more beers. The Locomotive was selected as the next port of call and when the darts match was over, we all climbed aboard a bus for the town centre at 8.30 pm.

The Locomotive was quite busy but we managed to locate a seating area in the lounge. Football dominated the conversation as we got comfortable and Stan said; 'The Toon got beat 1-0, at Man Utd last week. We should have got at least a point; both John Tudor and Wyn Davies missed good chances. Davies is having a lean time of it he couldn't score in a Bangkok brothel. Rumour has it that we are looking to sign Malcolm Macdonald from Luton Town, he has been banging the goals in apparently.'

'Never heard of him,' added Tom.

General banter on the prospects of our local teams followed until John called a halt to the proceedings; 'Listen, these buggers get too much bastard money for lumping a leather ball full of air around a football pitch.'

'That sounds like you are not a fan of the beautiful game then John,' said Andy.

'I would rather stand naked in the snow and have my genitals lashed with rusty barbed wire, by a Mongolian dwarf,' replied John.

'Now that is very original John, and I would pay good money to see that,' said Keith.

'It begs the question, why a Mongolian dwarf John?' added Norman.

'Well, firstly being a dwarf would mean he is just the right height, he would be at eye level and therefore have a better view of the aforementioned sexual organs. Secondly, Mongolians have a reputation for inflicting barbaric torture on their victims,' replied John.

'You know what, I am beginning to come around to John's way of thinking on this one fellas. It is obviously a personal fetish, that John has revealed to us today. However, there is a far more significant aspect to this story. The need for sexual gratification takes on many forms gentlemen, I have heard of bizarre and worrying anecdotes regarding the lengths that some people will go to in order to gain sexual pleasure. I have it on good authority, that some partners even take their clothes off when performing sexual intercourse. Of course, there is the dilemma of erectile disfunction and the anxiety that produces.'

Some quizzical glances around the table as to where the conversation was heading until Geordie broke the impasse with another gem; 'Erectile disfunction, my old man had to deal with that, he had to go up on the roof.'

'He did what?' said Norman.

'He went up on the roof to fix the TV aerial, you know erectile disfunction, we couldn't get a bloody signal.'

We were all creased up in laughter and Geordie said; 'Alright, what's the joke then?'

I was helpless and could not speak, I was laughing so much my back started to ache. When the laughter died down, Malla said; 'Geordie, it's got nothing to do with your TV aerial. It refers to the problems some blokes have when they don't have any lead in their pencil.'

Even Geordie had to laugh now and Stan added; 'That was bloody funny though, even if it was at your expense Geordie.'

'There is an easy solution to erectile disfunction, just jam your todger in the door, it will bloody swell up then,' joked Andy.

Norman continued with his oration relating to the wearing of clothes during carnal activities; 'It is a well-known fact that some lovers prefer to perform in the presence of others and will even carry out sexual proclivities in front of their neighbours.'

'Wait a minute, that might happen in Westoe Village; but I have never seen any bugger doing it in Eldon Street,' joked John.

'You would not want to be performing outside in this weather, it's bloody freezing,' added Keith.

'I always leave my socks on anyway,' added Malla.

'What, even in the house?' asked Keith.

'Even in bed,' he replied.

'This conversation has yet again descended into anarchy. Has anybody got anything to say, that bears any relation to reality?' said a disillusioned Tom.

'Yes, I have an admission to make,' said Andy.

'Oh no, take care Andy; walls have ears,' added Stan.

'It relates to my first sexual encounter.'

'Yes, we know about that Yorkshire Terrier Andy, it was all over the *Shields Gazette*,' joked John.

John was shown the finger as Andy went on; "Me and a former girlfriend were performing the deed on her mother's couch and having completed the activity; I stood and rearranged my tackle, I then started to pull up the zip of my Levi jeans. Disaster, I got halfway up and caught my todger in the zip. It was well and truly jammed and it hurt like hell. My female partner in the activity asked if she could help. I quickly replied that I would deal with the emergency. I tried to pull the zip down, but it would not budge, I then tried to carefully pull the skin from the zip; again failure. She began to panic; My mother will be back soon, I better ring for an ambulance. No, you will not. I will go home if I have to, I replied.

Then I had a thought, in order for the skin to escape the zip, it needed to be stretched. The natural way would mean that my todger needed to grow in size. Well, how the hell do I get that to happen? As yet, I had not cut any tissue but further tugging of the zip would no doubt cause bloodshed. Thankfully, my partner brought some Stork margarine from the kitchen, and after I had applied a generous amount of the lubricant, I managed to free my member.'

'Have we a name for this partner then Andy?' asked Tom.

'Hang on, let me guess, is it Rex or Patch?' I asked.

'Shite off Harry, no names, no pack drill,' replied Andy.

As we sat and insulted one another in a jovial way, a couple arrived and sat opposite. They appeared to be in the process of swapping tongues. Within seconds of sitting down they began snogging and were not bothered who was watching. It got really intense and Tom felt the need to comment; 'If this continues, his trouser snake will be making an appearance.'

'We will have to ask the landlord for a bucket of water soon,' I added.

'They eventually took a breather and looked over to our table and the fella said; 'Sorry guys, we just got engaged to be married today.'

'Well congratulations to you both, when is the baby due,' said Andy.

We all looked at Andy in astonishment and the fella took exception to the slur; 'I beg your pardon; how dare you make such an assumption.'

Again, we fixed our gaze on Andy, anticipating how the hell he was going to extricate himself from this situation and he said; 'Well, around here you don't get married unless your bird is up the duff.'

We fully expected Andy to cop for a punch in the gob at this stage, but the guy thought better of it; 'That may be the case, but I can assure you where I come from it certainly is not.'

Stan felt the need to interject at this stage; 'Can I on behalf of my friends inform you that none of us share the misgivings of this neanderthal sitting with us. He is educationally subnormal and at times he astounds us with his lack of common sense and manners. As a measure of our respect can we buy you both a drink to celebrate your good news?'

'Thank you, that would very kind of you, I am Paul and this is Ruth,' he replied.

'Please to meet you both and now Andy will go to the bar to get your drinks, won't you Andy.'

Andy looked like he was going in front of a firing squad, but rose to his feet; 'Well, sorry about all that, I blame the company I keep, what are you both having?'

Ruth asked for a gin and tonic and Paul requested a whisky. This brought smiles all round as Andy trudged forlornly to the bar. While he was there, Stan introduced us individually and we made pleasant conversation. Paul informed us that he was thinking of joining the army. He had already undergone an interview at the Army Careers Office in Fowler Street. Ruth worked at Barclays Bank in Newcastle and she lived in Jesmond. Andy returned with their drinks and placed them on their table as Geordie asked; 'Andy, you haven't forgotten the crisps and nuts, have you?'

'I think he has suffered enough, don't you?' added Ruth.

Andy gave Geordie a look that suggested, there would be serious consequences that just might result in Geordie needing hospital treatment. Having finished their drinks Paul and Ruth bid us farewell and departed.

Andy was quick to admonish Stan for his less than supportive comments relating to his earlier observations regarding the two lovebirds; 'That was a bit over the top Stan, I only said what you were all thinking.'

'Yes, well there you have it in a nutshell Andy. One has to be careful not to say what you are thinking sometimes, less you upset the other party. This is what you did to great effect, you brainless jumped-up son of a dunderhead,' added Norman.

'And it cost you for the apology, you moron,' joked John.

'What the hell, bad eggs don't smell when scented with sweet perfume,' replied Andy.

'Now I have heard that before, but where?' replied Malla.

'I know, it's a song from the album *Family Entertainment* by Family,' I said.

'Well done Harry, you win a sherbet fountain,' replied Andy.

Before we departed, we agreed to meet again as soon possible, bearing in mind our working schedules. Communication would be through the telephone and word of mouth.

IT'S ALIVE AND LOOKING AT ME

It was a warm bank holiday Monday in May 1971; I was with two decent young fellows John and Geordie. We were enjoying each other's company and a splendid libation of Broon Ale in The Scotia, a popular hostelry in South Shields.

The pub was well-attended with folk of all kinds including; seamen looking for ladies to cool their ardour and a healthy smattering of us wiser guys, who were far more knowledgeable as to the condition of these 'ladies' and what you might catch as a consequence of any close relationship.

During the course of the afternoon a number of our pals arrived including Norman, Stan, Keith and Malla. They joined us and ordered various refreshments including, Broon Ale snakebite, lager, black velvet and Guinness. Stan suggested a new libation of Special Brew and Barley Wine. This did not have the attraction of a refreshing alternative, so I continued with the Broon Ale snakebite.

Then John pipes up; 'this pint is off.'

Despite the fact that he had drank half of it, he was determined to seek recompense from the manager. This was not the first time John had tried this. Just two weeks earlier both of us were asked to leave The Garrick's Head, after he complained that he had a dirty glass.

John had returned to the bar claiming that the glass was dirty. The barman's response was not what John had expected; 'It's not the dirtiest thing you have ever had your lips on, I have seen your girlfriend.'

John took exception to this slur and demanded an apology, which never arrived.

John's response was really funny and it captured the mood perfectly, when he said; 'Now then folks,' and he turned to address all those in the pub. 'I have an urgent message from the management; all glasses have to be returned immediately. Due to the manager's cat having a piss in a tray of glasses this morning. Sadly, he forgot to tell this cretin behind the bar.'

Then a customer shouted out; 'It won't make a lot of difference to the shite he serves up anyway.'

Both of us were promptly told to leave and as we left, I said, 'We have been thrown out of better places than this.'

'No, we haven't Harry,' said John.

IT'S ALIVE AND LOOKING AT ME

'Yes I know that, but he doesn't.' I replied.

Well, that was two weeks ago, back to the present. The manager's approach to John's complaint was expected when he said; 'You have supped half of it, you swine.'

'Yes, but it now looks like someone's had their knob in it,' John replied.

'Well, you're not getting another one, bugger off you are barred.'

Here we go again I thought, and we all left and crossed the road to The North Eastern, another drinking establishment. However, the manager of The Scotia had already phoned ahead warning the manager of The North Eastern of our imminent arrival. As we entered the pub the barman shouts; 'You lot are barred.'

'What now?' said Geordie.

'The Criterion,' replied Malla.

So off we went and thankfully no forwarding message had been sent from that git in The Scotia and we all ordered our drinks and sat down. The main talking point for discussion was who was the best guitarist in the world?

I suggested Eric Clapton and Malla nodded in agreement. Various contenders were named including; Carlos Santana, Alvin Lee, Rory Gallagher, B. B. King, Buddy Guy, Lesli West, Jimmy Page, Frank Zappa and Jeff Beck. We all agreed that Jimi Hendrix outshone them all, but sadly he was no longer with us.

Then it appeared, at first all we could do was stare in astonishment.

'It's rude to stare,' said Norman.

'Jesus Christ, what the hell is that?' said Keith.

It was an incredible sight, as yet undefined, was it animal, vegetable or mineral? As it drew closer you could see that it was dressed in female garb. I will now give you a detailed account of what we all saw on that warm May afternoon.

As it shuffled across the floor towards the bar, we caught our first breath of the aroma that permeated from it. It was a repulsive odour that smelt of stale urine, vomit, with a hint of fish.

'Smells like a pox doctor's apron,' said Norman.

'You would know,' replied John.

As it glided to the bar, I could see the barman getting a little nervous. I suspected he had lost his RP9 respirator. Then it spoke, yes folks! It could talk.

'A half of Guinness,' it snarled.

'My husband will be here in 5 minutes; he will pay you.'

We all looked at each other in disbelief, a husband! 'He must be a bonny sight,' said Keith.

Then Stan injected a certain amount of doubt into the conversation when he said; 'Listen, how many blind mountain Gorillas with no sense of smell have you seen in Shields lately?'

We all creased ourselves laughing at this funny yet realistic quip. Having received its Guinness, it turned toward our table and smiled. Well, we think it was a smile, due to the absence of teeth it was hard to tell. It could have just farted. She (we think) did have one solitary tooth in the bottom of her gob. It was black in colour and it resembled a chunk of burnt plywood.

Now we were nervous, was it coming to join us? Thankfully, it chose a table some six feet away and waited for its husband to arrive. I will continue to provide a pen picture of this revolting apparition before us. Working from the top down, it had hair that appeared to be growing from every available orifice; her eyelashes were like rusty barbed wire. The eyes were dangerously close together and were at the point of swapping positions. They were so sunken that they must have been touching the back of her head. The nose, well the only comparison I could make would be a saveloy without the skin on.

At this stage, it would be impossible to put an age to this phenomenon, but the extensive growth on the chin may suggest that it was in its twilight years. The remainder of the body was wrapped in clothing that was stained in what can only be described as 'stuff', hence the smell. It looked like it had a hump on its back, but it may well have been one of its offspring sleeping. Even at a distance of six feet the smell was overpowering and we made a joint decision to depart to the Stags Head and leave this vision of loveliness to her 'husband'.

John wanted to stay, just to see the husband, but our respiratory system could not take it and as we left, Malla shouted to the barman; 'This young lady would like a beer mat barman.'

The barman's response was immediate as he silently mouthed; 'fuck off.'

I gave my pals a word of warning when I said; 'Now gentlemen that is what you will look like if you take drugs.'

'Bollocks, she has been ugly all her life,' replied Stan.

RITUALS AND RECOMPENSE

It was Friday and I glanced at the clock on the wall, it was 3.45 pm. I will finish brazing this water tank and that's it for the day. I was now completing a tank in ten minutes and that was some achievement. However, I was still second best to Dodger Brown he could knock one out in seven minutes and nobody managed to achieve that. Nevertheless, I was content with my progress, I was in the first year of my apprenticeship as a sheet metalworker. Having washed up, I clocked out at 4 pm and left work to walk the short journey to my home in Bainbridge Avenue. During that walk I bumped into one of my pals Malcolm Carpenter, more commonly addressed as Malla by his mates. It was unusual to see him at this time of the day and I said. 'You are finished early mate, what's up?'

Malla was a second-year apprentice plater at Middle Docks, a ship repair yard in South Shields.

'Accident at work, we were all sent home. It will be on *Look North* tonight Harry,' he replied.

'Why what happened?' I asked.

Malla told me what he had gleamed from witnesses at the scene. It was common place in engineering and other industrial organisations that new apprentices would be subjected to some form of initiation ceremony within their first week at work. These activities included, suffering a blackballing; this involved the unfortunate individual having his pants removed and then black grease was applied to his genitalia. He was then hung on a crane or chained to a vice.

On this occasion, the apprentice on the receiving end of the initiation was to undergo a horrific ordeal. His fellow apprentices decided to use compressed air as a means of power to enhance the embarrassment on their new workmate. Compressed air was and still is an effective power source for machinery like drills and grinding machines. It is extremely powerful, the air travels at 50 psi.

Malla gave me his account of what happened next; 'They grabbed hold of him and removed his overalls and underpants; then they stuck a compressed airpipe up his arse and turned it on. They had no idea what they were doing to the poor sod and when he was carried past me on a stretcher he was in bloody agony.'

'What time did this happen then?'

'It was after dinner about 1.30, I think. They carted him off to hospital, but I don't know how he is.'

'The buggers who did this will do porridge I reckon. Who was he, did you know him?' I asked.

'No, but I heard from a welder on the bus that he was from Whiteleas and he was a good footballer. Apparently, he had trials with Newcastle and Derby County.'

I changed the sombre mood; 'So, what is the script for tonight then?'

'Locarno for 8.30 pm, but if you fancy a livener or two; John, Stan, Geordie and me are meeting in The Garrick's Head at 6.30 pm.'

'Don't think I will make it Malla; I have some chores to do. I told my old man I would help him lift some spuds tonight. I will just see you all in the Locarno.'

We parted company and set off for our respective homes. When I arrived in the house, the smell of home baking filled the place. My mother had been creating a pastry extravaganza. This included all manner of sumptuous fayre including, scones, bread buns, cakes and her legendary 'kneeling bags'. These were corned beef and potato pasties and my old man renamed them due to their size, because my mother could only fit three in the oven. This would be the evening meal accompanied with homemade chips and peas. As I entered the kitchen, my attention was drawn to two of the aforementioned 'kneeling bags' that were on a baking tray on the table.

My mother was quick to notice my enthusiasm and said; 'Hello son, and don't even think about it. You will eat at 5 pm with the rest of the family. As you are the first in, would you go to the shops and buy a pint of milk please. You can pay for it out of my allowance.'

I gave my mother half of my wages every week, this amounted to £4.50p and she was always grateful for it. Money was tight and my allowance was a big help in 1971. On my way to the grocers, I met Jean Gibson who lived around the corner in Drummond Crescent.

'Have you heard about the lad who was killed in the shipyard? He had his head blown off,' she said.

Word gets around bloody quick I thought, and then I corrected her with regard to his injuries; 'It was the result of compressed air being forced up his back passage and it did not blow his head off. He was still alive when he went to hospital.'

'Did you know him?' I enquired.

'Not really, but he was going out with Joyce Hudson, who lives in Monkton Avenue.'

'What was his name then?'

'I think he was called Michael Dennison,' she replied.

When I returned home with the requisite pint of milk, I told my mother about the incident at the shipyard. She was very shocked; 'The boys who did this should be made to go and see the parents of this poor lad and face the music, I do hope he recovers.'

I then ascended the stairs and sought sanctuary in my bedroom. I put *Blues from Laurel Canyon* on my record player and listened to John Mayall and the Bluesbreakers. I lay on my bed and contemplated what it must be like for the family of that apprentice. I must have dozed off and was awoken by a familiar voice shouting up the stairs. 'Harry, your tea is ready you lazy knave.'

That was father, always full of compliments. I descended the stairs and joined the bosom of my family at the kitchen table. My brother Jack had just turned up after playing football for the school team. My mother banished him to the bathroom to clean up before he sat at the table. My father had removed his overalls, which did nothing to improve the ambience of the scene and he was told to wash up in the kitchen sink. The main problem lay with his feet and when he removed his boots, we were all subjected to the odour permeating from his socks. The smell would have stopped the traffic. She insisted that he remove the offending garments and put them in the wash basket. This he did with a comment that fell on deaf ears as far as mother was concerned when he replied; 'Well, I think the smell of these socks gives me an appetite.'

My mother just gave him a look of disgust; 'They are revolting, they belong in the bin.'

The tragic story of the apprentice was touched upon and my old man said those responsible should be jailed for life. My brother Jack asked how he could be seriously injured with an air pipe. My mother looked at my old man for guidance, but he seemed uncomfortable about expanding on the topic and answered abruptly; 'Eat your tea and shut your trap Jack.'

A contradiction in terminology I thought to myself, as my mother raised her eyebrows and deposited a ladle of peas on my plate alongside the chips and the mother of all kneeling bags. After tea we all gathered around the TV and watched the local news and sure enough the shipyard incident was the lead story. Sadly, the apprentice died in hospital. His name was not revealed, but he was an only child and this was his first day at work. Three of his workmates were helping police with their enquiries. Other items on the news included a piece on the Tyne Tunnel, which had been opened by the Queen in 1968. The news item concerned the disruption caused by a posse of gypsies and their horse and carts. Two horses had broken free from their reins and created mayhem, resulting in the closure of the tunnel for two hours.

My father made an observation; 'If those horses had managed to gain freedom in North Shields, they would eventually end up on Sunday dinner plates.'

After the news of the day had been divulged, I accompanied my old man to the garden to extricate the spuds. As we dug them out, he regularly threw worms in my direction in the hope that they would fall down my shirt front. He was only successful on one occasion. I had no such luck with my attempts to do the same to him. We lifted a healthy crop of spuds and then turned the soil in readiness for another crop.

It was now 7 pm and in preparation for this evenings entertainment I asked my mother to iron a new white corduroy Levi shirt I had purchased the day before. She had carried out this task so that her first born would look spectacular for the evening. After the horticultural chores I had a long soak in the bath listening to the wonderful vocalisations of Jack Bruce singing *We're Going Wrong* from Cream's second album *Disraeli Gears*.

Please open your eyes, try to realise
I found out today, we're going wrong
Please open your mind, see what you can find
I found out today, we're going wrong

Having soaked my bones and washed my hair, I dried myself and put on my ensemble for the night. Levi shirt, Lee Cooper denim jeans, desert boots and a black velvet jacket. This was the look in 1971, so look out girls. Was I in for a surprise?

I left the house at 7.45 pm and caught the bus to Westoe and from there the bus to Sunderland. I disembarked at the Wheatsheaf pub and had a cool bottle of Double Maxim. I arrived at the Locarno around 8.30 pm and wandered around in search of my pals. I could not find them, so I bought another bottle of Double Maxim. There I was standing under the balcony that extends all the way around the Locarno and then I spotted a familiar face. Three weeks earlier I had decided to end a relationship with a girl called Rachel who hailed from Gilley Law in Sunderland. We had been seeing each other for about a month, without any real commitment. So, I decided to end it; she was somewhat disappointed and suggested that we should give it more time. I had made my mind up and that was that.

I noticed that she was standing with three guys having a conversation. What raised my concerns was that she continually pointed at me during this dialogue. After a couple of minutes, the three protagonists walked in my direction. I had a feeling that they were not going to exchange pleasantries and offer me a drink. I guessed that some delicate negotiation may be required to avoid any unpleasantness. I placed my beer on a shelf some two feet away. As they approached, they moved into a pincer movement. They stood and the guy facing me began the conflab saying; 'Rachel said you dumped her and told her to piss off.'

'Well, that's not the real story is it? I decided to call it off yes, but I did not tell her to piss off. Anyway, what has any of this got to do with you?' I replied.

'Rachel is my fucking sister, you faggot.'

I was in a bit of a sticky situation here. The way they were positioned suggested that I would soon be on the end of a punch. The two at my right and left had their fists clenched so I decided to take action. Running was out of the question and there was still no sign of my buddies so I leaned back and launched my head into the face of the guy in front of me. There was a loud crack as I connected with his nose, which probably meant I had broken it. Then the guy on my left connected with a punch that sent me backwards. Another blow floored me and from then on it was a free-for-all as they pounded me with fists and feet. I did my best to protect my head and tried to curl into a ball. They still managed to give me a real hiding that seemed to go on for a long time. When the assault finally ended, I was in some pain, my ribs were sore and I knew my face had received many blows. I managed to get to my feet and make my way to the toilet to clean up. During this whole ordeal, no one offered any help. I washed my face and sought refuge in a cubicle. My right eye was virtually closed and I was still bleeding from numerous cuts and abrasions. After sitting and gathering some strength, I left the toilet and made my way to the exit. A bouncer stopped me as I got to the door; 'Whoa there fella, what happened to you?'

I just looked at him with one eye and walked out into the cool night air. My head was pounding and I could taste blood running down my throat. I arrived at the bus stop and after five minutes I boarded the bus for Shields. The conductor on the bus said; 'You need a hospital son; we will drop you off.'

'No, it's alright. I just need to go home; my mother is picking me up in Shields and she is a nurse.'

I am sure he knew I was lying and added; 'Are you sure son, you look pretty bad to me.'

'It's OK, I will just sit at the back,' and I attempted to pay for a ticket.

'No, I don't want your money son, just take a seat,' he replied.

When I returned home, I put my red and white Levi shirt in a bowl of cold water, but I knew it was ruined. My mother was out visiting a friend and would not be back for another hour. I took two aspirin and went to bed. The next morning, I gave my brother Jack one hell of a fright. We shared a bedroom and when he saw my face, he failed to recognise me and I said; 'It's me you idiot.'

'What the hell happened to you.'

'This is what happens, when you dump a lass from Gilley Law.'

Facing my mother was the next hurdle and when I entered the kitchen, she too was shocked; 'My God, what happened to you son? You need to go to hospital Harry.'

She then spent the next twenty minutes checking my wounds and applying the requisite medication. She asked me how it happened and I relayed the story back to her. 'Someone should have rung the police and you should have gone to the hospital. God knows what your father will say when he finds out. You know what he is like, he warned both of you about bringing trouble to the house,' she added.

'I think I am the innocent party in all this mother, anyway, just tell him I fell off the bus.' I spent the weekend lying around the house and contemplating why me? In addition, where the hell were all my mates that night? However, I still thought about that apprentice who would be buried in a weeks time.

THE CONVERTED

Religion was a peripheral aspect in the lives of both myself and my peers. As young men embarking on their futures, religion was not a topic discussed at any length during our many get-togethers. That was to change on a warm Saturday in September 1971. Our band of brothers had gathered at the West End Vaults, a boozer that sat opposite Holy Trinity Church in the Windmill Hill area of South Shields. In attendance were Tom, Norman, Andy, Geordie, John, Keith, Stan, Malla and yours truly. We had acquired our drinks and the pub was reasonably busy as we all sat at tables in the bay window. The conversation was focused on the current music scene and a debate had started on what was the finest LP currently in circulation. Much praise was heaped upon Frank Zappa's *Hot Rats* by me and Malla. Other albums were mentioned including; *Parachute* by the Pretty Things, *Blind Faith*, *Led Zeppelin II* and *Bare Wires* by John Mayall. Then Andy added; 'What about the best single of all time? Mine is *Sunshine of Your Love* by Cream,' he said.

Stan nominated *Honky Tonk Woman* by The Rolling Stones; Norman plumped for *Pinball Wizard* by The Who. John suggested *Revolution* by the Beatles and Tom voted for another Beatles song, *Paperback Writer*.

'What about you Harry, what is yours then?' asked Tom.

'It has to be *Voodoo Chile* by Jimi Hendrix; may he rest in peace.'

'What a loss he is to the music scene,' I replied.

'Well Malla, Keith and Geordie come on then; who are you plonkers voting for? asked Stan.

Geordie gave it a little thought and said; 'My favourite is *Good Vibrations* by the Beach Boys,' he replied.

Keith opted for *Satisfaction* by the Rolling Stones.

'It's all down to you now Malla,' I said.

'Gentlemen, there can only be one outright winner in this musical reflection. It is of course the one and only *Roll Over Beethoven* by Chuck Berry,' he replied.

I continued my comments relating to Jimi Hendrix saying; 'I bet when Bob Dylan first heard his song *All Along the Watchtower* played by Hendrix; he must have thought; what the hell is that? He could not have imagined the song sounding like that.'

'Damn right Harry, it is incredible what Hendrix did to that song,' added Keith.

As we mulled over the music scene, the pub door opened and in walked a man of the cloth and with singular purpose he strode to the bar and ordered a pint of Guinness. Andy then said; 'That's the Reverend Johnson from Trinity Church.'

Having received his libation from the landlord, he turned and noticed our little band of revellers approached and asked; 'How are you fellas today? Do you mind if I join you?' Spoken in a thick Irish twang.

We were all slightly surprised and then John said; 'Well, if you are happy to share your conversation with this bunch of morons, you are most welcome Vic. However, I must warn you that this here group of deranged chimps don't have an intelligent thought in their heads and I am a little fragile after last night.'

The reverend pulled up a chair, sat down and said; 'Everything in moderation my son, then you will serve the Lord your God to his liking.'

'I thought men of the cloth were not allowed to drink,' added Andy.

The reverend's response was met with a little surprise when he replied; 'The hell with that, I need this for medicinal purposes or I will crack up. You haven't seen the congregation I have to preach to.'

This brought polite subdued laughter to the situation and created a more relaxed atmosphere. 'So, Reverend Johnson, where in Ireland do you come from?' asked Keith.

'Call me Patrick, I am not on official duty. I was born in County Cork and I have lived in South Shields since 1937,' he replied.

Then Geordie provided another one of his gems when he asked; 'Are you a Catholic then?'

'How can he be a Catholic you daft sod, Trinity Church is a Church of England,' added Stan.

Geordie just looked at Patrick; 'Oh yes, I forgot, sorry Patrick.'

'You are one knucklehead Geordie,' said Tom.

Patrick was amused at Geordie's error and chuckled with laughter. This caught the attention of the landlord who gave us a look of bewilderment. Patrick rose to his feet and asked what drinks were required but was halted by John who said; 'No no Paddy, let us buy you a drink. Norman it's your round.'

Norman shot John a filthy look as he left his chair to purchase a round of drinks for this party of new theologians. Norman took the

THE CONVERTED

opportunity to subject the landlord to one of his monologues. Before requesting the drinks, he positioned himself at the bar counter and with his arms outstretched on the bar rail, he began his oration.

'It is with a heavy heart that I address you my fine fellow. I have been summoned by my contemporaries to purchase several beverages of an alcoholic nature to quench their somewhat inexhaustible thirst. In such an unforgiving economic climate, I am somewhat perplexed sir. I therefore have to implore you to look upon this son of England with pity and a degree of reverence. In particular I would be most grateful if you could introduce a discount in relation to this forthcoming financial transaction.'

Having listened to Norman's performance, the landlord cut to the chase and said; 'No credit, no tab and no bloody discount, what do you want?'

Norman was left with the impression that the landlord had failed to grasp the gravity of the situation; 'Then perhaps I can present a case for the accused.'

The landlord was becoming a little irritated now and we all felt any further drinking may have to be continued elsewhere. But Norman pressed on. 'My exposition may enlighten your demeanour and as Oscar Wilde once said;

> *The public is wonderfully tolerant. It forgives everything except genius.*

And it is my firm belief sir, that God is working on a much more ambitious project. You sir can be part of this wonderful spiritual journey. It is said that he who possesses wealth, is possessed by it and in that regard my dear landlord, I lay my case before you. However, should you refute my case and thus ignore my plea, I say with the utmost candour:

> *A map of the world that does not include Utopia is not worth even a glance, for it leaves out the one country at which humanity is always landing. When humanity lands there, it looks out and seeing a better country, sets sail. Progress is the realisation of Utopias my good man.'*

The landlord had now had enough; 'After talking all that crap, what do you want?'

Norman now conceded defeat and ordered the drinks, but he left the landlord with one final thought saying;

Allusions in humour involve extra linguistic knowledge. In other words, my good fellow; knowledge of the world. I am of the opinion that you sir, have not availed yourself of the desired panache in which to entertain our band of free-thinking intellectuals.

Norman returned to the comfort of his friends and Andy shouted; 'That nearly resulted in us getting barred you idiot.'

Patrick thought Norman's soliloquy was entertaining and said; 'You have a gift my son, I wonder if the landlord is aware that you have very cleverly insulted him?'

'I doubt it and I am now officially skint,' replied Norman.

Patrick suggested that Norman should seek a career in the theatre. And as a thank you for his efforts he bought Norman a tot of rum.

Andy dropped himself in it yet again when he said; 'Anyway, what does panache mean?'

'It's a French pancake,' replied Malla.

Patrick was in mid-swallow and nearly sent a mouthful of Guinness flying from his mouth as laughter ensued at Andy's expense. The banter returned to Patrick's life and Geordie asked him about his early years in Ireland.

'Well, where do I begin?' said Patrick.

'At the start,' joked Stan.

Patrick smiled and began; 'I was born in a small village called Skibbereen, in County Cork. My father died when I was four years old. My mother had to take washing in to make ends meet. Skibbereen is now a small town and a lovely place to live.'

'Is it bigger than Shields?' asked Keith.

'Oh no it's much smaller than South Shields,' he replied and went on; 'I attended the local school and gained a decent education. When I was ten years old, I saw the mayor of Cork shot by the Black and Tans during the unrest and civil war in 1920. I had a few farm jobs as a youth and in 1928, I was fortunate to be offered a place at the Theology College in Dublin.

'Who were the Black and Tans?' asked Malla.

'The reverend smiled and said; 'They were ex-soldiers brought in by the British government, to keep the peace, which was a complete disaster. My first ministry was in Dublin, that lasted three years and then I was given the posting at Holy Trinity Church in South Shields in

1937. I have seen the despair of conflict both in Ireland and in England. I was in the market place when the Luftwaffe dropped their bombs in 1941.'

'They had buses upside down and my mother had to seek refuge in the Golden Lion Hotel on King Street,' I replied.

'That makes you sixty-one years old then Patrick,' added Norman.

'Yes that is true, but I feel like a twenty-one-year-old in your company fellas,' he replied.

We were fascinated with Patrick's life story and looked forward to more anecdotes when events took a turn for the worse. The pub door swung open and in strolled 'Tommy the tramp.' He stood and surveyed the scene before him. He realised that the landlord was not at the bar and he selected a chair near the toilets. Tommy was well-known in the town and most of the time he was heavily intoxicated with methylated spirits. He was a sad sight to behold, standing no more than 5 ft 4 in. Starting from the top down; his head was covered with something like an explosion in a pubic hair factory. His skin was worn and pockmarked like an old leather satchel. He was the proud owner of two teeth, which had an uncanny likeness to two sugar puffs. His hands were badly gnarled and his fingers were encrusted with filth. His attire consisted of a heavy woollen overcoat tied casually around his waist with a length of rope. His trousers were trying to defy the law of gravity and were covered with all manner of stains.

His ensemble was delicately finished off with a pair of odd shoes, one old brown brogue and one grey loafer. Rumour has it that Tommy returned from serving King and country in 1945, only to find someone else getting their eggs fried in his frying pan. His wife had taken another man and Tommy was on his own. This led to a life on the streets and regular nights in Kepple Street police station, after numerous misdemeanours in the town. Tommy had a knack of upsetting the general public with his constant abusive language. To the younger generation he was just a figure of ridicule.

Having settled himself he expressed his anxiety and said; 'Where the fuck is that lazy bastard landlord?'

As if by magic the landlord appeared at the bar and said; 'Tommy, out you go now would you please.'

'Fuck off,' replied Tommy.

The landlord made his way to where Tommy was sitting. However, as he approached, he was subjected to the smell permeating from him and he stopped in his tracks. This was Tommy's defence mechanism and very powerful it was too. The smell would have curdled milk. Tommy scratched his matted hair and said; 'I want a drink you twat.'

The landlord seemed quite indifferent to this abuse; he probably had endured it on many occasions. Tommy would not budge and a stalemate was reached. Tommy then informed those gathered that he had shit his pants. One can only imagine what the inside of his trousers were like prior to this worrying announcement. To our amazement our new drinking buddy, Reverend Johnson rose to his feet and walked over to Tommy and said; 'Come on my son, I will give you a nice cup of tea over at the vicarage, then we will clean you up.'

Tommy was somewhat surprised by this intervention; 'See, God has spoken and he looks after old soldiers like me.'

As they approached the door, Patrick turned and said; 'Nice to meet you fellas, have a pleasant day now; the Lord has given me another task to perform today.'

We all sat and pondered for a short while, then Norman said; 'Well, we have been entertained today boys.'

'I bet he gives Tommy a hosing down in the churchyard before he gets that cup of tea,' added Stan.

The theme of religion continued and Norman seemed preoccupied with the experience we had just been party to and went on; 'Perhaps this is a sign for us.'

'A sign, what the hell do you mean?' replied Geordie.

'Yes, a sign Geordie,' and he continued; 'It may well be fine friends, that we have been chosen to follow in the footsteps of the apostles.'

Tom decided to go along with this theory and added; 'Yes, but can we perform miracles and convert the pagans, as did Peter and Paul.'

'Never mind miracles, whose round is it?' replied John.

Andy poured fuel on the fire; 'Tell you what, why don't we go to Trinity Church for Sunday service. Patrick will be surprised to see our ugly faces sitting there.'

'Splendid idea Andy,' replied Norman.

'This is getting bloody stupid; are you buggers serious?' quipped Tom.

'We will have to dress smart,' added Keith.

Both John and I were a little hesitant, we had arranged to meet our respective girlfriends on Sunday. I pointed this out, but I received little sympathy from my comrades and Stan said; 'There is more to life than birds Harry, we have been set a challenge and we must embrace it.'

John still had reservations and added; 'Stan you are talking shite, anyway I don't have any shoe polish.'

'Just wash your feet,' joked Andy.

Agreement was reached and we all met at 10 am outside the church. We were all dressed appropriately and Norman looked at John and said; 'I see you found the shoe polish then John.'

He was wearing a gleaming pair of black brogues.

John's response was predictable when he countered; 'Piss off Norman, you look like a dummy out of Burtons window.'

We found a pew three rows from the front. There were about thirty people present as we took our seats. Most of the congregation were older than us. When Reverend Johnson appeared to give his opening welcome, he spotted us and gave a welcoming smile and said; 'Good morning and a special welcome to our young friends in the third row. It is indeed a pleasure to see you. And may the Lord be with you.'

Sadly, our ignorance was self-evident, as we didn't give a response. Thankfully the rest of the congregation bailed us out. He began with a reading from the Acts of the Apostles. Norman who was sitting next to me whispered; 'I told you Harry, we are medalling with powers we cannot comprehend.'

John who was sitting to my left said; 'Jesus Christ this is spooky.'

'Mind your language,' I replied.

Patrick went on to tell his flock all about Peter and how he converted the centurion Cornelius to Christianity. We sang the three hymns and listened intently to his sermon. He concentrated on those in our society who have fallen on hard times, (a reference to Tommy no doubt) and how we must all show compassion. At the end of the service Patrick joined us and said; 'Does this mean that I have nine new members of the congregation?'

We all looked at one another and Andy answered; 'Well, I am not sure about that Patrick, but we might just call again.'

We all nodded in agreement. Patrick smiled and said; 'You have made my day fellas; the next Guinness is on me.'

As we left the church John said; 'I can't wait to get my Uncle Bob's shoes off, I am crippled.'

THE HORSE

When among friends, conversations can lead to all kinds of intellectual repartee. Sadly, with this band of Sundancer's, any intelligent discussion was very limited. It was a wet Saturday afternoon in November 1971. Those present were Tom, John, Keith, Geordie, Norman, Andy, Malla, Stan and me; all sons of South Shields enjoying a drink in The Garrick's Head.

Norman enjoyed a flutter on the horses and was scrutinising the racing page of *The Journal* newspaper when John said; 'Backed any winners lately Norman?'

Norman hesitated, but finally responded with; 'No not for weeks, but I think today could change all that John,' he replied.

'The last horse I bet on, ended up in a tube of Bostick,' quipped Stan.

Tom then suggested; 'When you consider the horse, it's a bloody thick animal. I mean think about this: A racehorse allows some midget dressed like a circus clown; climb onto its back, lash it with a whip and make it jump over fences for three bloody miles and what does it get in return? A nosebag full of hay.'

Norman, having chosen his equine performers, folded his paper; 'Tom that is a very interesting point you have so eloquently expressed, let's just consider the implications.'

'Oh, no here he goes again,' said Keith.

Norman gave Keith a look of disapproval and went on. 'The horse; what do we know about this animal?'

Malla joined the debate; 'Well, it has four legs, one in each corner. A long neck, big teeth and metal feet.'

Norman looked at Malla; 'I didn't realise you were an expert on the equine studies, have you been attending a college course on the subject Malla?'

'Now then Norman, sarcasm does not become you,' added Andy.

'Cheeky bastard,' replied Geordie.

Norman smiled; 'Come on what do we really know about the horse, what does history tell us about this odd-looking creature?'

Andy suggested that they can be very clever when he added; 'Well, what about Ed the talking horse on the tele.'

Stan looked at Andy; 'I don't believe you, it can't talk you idiot, and it's all special effects.'

THE HORSE

Andy would not be swayed; 'Ok, how do they make the horse move its gob to simulate the sound?'

Keith intervened; 'Andy, it is all done with clever camera work, the bloody horse can't talk.'

Norman steered the debate back to the original question, leaving Andy to ponder on Ed the talking horse; 'Let's examine the knowledge about the horse; it has been with us for thousands of years. It takes many forms; the shire horse, mule, donkey, pony and the zebra.

John joined in; 'Listen to this, I knew a lad that worked at the stables in Boldon. His girlfriend worked there as well and one day they decided to embark on some sexual activity in a stable. The horse was untethered and munching on a pile of hay. As the activity progressed to the missionary position, the horse manoeuvred itself with its arse over the two lovemakers and dropped a hefty turd on the pair of them.'

John laughed and added; 'The shite was all over his back and splashed her in the face, lovely.'

Norman joined in the laughter and added; 'John, trust you to come up with that little anecdote, but what does that tell us about the horse?'

'Don't hump in my stable,' said Stan.

Norman continued with his study of the horse and went on. 'Did you know that horse is still eaten in parts of Europe, in France it is considered a part of their 'stable diet' and is called *le cheval*.'

'Very funny,' quipped Keith.

John joined in the humour. 'These racehorses that go around the course with this dwarf on their backs and all of a sudden they think; bollocks I'm not going to jump over this and then hurl the jockey over the fence. Then the daft buggers still run until the race is over.'

Norman would not be put off and continued with his speculation of this much-maligned animal adding; 'Gentlemen, many of the great historical figures have used the horse not only as a mode of transport, but as a symbol of power. Think about Lady Godiva, who rode through Coventry buck-naked on a horse. Napoleon had a horse, the lone ranger had Silver. Harold Steptoe has Hercules; Roy Rodgers has Trigger and what about Muffin the Mule.'

'I thought that was illegal, bloody perverts,' said John.

A chorus of laughter ensued and Geordie joined in with; 'Dick Turpin had Black Bess.'

Geordie then said, 'Here is a question, and you have five minutes to answer. If you don't come up with the answer, you all chip in and get me a whisky; what is the name of Tonto's horse in *The Lone Ranger*?'

After some blank looks around the table, Tom moved the conversation on; 'Anyway, I read it somewhere that horses don't have a very big brain in relation to their body mass.'

'Thank you Tom, now we are getting somewhere,' replied Norman and he added; 'Look at the length of a horse's neck; I can only think that it must take ages for any horse to make a conscious decision. The time it must take for the information to travel the distance. Let's say it wants to lift its tail in order to have a crap, it could take up to three minutes for the message to arrive. Bear in mind that its bowels are closer to its brain in relative terms, it would suggest that all too often it shits on its tail.'

Geordie chirped up; 'Your times up lads, what's your answer?'

'Does anybody know?' I said.

The silence indicated that it was likely that Geordie would soon be enjoying his complimentary whisky. Then Tom shouted over to the barman; 'What's Tonto's horse called?'

The barman stood and contemplated the question and Geordie said; 'He won't know.'

'Scout,' shouted the barman and Geordie's face was a picture as he whispered 'bastard' under his breath. All present raised their glass to the barman and bowed to his superior knowledge.

'We forgot about *Champion the Wonder Horse*,' said Malla.

Keith provided another interesting point when he said; 'I believe it is still legal to marry a horse in some states in the USA.'

Andy was intrigued by this statement and added; 'Hang on a minute, how the hell can you marry a horse? You lot said that horses can't talk remember. So how the bloody hell is it going to say I do?'

'Ah well, what happens is that the vicar gets the horse to answer by stamping its foot, once for yes and twice for no,' said Tom.

Andy would have none of it; 'We are now talking a load of bollocks, time to change the subject.'

Norman wanted to maintain the theme of horses and asked for any ideas on this topic. 'What about them Greek fellas?' replied Keith.

'What Greek fellas?' I asked.

'Remember the Trojan Horse of Troy,' said Keith and he went on.

THE HORSE

'Them Trojans must have been thick buggers; they watched the Greeks build this giant wooden horse outside the city and see the Greek army walk away as if accepting that they were defeated. Then the idiots drag this wooden monstrosity into Troy claiming it as a sign of surrender. What happens next? Well, the Greeks have only filled the bloody great thing with thirty soldiers, who open the gates of Troy as the Trojan army sleeps and hello there, in sweeps the Greek army and kills the bloody lot of them.'

'Hence the saying. Beware of Greeks bearing gifts,' added Tom.

'Even Ed the talking horse would have worked that one out,' I added.

'We forgot the pantomime horse,' said Andy.

Geordie had a somewhat negative slant on this when he said; 'That's just one bloke sniffing the arse of another bloke.'

More laughter and then John introduced the zebra into the conversation; 'What about zebras then, they are not the full shilling are they? Listen to this, a zebra has moved away from the rest of the herd and it's grazing in a patch of tall grass. Then it spots a lioness stalking it some 200 yards away. Now the zebra knows it can outrun the lioness if it gets a head start. But it is a member of the horse family so it is educationally challenged. It thinks to itself; I will let it advance another 100 yards then I will leg it. Then it thinks, where is that big male lion with the crazy hair and thinks; it will be lying down somewhere it's a lazy sod. Now the lioness is only 100 yards away and the zebra says that's it I'm offski. Well, the zebra has done 20 yards and is chuckling away to itself thinking these lions are stupid, when bang! Lenny the male lion with the big hair, who has been lying in the tall grass behind the zebra pounces and clamps its jaws around the zebra's throat. Within seconds the lioness is joined by the rest of the pride and they begin to disembowel the zebra while it still breaths, thick as tar.'

'That's an interesting point,' replied Norman and added; 'However, you don't see zebra's jumping over fences with some circus clown on their back, do you?'

'Point taken, clever shite,' replied John.

Geordie felt the need to bring religion into the debate when he said; 'Jesus rode a donkey when he went to Jerusalem on Palm Sunday.'

'That's only because he missed the number 35 from Easington Lane,' joked Tom.

'Very funny, what about;

A horse, a horse, my kingdom for a horse.

Larry Oliver, *Henry V,*' replied Geordie.

'I think you mean Lawrence Olivier,' I said.

'Never mind that rubbish, I have got a great idea,' said John.

'For next week, why don't we each practice an animal impersonation and have it perfected and come back here at the same time and give a performance, it will be as funny as hell.'

'I am doing my hippo,' said Geordie.

'Alright you mindless idiots what are the rest of us doing,' replied Norman.

'I will do a wolf,' said Tom.

'I will do a crow,' added Andy.

'I am doing a chimpanzee,' said John.

'Ok, I am the sheep,' added Malla.

Norman considered the options; 'What animal are you doing Harry?'

'I will do an owl,' I said.

'This is lunacy, but I will do a chicken,' added Norman.

'Right Stan what member of the animal kingdom are you doing?' said Malla.

Stan considered the question and finally said; 'I will be the snake, it's easy anyway. I will just talk with a lisp,' he joked.

That left Keith and while not wishing to let the side down, he felt somewhat reluctant to volunteer and after a lot of verbal abuse he relented and chose the topic of the day, the horse.

The scene was set for the following week and this band of young animal impersonators left The Garrick's Head in reflective mood aided by a rendition of Geordie's splendid hippo at the waterhole.

One week later

The day had arrived and the nine animal impersonators duly assembled in The Garrick's Head. Andy was the last to arrive at 1.05 pm. Drinks were ordered at the bar and a table selected to maximise the acoustics of the lounge bar. Some good-humoured banter was exchanged with the barman on his knowledge of the lone ranger, much to the annoyance of Geordie and seats were taken in readiness for the performance.

THE HORSE

Norman opened the proceedings with; 'I do hope you have all perfected your chosen animal my good pals.'

'Oh yes, I have had my mother round the twist with my howling wolf,' replied Tom.

John suggested a sound check just to fine-tune the performance. Andy began with a very realistic crow. The barman gave us a puzzled look as John did his chimpanzee. Norman was a little concerned that the barman might react in a less than positive way and suggested that they should tread carefully; 'After we have done our demo, we should wait a short time before launching into the full symphony. At 2 pm the pub should be reasonably busy, so at exactly five minutes past, we all stand up and do our show.'

Agreement was reached and one by one each artiste gave a rendition of the chosen animal. The other customers present considered the side show to be just daft banter at this stage.

At five minutes past the hour Keith said; 'Right when the next person walks through the door, we do our thing.' We all nodded in agreement and waited. Then as the door swung open, we all stood and in unison did our thing.

A bloke standing only a few feet away got the shock of his life and dropped his pint. Norman slipped on his arse and got drenched as the beer cascaded up his leg. However, this was just the tip of the iceberg, there standing in the doorway was none other than the local copper, PC Jack 'the bastard' Brown. Sadly, John had as yet not noticed our esteemed law enforcer and carried on with his chimpanzee impersonation.

Jack made his way to our table and snarled at John; 'Hey you shut it or I will wring your neck.'

John did as he was told.

Jack looked over to the barman; 'This lot giving you any trouble?'

'Not until you walked in,' replied the barman.

Jack gave the barman a look of utter contempt, then the bloke who dropped his pint chirped up. 'I got such a shock, that I dropped my pint.'

Jack looked at the floor and managed to negotiate himself around the mess and approached the table. He was a formidable figure, standing about 6ft 4 in and with the build of a seagoing tug boat. He surveyed the scene in front of him, the pub was very quiet and you could have heard a pin drop when he said; 'Right you bunch of farmyard creatures, chip in and get this man two pints for his loss.'

'I would rather have a pint and a short,' replied our new drinking partner.

Money was collected and Tom said; 'I will go to the bar,' and our new drinking buddy accompanied him.

'Any more jungle noises from you lot and I will lift you for disturbing the peace, do you understand?' said Jack.

A sense of relief appeared on the faces of our farmyard thespians until Andy said; 'Will do Jack.'

The general impression was that this familiarity would not go down too well with our distinguished officer and it proved to be the case, when he looked at Andy; 'Oh, what animal were you impersonating, stupid?'

Andy now looked somewhat troubled and could feel the tension mounting, not least from his fellow performers. 'I was a crow,' replied Andy.

'Excellent, now stand on your chair and give us all an example of that fine bird the carrion crow. I also want you to flap your arms to give the performance that air of reality. I am sure all these nice people will be more than pleased to witness such a sight, do you agree?'

Andy nodded and climbed up on his chair and performed his flying crow. Jack made him stand there for at least two minutes, much to the amusement of all the other customers.

Meanwhile our new drinking buddy was at the bar with Tom collecting his pint and a shot of Bells. With a smug look on his face, he said to Tom; 'You lot should be on the stage; it leaves in ten minutes,' and he began to laugh.

Tom took the opportunity to give him a little advice; 'Is your dentist local?'

'Why do you ask?' he replied.

'Because if you are still in the pub when Jack has gone, you will be chasing your teeth across the bastard floor,' said Tom.

Back at the table Jack was supervising the cleaning and watching as Keith and Geordie cleared up all the broken glass and mopped up the beer on the floor. When all this was done Jack slowly walked to the bar and said to the barman; 'Have you checked the age of any of these customers? Because I wouldn't want you to lose your licence, especially as you're putting on such talented entertainment.'

'I know these to be of drinking age constable, they are just daft at times,' replied the barman.

Jack then walked out of the pub, closely followed by a man that was looking to avoid any dental treatment in the near future.

Back at the table Norman summed up the events of the last hour by saying; 'How about that for timing, the one person you don't want to walk in through that door, Jack 'the bastard,' Brown.'

John put the whole experience into perspective when he said; 'I have a sore throat; I am feeling a little 'hoarse.'

'Pervert,' I replied.

Andy returned to last week's debate on the horse and reflected on another animal, the giraffe. 'It must take about an hour for a giraffe to have a turd, their necks are about nine feet long.'

'Very observant Andy,' replied Norman.

Geordie then added; 'That's why horses can't sit down, because by the time the message from the brain gets to its muscles in its arse. It has forgotten what the message was.'

'Brilliant, you will make one hell of a zoologist Geordie,' I answered and everyone burst out laughing.

BISCUITS TO BOLIVIA

Another Saturday and eight of South Shields finest young men, our *dramatis personae* were gathered to chew the cud over their respective hopes and aspirations for the future. After the incident at The Garrick's Head, it was decided that an alternative venue should be used for the latest conclave. The Stags Head was chosen and the usual time of 1 pm was selected. John, Norman and I arrived first, closely followed by Geordie, Malla, Tom, Stan and Andy.

Andy asked Norman; 'Where is Keith?'

'With his girlfriend, he has gone to the flicks to see *Love Story*,' replied Norman.

Tom suggested that Keith was beholden to his latest squeeze when he said; 'Well he is definitely hen-pecked; he could be here really enjoying himself.'

John provided an argument to the contrary when he added; 'Have you seen his new bird, what a doll? She ticks all the boxes this one, the lucky bastard.'

Norman brought a touch of reality to the occasion by saying; 'Now my good chums, I am sure Keith has made the correct decision, bearing in mind what John has told us.'

I was having none of that; 'Hang on, we are basing this decision on the fact that John thinks she is gorgeous. This is a man that would sleep with a warm scarf.'

'Cheeky swine, but it's true you know,' replied John.

Laughter lightened up the atmosphere as we sat down in the window seat of the pub and Norman asked all present what they wanted to drink. A unanimous cry of Brown Ale from all present. Drinks were served and Norman joined his friends at the table in the bay window.

Tom then said; 'See that young lad at the bar with the manager, that's 'Bucknut' Bob.'

'Who the hell is Bucknut Bob?' I asked.

'That lad behind the bar,' said Stan.

'Funny bugger,' I replied.

Tom continued; 'He used to work in The Jester. He got the sack because he can't add up. So, all he does is pour the beer.'

'That's why the manager took my money at the bar,' added Norman.

Tom went on; 'Yes, he was always getting ripped off and he couldn't keep a record of who ordered what.'

John could see an opportunity and he said; 'We could be on to a winner here boys.'

'Not while the manager is around,' I replied.

The pub was starting to fill up and the conversation at the window seat revolved around the impromptu appearance of Jack the 'bastard' Brown the previous week.

'I hope that swine stays clear of us today,' said Stan.

'Oh yes, and if that bugger, who got the free drinks out of us comes in here, he will get a good punch in the gob,' added Tom.

Then the manager appeared to be putting his coat on and while doing so he seemed to be instructing Bob on the importance of recording the sales at the bar. John was taking a keen interest in this as Malla said; 'Next round of drinks.'

'Let me get these,' replied John.

'Are you in the money then?' said Stan.

'Just watch and learn, when I give you the nod Norman, come and collect the Brown Ale,' replied John.

John saw the possibility of saving money and possibly getting the drinks free. The manager was still engrossed in instructing Bob on how to record the sales when John approached the bar. John waited for the manager to leave before ordering the required beverages. 'Five bottles of Brown Ale please.'

Bob picked up his seating plan and marked five brown against the table in the bay window. Bob also had a list of prices and put five ticks against the bar chart giving him a grand total of £3 at 60p a bottle.

John asked Bob the cost of the drinks and Bob replied; 'That will be £3 please,' said Bob.

John then asked if the manager was going home?

'No, he is just off to Makro to get some spirits,' replied Bob.

Then John said; 'You know I can't really afford to pay for these drinks.'

Bob looked puzzled. John went on; 'It's Bob is it; you don't mind me calling you Bob, do you?'

'No that's fine,' replied Bob.

'My name is Geordie by the way,' John said quietly.

'Have you got the money then?' asked Bob as he removed the top from the last bottle.

'Oh yes,' replied John as he turned to give Norman the nod to collect the drinks, which he did and returned to the table.

As Norman regained his seat at the table with the rest of us, John commenced to relay to Bob his financial predicament.

'Well Bob, I have been saving money for my brother's operation.'

'Operation, what operation?' replied Bob.

Now John had his full attention and continued; 'I don't really want to talk about it, but you look like a caring person, so I will tell you. My brother had blood clots in both his arms and had to have them amputated. The thing is Bob; he had to go to Bolivia to have the operation.'

Bob looked surprised and asked; 'Bolivia where the hell is that?'

'South America.'

'Why.'

'Well Bob, there is a special hospital high up in the mountains, some 3,000 feet above sea level, where the air is very thin and this aids recovery.'

'Never in the world.'

'Oh yes but listen to this Bob; when they operated on my brother the lights and power were cut off and they had to switch to the emergency generator. Well, because of the poor lighting they put the false arms on the wrong way; left onto right and right onto left. Worse still, they also had the hands facing the wrong way.'

Bob had a look of amazement on his face; 'What happened and what caused the power cut anyway?'

'You won't believe this Bob, but a llama had chewed through the power cable and got electrocuted.'

'What's a llama?' asked Bob.

'It's like a small camel, without the humps.'

This was taking longer than it should but Bob was enthralled and John was expecting the next question to be 'what's a camel?'

But no, Bob had another question that was just as stupid; 'How did the llama get into the hospital?'

Andy shouted out; 'Are you going to join us John, our company not good enough for you?'

'I thought your name was Geordie,' said Bob.

'No that's my middle name, he is just taking the piss.'

John was conscious of the time now and wanted to wind this up and leave without paying and so he continued with his tragic tale.

'No Bob, the llama was outside the hospital and must have dug the cable up with its hoof and chewed through it.'

'What's going to happen now?' asked Bob.

Before John could answer, the phone at the end of the bar rang. Bob answered the phone and said; 'Yes, boss it's me, everything is fine. Alright see you in an hour,' and hung up.

Brilliant thought John, the manager will not be back for ages and he carried on; 'well my brothers back home now, but he has to go back in a months time, which is going to cost another £5,000.'

'Bloody hell, that's a lot of money,' replied Bob.

'Yes, it is, and to add to that my dad died three weeks ago, he got killed in the war.'

Again, a look of bewilderment on Bob's face. 'In the war, what war?' he asked.

'The Vietnam War.'

'They are yanks, aren't they?' asked Bob.

'Yes, but my dad was Vietnamese and he was fighting with the Viet Cong. He was born in North Vietnam.'

Bob was now totally confused, but tried not to look stupid; 'What does your mother do?'

Perfect, thought John a change of focus; 'She has a highly skilled job at Wright's Biscuits factory.'

'Is she a manager then?' asked Bob.

'Oh no, a much more important job than that Bob.'

John went onto explain the complexities of biscuit manufacturing; 'You know Rich Tea and Digestive biscuits Bob?" he nodded. "Well, my mother has the job of putting all the holes in them with a very fine prong, just before they go into the oven. But remember it has to be done very quickly, as they are on a massive conveyor belt and she does something like 200 a minute.'

'Christ that's incredible, have they not got a machine to do that?' asked Bob.

John was thinking how stupid this bloke is but carried on. 'No, they had one which they bought especially for the job, they tested against my mother and she even beat the machine. The machine could only do 150 a minute.'

'Your mother must be good then?' replied Bob.

John needed to enhance the problem of finance so he moved the conversation on; 'As I said Bob, we are struggling to get enough money to pay for the trip to Bolivia for my brother's operation. People have been very good and donated money and even Wright's Biscuits factory have had raffles to help generate cash for us. They even sent ten boxes of biscuits to Bolivia for the doctors and nurses at the hospital,'

'That's great,' said Bob.

The rest of us were now getting impatient and started to barrack John at the bar and Stan shouted; 'Come on, join your mates you ginger pisspot.'

John turned, smiled, and began to count the money he had taken from his pocket, taking particular care to count out the coins. It worked and Bob said; 'Look, you don't need to pay I will tell the boss about your brother Ronnie, it's fine.'

John took a long drink from his schooner of Brown Ale; 'That's very kind of you Bob, I appreciate that, but can I ask you not to mention it to the boss until we have gone, I am starting to get a little upset talking about it. I am starting to fill up.'

'Look, I will put the £3 in and get it later from the boss,' said Bob.

John returned to the table and his pals and Norman asked; 'What the hell have you been up to with Bamber Gascoigne at the bar?'

'Well, let me tell you that Bucknut Bob is as thick as a hod carriers sandwich, if brains were made of dominoes he would be knocking,' replied John.

'I told you he was stupid,' added Tom.

'Damn right, he adds another dimension to the word stupid, I just got a free round in boys and I would suggest that after we have had these drinks, we should move on.'

I sensed that all was not well; 'Have you been implicating us in one of your tall stories then John?'

'Let's just say it would be a wise move to vacate the premises before the manager returns, *veni, vidi, vici,*' John replied.

'Bollocks another pub we will have to stay clear of,' added Malla.

As we were finishing our drinks John asked; 'Hey Harry, where is Bolivia?'

'South America, why?' I replied.

'Well, I got that right anyway,' said John.

Geordie gave him a confused look as we left the pub and John shouted across to Bucknut Bob. 'Thanks Bob, I will bring some biscuits next time.'

Bob said; 'Thanks and I hope your brother's operation goes well in Bolivia.'

Stan looked at John; 'You don't have a brother.'

John had a wide grin on his face; 'No but Geordie has.'

Tom suggested the Station Hotel for their next libation and Andy said; 'Why don't we get something to eat at Dickson's on the way?'

So, we all piled into Dickson's and washed our faces with a saveloy dip and arrived at the Station Hotel ready for another bottle of the Broon Dog.

MONEY

Our band of revellers once again congregated for their weekly rendezvous to enter into a discourse on the topics of their adventures relating to the last seven days. After John's performance at the Stags Head, it was decided to choose yet another venue for this pow-wow.

Our band of revellers gathered at 1 pm, on a damp Saturday at The Grey Hen, an out-of-town boozer in the Harton area of South Shields.

John, Tom, Geordie, Andy, Malla, Stan, Keith and I were all present at the designated time, but as yet Norman had not appeared. Drinks were ordered at the bar and my seven associates and I took their places in the lounge. Andy was intrigued to see that Tom had broken from tradition and instead of his usual bottle of brown ale he had chosen to begin the session with a black velvet; 'Black velvet, that's a change Tom, what's the script?'

Tom took a long drink of the dark elixir; 'Well I am a little fragile after last night, I was in the Neptune Hotel with a bird and I was well-oiled. I can't remember taking her home.'

'I bet someone else took her home you daft swine, if you were that pissed,' quipped Malla.

Tom just gave Malla a look of contempt and continued; 'I can't remember walking out of the pub with her, but I definitely arrived with her. I have no recollection of what she was wearing,' he added.

'Well, that's the end of that relationship, she will give you the bullet after that mate,' said Geordie.

Stan joined the conversation and added; 'What the hell were you drinking to end up in that state?'

Tom sat back in his chair gathering his thoughts and said; 'I started on brown ale, but they ran out of it. So, then I started drinking Carlsberg Special and Barley Wine chasers.

John asked, 'Christ! What time was that?'

'8 pm,' replied Tom.

'What time did you leave the Neptune?' added Andy.

'No bloody idea,' Tom replied.

'I am surprised you could still walk after drinking that combination all night,' said Andy.

Keith saw the opportunity to put Tom to the test and asked; 'I bet you can't remember her name.'

'Whose name?' replied Tom.

'Your bird's name, you moron,' replied Keith.

'It's Maureen,' answered Tom.

John laughed, 'that's your mother's name you idiot.'

'Oh yes, her name is Margaret then,' replied Tom.

'Are you sure about that?' added Geordie.

John continued with his ridicule; 'Tell you what, why not ask the lad behind the bar what her name is, because he told me that he was in the bath with her the night before, scrubbing the coal dust off her back.'

Raucous laughter then ensued, at Tom's expense.

'Anyway, where is Norman?' asked Andy.

'Probably in the library, he works there on a Saturday morning remember,' said Geordie.

'Just to read the papers, the tight swine,' said Stan.

'No, he will be revising for his A-level English literature exam,' added Tom.

Right on cue, Norman appeared and walked to the bar where he was greeted by a rousing cheer from his drinking companions. He collected his bottle of broon and joined the conclave.

'Have you attended the library my dear fellow, to enhance ones standing in the literary world?' asked Andy.

'Indeed, my fine fellow, I have advanced my knowledge and understanding of the written word. An experience you would do well to contemplate if you are to make progress on this earth,' replied Norman.

'I gain all the wisdom I need from reading the *Fiesta* and the *Razzle*,' said John.

Norman looked at John; 'There we have it gentlemen, forget Keats, Wilde and Shakespeare and let us bury our faces in glossy magazines, revealing scantily clad females exposing their wares. Let us rise to the summit of greatness and enhance our wrist action and in doing so, somehow embellish our understanding of life.'

He continued; 'Tell me my bosom friends, what if any books have you read lately?'

The silence was deafening, until Andy answered; 'I have just recently read the *Beano* annual.'

Norman shook his head in despair and asked; 'What about you Tom?'

'This might surprise you, but I have just finished reading *Kipps* by H.G. Wells,' replied Tom.

'Excellent Tom,' added Norman.

'What's it about?' asked Andy.

'It's the story of a simple man who looks to better himself, after he inherits wealth,' answered Tom

'Sounds like that nugget in the Stags Head last week,' said John.

'What about you Malla?' asked Norman.

'The Highway Code, I am learning to drive,' he replied.

'Well, the British Literary Society can be secure in the knowledge that this group of intellectuals are doing our bit for literature in this backwater of the British Isles,' added Norman, with just a hint of sarcasm.

Then attention focused on a young couple entering the pub, making their way to the bar. 'Take a look at that bloke in the threads with the bird on his arm?' I said.

'It's Long John Silver, Harry,' joked Tom.

'He looks like an ironing board in a suit,' announced John.

'His bird is a bit of alright,' added Geordie.

'Money has just walked in the pub,' said Tom.

'Well, you must inform this auspicious gathering of the details surrounding the wealth that is now in our presence,' added Norman.

Tom continued; 'That long tall drink of water is the son of a local scrap metal merchant; he has more money than Soft Mick. He also has a couple of racehorses that train up at Morpeth.'

'What they training as, electricians?' joked Keith.

'Whose Soft Mick?' asked Stan.

Tom gave Stan a look of disgust and added; 'He drives an E-Type Jaguar; he is a right flash git and drinks in The Cottage in Cleadon Village.'

At that point, the tall drink of water acknowledged Tom's presence by waving in our direction.

'Are you a pal of his?' asked Andy.

'Not really, he is a friend of my uncle Bob,' replied Tom.

'His bird is sweet; her legs go up to her neck,' said Andy.

At that moment, she glanced across to our table, smiled and tossed her long blonde hair back over her shoulders. Andy was lost in her beauty; 'I would love to spend a little time with her boys.'

John took the opportunity to bring Andy back to the real world; 'For you to get close to any kind of sexual activity with anything as sweet as that, you would need to slip your member in a jar of your mother's lemon curd.'

More laughter from those gathered.

'What's his name then?' asked Geordie.

'Ben Mullen,' replied Tom.

Having collected their drinks Ben and his bird walked over to the testosterone fuelled table and pulled up a couple of chairs. 'Hi Tom, how is life treating you?' asked Ben.

'Very well thanks,' replied Tom.

Andy looked like he was suffering from an out-of-body experience, and he asked the girl her name. But before she could answer, Ben said; 'I must apologise fellas, this is Iris my girlfriend. I only know you Tom, are these guys your friends?'

Tom duly introduced all those present and added; 'This is our regular Saturday gathering.'

Norman moved the conversation on and asked Ben about his horse racing connections, in the hope of a tip for the afternoon meeting at Kempton Park.

'Well, I plan to put a few quid on the winner of the 2.30,' replied Ben with a wry smile.

Norman returned the smile and added; 'Have you placed money on it?'

'I have indeed, £30 to be precise,' replied Ben.

John said; 'Jesus Christ, that would keep me going for three weeks.'

Iris seemed to be a little uncomfortable sitting as close as she was to Andy. But Andy was now gaining confidence and slowly coming out of his spell and asked; 'What is your profession Iris?'

Iris shifted awkwardly in her chair; 'I work at Longbenton for the civil service.'

'Really, are you a colleague of Dave Smith then?' asked Andy.

'No, the name is not familiar, but it is a very big site you know,' she replied.

Norman continued pressing Ben for the name of the horse in the 2.30 at Kempton and finally the flash git relented and said; 'OK, put your money on Viva Campari.'

'Splendid, I am off to the betting shop,' said Norman.

Not to lose out Geordie, John, Andy, Keith, Malla, Stan and me asked Norman to put £1 win on for each of us. Tom did not commit himself to any further expenditure and declined the offer. Norman left for the betting shop.

Geordie then said; 'Viva Campari, that's a car is it not. My old man used to have a Vauxhall Vulva.'

Iris gave Geordie a look of disgust and explained what a vulva was, to the amusement of all present, Geordie laughed; 'That's why it was hard to climb into.'

Again, Iris gave Geordie a look of contempt and said to Ben; 'Should we go, I want to go to Newcastle to look for new clothes.'

'Yes, I think that is a wise move love and leave these guys to their little soiree,' replied Ben and they both rose to their feet and headed for the door.

As they were going out Ben turned and shouted; 'The best of luck with Viva Campari.'

Tom was less than impressed with Ben and said; 'Viva Campari my arse, flash git.'

Andy was still besotted with Iris and said; 'Iris, I would swim buck-naked through a river full of crocodiles and have my nuts heavily beaten by a cricket bat wielding deranged chimpanzee, if it meant that I could spend an hour in your presence.'

It was now 2 pm and Norman returned from the betting shop, with the news that Ben's hot tip was 20/1 in the betting.

'I could be £20 better off if it wins,' said John.

'Not exactly the favourite,' added Tom, with a touch of cynicism.

Andy was still dreaming of Iris; 'If you had shown a little more decorum Geordie, she would still be sitting here next to me, you useless git.'

Geordie brought Andy back down to earth; 'Andy, she is way out of your league mate, you have no chance with the likes of her, she follows the money that one.'

'Never mind that bollocks, your race will be on the telly in the bar any minute,' said Tom.

'Not for another ten minutes,' replied Norman.

Norman then sought to provide Andy with a degree of hope in relation to his aspirations on the fairer sex; 'Andy my friend, it must be said that you should never accept second best when you are searching for radiant beauty. Iris may well be out of reach at the moment, but fate may yet intervene in the game of love. Avoid the pain of a rebuttal in the stakes of love Andy, as the Bard once said;

> *A woman sometimes scorns what best contents her.*
> *Send her another; never give her o'er,*
> *For scorn at first makes after-love the move.*
> *If she does frown, tis not in hate of you;*
> *But rather to beget more love in you;*

'What tripe are you prattling on about now,' said Malla.

'Shakespeare my fine fellow, Shakespeare,' replied Norman.

'I will be glad when you pass that sodden A-level, then we will not have to put up with all this bullshit,' added John.

'*Nil desperandum* John, I will continue and start a degree course in literature at Newcastle University,' replied Norman.

Tom joined in the debate; 'Harry was at university you know Norman.'

'Is that a fact?' replied Norman.

'Yes indeed, he spent five years in a pickle jar,' answered Tom.

'Alright enough of that shite, let's transfer into the bar and watch the money roll in,' I replied.

'That's confidence for you,' said Andy.

So, Tom along with the rest of us trooped into the bar to watch the hot tip Viva Campari in the 2.30 at Kempton.

'Shit, I didn't know it was over the jumps,' said Keith.

'Yes, it is a hurdle race you fool,' replied Norman.

'How far is the race?' asked John.

'To the end,' quipped Geordie.

'It's a three-mile steeplechase,' replied Norman.

'How many horses are in the race?' added Andy.

'Twelve in the race; now shut your trap, they are under starters orders,' barked Norman.

'Don't like the look of our jockey, too shifty looking,' said Malla.

'There they go, start galloping Viva Campari,' shouted Geordie.

The bar was at fever pitch as the punters were glued to the TV screen. Viva Campari easily negotiated the first fence, then disaster. The hot tip pulled up at the second fence. 'What the hell is it doing? Jump over the bastard fence,' shouted Geordie.

'Watch your language,' said the barman.

'I have £1 on that bloody horse,' replied Geordie.

'I don't give a toss how much you have wasted on that nag, keep the language down,' the barman added.

'Look it's having a dump; I don't believe it. Why does the jockey not give it a lash of the whip,' shouted John.

With a look of resignation Norman said; 'That's it, it's not going to jump, money down the pan.'

'I had that £20 spent, the bastard,' said Andy.

'Flowers for Iris,' quipped Tom.

'Bollocks, it's your round for the beers Tom,' replied Andy.

The barman had a cheeky smile on his face; 'That lad that was in earlier with the blonde. Are you aware of who he is?'

'I know him, it's Ben Mullen,' replied Tom.

'Do you know his brother?' added the barman.

'No why, should I?' replied Tom.

'Oh yes, he owns the betting shop you lot have just wasted your money in.'

'The bastard, that means Ben the flash git gets added to the list for facial reconstruction,' said John.

Geordie reflected on another harsh lesson; 'Well, money is not everything, health, happiness and the love of a beautiful woman. Or, in Andy's case anything with a pulse; is much more important.'

Then Tom changed the focus of the conversation; 'I remember now, her name was Linda.'

'Who is Linda?' replied Stan.

'The lass I was out with last night,' said Tom.

'That's a hell of a difference from Margaret,' I said.

'Well boys, here we are once again contemplating our plight. Andy has fallen in love; Tom has saved himself £1 and his memory has returned and the rest of us have succeeded in making the local bookmaker a little richer,' concluded Norman.

'I am sure my old man had a Vauxhall Vulva,' said Geordie.

LOVE AND WAR

Two weeks after the sting at The Grey Hen, our band of intrepid socialites had once again agreed to muster at the Station Hotel for our regular confabulation on the respective personal events and the future of mankind. Keith was the first in the pub, anxious to avail himself of a pint of snakebite.

It was 1.30 pm and the resident barmaid Hilda had just served him with his pint, he lit a cigarette and turned to find a seat, when his partners in crime burst through the door. John, Tom, Andy, Geordie, Malla, Stan and me stumbled in laughing and Andy said; 'Tom has just spoilt a bus conductor's day, God it was funny.'

'Never mind that, Andy it's your shout, broon ale all round; please Hilda,' said John.

'What's happened?' replied Keith.

'Let's order the beers and sit down first,' said Tom.

Drinks were served and a table and chairs selected in the bay window. It was a wet December day in 1971, and today one member of the team would make a life-changing announcement.

'Well, what happened on the bus?' asked Keith.

'Tom, you will be stopped from using public transport after this mate,' replied Stan.

'Come on what the hell happened?' said Keith.

'Let me tell this one,' said John and he continued; 'We had all been to the Handy Shop in Frederick Street, looking at LPs and then jumped on the bus at Laygate. The gang boarded and paid the fare to Mile End Road, Tom was last to get on and he paid his fare in pennies and halfpennies. The conductor was not best pleased about this and said to Tom. 'You have nothing smaller than that, you swine?'

'Tom responded with. 'Are you for real mate? You can never win with you lot, if I had given you a £1 note you would have a right to be annoyed.'

The conductor then said, 'I have to count all this up at the end of my shift you nugget.'

So, Tom said, 'Listen here you bonehead, I could train a baboon to carry out this task and the chances are that he would be a better performer in the bedroom athletics with your wife as well.'

'What did he say to that?' replied Keith.

'He just looked at me and said I will remember you, cheeky swine,' said Tom.

'Tell Keith what you said after that Tom,' quipped John.

Tom continued; 'I said; if you need to know my details, in particular my physical dimensions, just ask your wife and her sister. They had me exhausted last Saturday night.'

Andy joined in; 'Some people on the bus thought it was hilarious, but the conductor was really pissed off and he went upstairs on the bus to collect more fares and cool off.'

Tom continued; 'Well if you are going to dish it out, you have to be able to take it as well.'

'Very true my son, very true,' I replied.

'What's the news, has anyone heard any scandal then?' asked Geordie.

'Never mind that where is Norman?' asked Keith.

Tom reminded Keith that Norman was ensconced in the public library; 'Now you know our 'man of letters' is studying all things Shakespeare, don't you?'

'Oh, yes I forgot,' replied Keith.

'He should be here soon, it's only a short walk from the library,' I replied.

Tom and Keith were discussing the sting at The Grey Hen the previous week when Norman walked in and acknowledged all those present with; 'Good afternoon my bosom chums, how are your bellies for spots?'

He then approached all those seated, smarting one hell of a black eye.

John said; 'Your little brother lamp you again Norman?'

Norman ignored the insult; 'I will give you the full story when I have purchased my beer.'

He turned and strode to the bar where Hilda poured him a pint of Guinness. On his return to the table, he sat and said; 'I dedicate this pint to William Shakespeare and unrequited love.' He raised his glass saying; 'A toast to the innocence of romance and the ignorance of faith.'

His peers were a little perplexed, but as ever with Norman, his comments heralded a quick rebuff and today was no exception as Tom said; 'Here we go, more verbal excrement.'

Norman was undeterred by Tom's rebuke and continued; 'This

black eye is not what it seems gentlemen; it is a love token.'

Geordie was a little more forthright when he commented; 'Tell the truth, you chatted up the wrong bird and the boyfriend clocked you one.'

Norman smiled and said; 'Geordie, one should have a little more faith in me, for have I not shown you the path to the love kingdom and its romantic delights?'

'Bollocks,' replied Geordie.

Norman continued; 'It all began last Sunday evening; I was enjoying a libation with a fellow student called Arthur in the County Hotel. As we stood and chatted, two fair maidens arrived.'

Andy chirped up; 'Maidens in the County, you are joking mate. The last bird I took home from that place was a sex maniac, she will be buried in a Y-shaped coffin.'

Hoots of laughter ensued, but Norman pressed on; 'They were two fine exhibits, my friends and I caught the eye of the smaller of the two. She responded with a very pleasant smile and I therefore introduced myself and asked her if she lived local. After chatting, I bought her a drink and the four of us sat at a table to continue the discourse. Arthur and her friend were chatty but I could see that there was very little attraction on either part, but it remained polite.'

'What's her name?' asked Malla.

'Her name is Laura and she is studying economics at Newcastle University,' replied Norman.

Another interruption, this time it was Geordie and he said; 'Well let's have her figure then, what are her measurements?'

'OK just to keep you interested I would say she was, 36-24-32 and very attractive with long black hair, standing about 5 ft 8 in.'

'Is she better looking than Iris?' added Andy.

'Ringo Starr is better looking than Iris,' joked Tom.

'Never mind that bull rot, proceed with the story,' said Keith.

Norman continued; 'We enjoyed each other's company and she agreed to see me the following Tuesday. I met her outside The Mariner, in Mortimer Road. She told me that she had just finished a relationship with another guy, who had turned out to be a real swine.'

'In what way?' said Malla.

'Well, he was caught stealing money from her dad's wallet, while it was on the kitchen table. Her old man threw him out of the house. She wouldn't tell me his name, but it all ended there. Anyway, we had a long chat and I walked her home to Stanhope Road. They have one of those huge, terraced houses opposite the West Park.'

'Did you take her in the park for a snog then,' quipped Stan.

'Oh no, this is the best bit. We arrived at her door and had a bit of a neck on. Then the front door flew open and her old man belted me right in the eye and I went flying, luckily I avoided the metal fence and fell in the garden.' I was sitting on my arse nursing my head and I heard her old man say, 'I told you never to darken this doorstep again, you thieving swine.'

Then it dawned on me and Laura shouted; 'Dad it's not him. I have only just met Norman.'

'He helped me up and was very apologetic, then he took me in the house and asked Laura's mother to bathe my eye. It was bloody sore and it started to close up. Her mother was not happy and give him a hell of a bollocking. But boys think of the brownie points I have accumulated.'

'You lucky git,' I said.

'What did your folks say when you got home?' added Keith.

They were in bed so they didn't see it until after college the next day, I just told them it happened playing football that afternoon,' replied Norman.

'Looks like you may have landed on your feet rather than your arse Norman,' added Andy.

Norman then took the opportunity to give us a cultured interpretation of this new aspect of his life; 'Here it is my learned friends, in the face of adversity I have triumphed. Let us not be bereft of compassion, but let us savour the outcome. For it might indeed lead to greater prospects for this honest Shields man.'

He then gave us all a quotation saying;

> *When the devout religion of mine eye*
> *Maintains such falsehood, then turns tears to fires;*
> *And these, who often drowned, could never die,*
> *Transparent heretics. Be burnt for liars!*
> *One fairer than my love! The all-seeing sun*
> *Ne'er saw her match since first the world begun*

'That was from *Romeo and Juliet* and it was Romeo's answer to

Benvolio's account of the fair Rosaline. Such is the power of the Bard that hope springs eternal even for you bunch of losers.'

'36-24-32 that sounds pretty impressive to me,' replied Andy.

Tom suggested that Norman was destined for greater things when he added; 'Norman, I think you are bound for a life in the theatre my son, to tread the boards and command the stage.'

'What's the script with you Keith?' said Tom.

'Boys, I have to enlighten you with earth-shattering news,' he added.

Curious looks around the table as Keith continued; 'I am joining the army.'

'For us or the enemy?' I asked.

'For us, daft bugger,' replied Keith and went on; 'I am joining the Royal Engineers as a junior leader and have signed up for three years. I start basic training in two weeks time at Catterick Garrison.'

'I bet they give you a catapult, oversized boots and two tins of bromide for your tea.' John added with a wry smile on his face.

Tom went on to tell us about his uncle Sid and his exploits during the war; 'When he was called up in 1940, he had to go to Catterick for his basic training. First, he had to undergo a medical check, along with the rest of his company. The medical officer had them lined up a dozen at a time and informed them to drop their trousers. The MO had an orderly and the company sergeant in attendance to maintain a level of discipline.

The MO said to the first bloke in the line; 'Cough'

The bloke said; 'No it's just a cold'

'The sergeant was not amused and said; 'No you idiot, you have to cough.'

'Then the MO carefully lifted his genitalia with what can be best described as a large wooden spatula.'

What for? asked Andy.

'Testing for hernias,' replied Tom.

'The MO then asked him to pull back his foreskin, to check for any sexual transmitted disease. The MO worked along the line to my uncle Sid who was the last to be examined. As the MO looked at my uncle Sid's todger, he said; 'Dear oh dear, what have we here? Your penis appears to be heavily swollen; can you pull back your foreskin for me, my good man?'

'Well, when my uncle Sid pulled back his foreskin, to the

amazement of all those present. Various items fell out including; a packet of cigarette papers, a box of Swan Vesta's and a pair of gold cufflinks.

The MO said, 'What are they doing there my good man?'

My uncle Sid said; 'You can't trust anybody these days sir.'

'The sergeant was not impressed; 'Pick this lot up you spineless moron and then get into the barracks, with the rest of these sad excuses for human beings.'

'His knob-end must have been sore with that lot hidden behind his muffler,' added Geordie.

'That is war, it's a dirty business indeed,' said Norman.

John brought the debate back down to reality; 'The army are not worth Moose shit; I'll take my chances with the Parks and Gardens Department.'

Norman chose the moment to evaluate the discussion and cogitate the tangible evidence; 'Love and war gentlemen, how they are such enemies to one another. Our dear friend Keith embarks on a challenging journey that is fraught with danger. Yet each of us has our own odyssey in which to navigate. I am at the station waiting for the love train to Laura and a mystic carnality, I so much desire.'

'Here comes more bilious baloney,' said Malla.

Norman as ever ignored this insult and carried on; 'You may pour scorn on my sentiments boys but I tell you this; *ecce homo, adsum primus inter pares*. For your information that can be loosely translated as; Behold the man, I am here and I am the first among equals.'

'First among arseholes,' joked John; 'Listen to this, I was at a wedding last Friday. A cousin of mine married his bird at Gateshead Registry Office, it was a shotgun job. She was six months gone. Just married and it sticks out a mile.'

Vociferous laughter all round and John continued; 'My cousin's name is Bob Burn and the bird he married is called Nichole Tracey Wood. I was sitting in the registry office and started to think.'

'Steady John, you know the doctor said that could be dangerous for a man in your condition,' added Norman.

'Shite off Norman,' he replied and went on; 'Well, her name is Nichole; get it! Nee coal tee burn (nee Wood) either.'

Norman took the opportunity to give all those present a hypothesis regarding John's witticism; 'The human mind is a cornucopia of emotions and extrasensory thoughts and yet again John has not disappointed us. He truly is an enigma, sometimes lewd, radical but never despondent. He is *bel esprit;* a man of wit and he is ours to cherish. So, to you dear John I say this, it's your turn for the beers.'

Andy had been contemplating the recent gathering at The Garrick's Head and the topic of horses and said; 'Do horses lay eggs?'

The rest of the team looked at Andy with a sense of bewilderment and Tom replied; 'Are you for real Andy? Horses don't lay eggs you plonker.'

Andy would not be swayed and said; 'What about Pegasus, that was a flying horse and birds fly and lay eggs.'

Amid all the disparaging laughter and ridicule, I responded with; 'Andy, Pegasus was the Winged Horse from Greek mythology, it didn't actually exist. You really must stop smoking banana skins.'

THE SHAPE OF THINGS TO COME

It was a miserable wet Saturday in December 1971, and I was sat with my friends in the Station Hotel on Mile End Road in South Shields. Me and my eight pals had convened for another convivial soiree. The clock above the bar indicated that it was 1 pm and we had all furnished ourselves with our libations. Geordie was providing us with a resumé of his duties as an apprentice plumber working for a local ship repairer called Brigham & Cowan and added; 'Working as a plumber in a shipyard was like being a shepherd in charge of a submarine.'

He felt his skills were not fully utilised and he was considering a career change. John offered some dubious advice; 'Now just think about it you docile idiot, when you have served your time and you start your own business; you will have all those lonely housewives begging for your services.'

A wry smile appeared on Geordie's face and he replied; 'Is that all you think about John?'

'Oh yes, I can imagine that you will have loads of boilers to service,' joked Tom.

Norman created a compromise and spoke of an alternative course of action saying; 'Sound men of Shields, do not despair, for I have a great plan that will bring untold riches beyond your wildest dreams.'

'Bollock's here he goes again,' moaned Geordie.

Norman would not be deterred and continued; 'Dear friends, we are gathered here today reflecting on our lives and contemplating on our opportunities for the future. I have considered much having sat here and listened to Geordie's discourse. I believe nirvana is just around the corner.'

'That's the Mile End Club, you bonehead,' said Tom.

Norman just gave Tom a look of desperation and went on; 'You may not realise the importance of this morphology, but hear this my fine fellows; I Norman Kennedy claim this moment in time as a gateway of opportunity.'

'What the hell are you chuntering on about Norman?' I replied.

'I will knock him out if he doesn't shut his trap,' added John.

Norman was not discouraged by the threat of violence and carried on, saying; 'We are all artisans in a number of bespoke disciplines is that not so? Why not set up our own organisation and project ourselves onto the world stage.'

'You should be on the stage, sweeping it Norman,' joked Keith.

'How the hell, does that work out?' asked Stan.

'Listen carefully Stan and give your somewhat limited brain the chance to soak up this information,' he replied.

'What the hell are you prattling on about Norman?' asked John.

'Well, in our midst we have a plumber, a plater, an electrician, a welder, a sheet metalworker, a gardener and a man of letters,' he replied.

'A man of letters, who would that be then?' asked Malla.

'John has loads of French letters,' joked Andy.

That raised the hilarity within our little band of miscreants, but Norman pressed on and added; 'Gentlemen, this august body has a cornucopia of talents at our disposal and I believe we must explore all avenues to realise our dream.'

'Hang on Norman, this is your misguided attempt to convince us that there is a future in your dream. Go and boil your head,' added Andy.

Tom decided to change the subject and he enlightened us on a recent event; 'I was standing at the bus stop in Fowler Street on Thursday night and this bloke with a boxer dog stopped and lit a cigarette. I asked him, 'does your dog bite?'

'No,' he replied.

'So, I bent down to stroke it and the bastard bit me.'

'The bloke or the dog,' joked Stan.

'Very funny, the dog you daft sod,' countered Tom.

'I thought your dog didn't bite,' I said.

'It's not my dog,' he replied.

Laughter ensued and Hilda the resident barmaid walked over to our tables and collected the empty glasses. Norman couldn't resist a comment; 'Here she is, the lovely Hilda; how are you, my darling?'

'Hello gorgeous,' added Geordie.

The greetings fell on deaf ears and she gave both suitors a look of derision. She did, however, offer Geordie some advice regarding his current hairstyle; 'It's about time you had your hair cut, you look like a raggy mat.'

Norman then attempted to woo Hilda with his romantic repartee; 'Oh Hilda, my luscious beauty. Join me and let us run along a deserted beach on a far-flung tropical island. We will fall in the warm sand and make mad passionate love. You must not fail me now my love, it is our destiny. What say you, my Juliet? Romeo doth fall at your feet.'

Hilda's response was typical but also humorous; 'When you were born, instead of slapping your arse, the midwife should have slapped your mother.'

More laughter at Norman's expense. Hilda although older than us, had something about her. She had a great figure and a smouldering demeanour of sexuality that was very sensual. This was enough for Norman to carry on with his romantic excursion; 'I have travelled across the wet wasteland of despair, mile after mile, just so I can cast mine eyes over your voluptuous body, my sweet marigold. Take my hand and off we shall go to spend endless nights in each other's arms. I will give you gold and the trappings of a princess, if you will join me on this quest for love.'

Hilda looked at Norman and stated; 'That rubbish does nowt for me son.'

'Well, God loves a trier,' replied Norman.

Malla asked Hilda for a further round of drinks and she walked off to the bar with the empty glasses. She knew damn well that every one of us watched her return to the bar with her arse oscillating in her black pencil skirt. Andy asked what the plan was for tonight and agreement was reached to meet at the Top Club at 7.30 pm for a couple of pints. From there we would go to Newcastle for further refreshment on the Quayside.

'Sounds like a splendid idea, but I bet we will all be walking home again. I don't know how many times that last bus from Worswick Street has gone without us on board,' added Stan.

Andy provided another joke before we departed the Station; 'This bloke who lives round the corner often sent his wife out on the street to make some extra cash around the docks selling her wares.'

'On the game, prostitution?' asked Tom.

'Yes Tom, they have five kids and he is on the dole. Anyway, she plied her trade on Saturday night and returned home with £12.50p. The husband was surprised and said; who gave you 50p? She replied, all of them.'

Hilda who was stacking glasses, laughed out loud and said; 'Now that is funny, which is rare for you lot.'

Keith expressed his confusion regarding the change to decimalisation earlier in the year saying; 'I can't get used to this coinage 50p, 10p and things have rocketed in price because of the change.'

'To quote Bob Dylan, *the times are a changing* my good fellow,' replied Norman.

THE EYES HAVE IT

There have been many books written about the language of humour, but when you are in the company of friends and situations arise without any prompting, then laughter is guaranteed. Sometimes hilarity is a result of a simple misunderstanding or a particularly funny joke or experience.

This story reflects on a situation that occurred one night in 1971, in The New Crown Hotel in South Shields. It was a Friday night in December and our little band of pals were sat discussing all manner of things while enjoying various alcoholic libations. The group consisted of Stan, John, Tom, Geordie, our resident literary scholar Norman and me.

We had moved onto health issues and Geordie was describing a delicate topic; his recent torrid time involving his bowels. It all revolved around his over-indulgence with regard to his mother's pea soup. On Tuesday evening, he enjoyed two very large bowls of the elixir along with the requisite suet dumplings, of which he had three.

Everything seemed fine until he got on the bus to go to work the next morning at 7.15 am.

Geordie then began his discourse; 'I got on the bus, which was quite full with seating limited. As I walked to the back, I felt an urge to fart. I thought the bus was full and as long as I dropped a silent one, I would not be singled out as the perpetrator. Just as I sat on the one remaining seat it happened. It wasn't silent and even worse, 'I followed through'. The smell was overpowering. My first thought was what if the torrent of turd moves north and makes its escape from my shirt collar? Thankfully gravity played an important part and the brown surge went south. The bloke I sat next to begin to wretch as if he was going to throw up. There were sniggers from some of the passengers at the front of the bus and I turned to the bloke next to me and said; 'that's my mother's pea soup,' and smiled.

His reply was quite funny, 'Jesus Christ, if I were you, I would tell her to get in touch with the Ministry of Defence and offer her services to the Chemical Weapons Division.'

Geordie continued; 'Well, the only consolation was that I had my overalls on, so there was a level of containment in relation to the movement of the shite in a southerly direction. I knew a few people on the bus and sadly, some of the women. One in particular, Helen Smith, a civil servant who worked at Wouldhave House.'

I always fancied her and I now suspected that I had gone down in her estimation as a possible boyfriend. As I got off the bus, I heard someone say;' 'I bet his underpants are like a corduroy cap.'

'I ignored the quip and made haste to the public toilets in the Market Square.'

'Having removed my overalls and jeans I began to remove the offending substance as best I could and sat on the pot, then flushed the toilet to remove any carlings and bean skins still attached. My undercrackers went in the bin, but my jeans were not too heavily soiled and I managed to remove any residue that had seeped through. I made my way to work, clocked in and thought at least none of my workmates at Brigham's knew what had happened.

Boy was I wrong; unknown to me a girl in the office had been sitting behind me and the news of my 'turdfest' had quickly circulated. This became very apparent when I entered the canteen at 10.30 am. I was given a raucous reception as those present shouted various comments including:

> *Here comes Strangely Brown*
> *Give him a seat by the window*
> *A bus in the Market Square has been quarantined*
> *Give him a cork*

This continued for a short period until the laughter subsided and I sat down to eat my sandwiches. Then one of the canteen staff brought me a toilet roll, 'You might need this love,' then she walked away laughing.'

Stan then spoke, 'I'm glad you mentioned it, because I was going to anyway, it was the talk of my place and I knew it had to be you on that bus.'

We all had a good chuckle at Geordie's impromptu evacuation and continued our debate about health issues. John brought up the subject of his eyesight and his recent visit to the optician. Norman was surprised at this statement; 'I didn't know you wore glasses John.'

John replied, 'I don't, you knucklehead.'

Norman responded in his usual imitable way; 'John, one has to appreciate that intelligence is often nurtured and you my good friend have not yet had the benefits of this phenomenon. Let me expand on that theme for you by saying; Experiences that are multi-sensory, dramatic, unusual or emotionally strong are remembered for longer and in more detail than normal mundane experiences.'

John looked perplexed by this comment; 'What the hell are you talking about, that sounds a lot of bollocks to me.'

Norman continued; 'Well, it is a known scientific fact that we remember fifty per cent of what we see and hear and therefore you will all take your intelligence to a higher plain by contemplating my discourse.'

Norman sat and waited for a response, but nothing of any great intellect was forthcoming, as we sat and looked in utter disbelief at our drinking buddy. Then Stan broke the silence by saying; 'Geordie, do your hippopotamus impression.'

He duly obliged and gave us a fine rendition to the amazement of the other customers in the pub.

Norman stood and addressed all those present; 'That was truly awe-inspiring and I must ask all those present to join me in a round of applause for our friend the Right Honourable Mr Geordie Pugsley Snott for that incredible performance.'

Most of those present just gave us a look of disdain, but one or two saw the funny side of it and joined in the applause.

Back to John's story about the optician, he continued; 'The optician is ready in room 2, if you would come with me please. So, I followed the receptionist into the room where the optician was sitting at his desk. Come in and sit-down Mr Telford, I will be with you shortly.

Both me and the assistant sat down. After a few minutes, he turned and asked. Well have you ever had your eyes tested before Mr Telford? I then thought I would inject a little humour into the proceedings; No, but I have had them blacked a few times. This did not have the desired effect and the optician looked at his assistant with a wry smile. He must have thought I have a right idiot here.'

He would be right on that score,' I uttered.

John continued: 'Anyway, I am going to ask you some questions regarding your medical history, is that OK? Yep that's fine, but don't mention the war, I replied. Another strange look, he had no sense of humour this bloke. He was a queer-looking fellow, he reminded me of Lurch from the Adams Family. He then began the inquisition.

'Have you any medical conditions? he asked. What do you mean conditions? I replied. Well things like diabetes, asthma, epilepsy etc.

No, but I had a boil on my nose two weeks ago and boy it was a big one. I thought I can't go to get my eyes tested because I won't be able to see properly. Anyway, are boils contagious? Because my girlfriend had one on her arse around the same time. The assistant looked totally lost at this point and left her seat to set up the apparatus. The optician then said; No, they are not contagious and you have no medical problems at present, is that correct? Yes I replied.

Can you sit in this chair and look at the chart on the wall in front of you? I did as I was told. Then he asked me to read the chart from left to, right? OK doc, I replied. I am not a Doctor Mr Telford; I am an optician. Oh, yes, and I stood up and walked over to the chart on the wall and began to read it.

No, no, no, you must try and read it from the chair. Ah oh yes sorry about that, mind that will take some reading it doesn't make sense. It looks like a foreign language to me and the letters are all spaced out.' I replied.

'You're spaced out, you retard,' stated Geordie.

Tom then added, 'I can't believe you said that, were you drunk?'

'No, I was as sober as a judge,' John replied.

Norman then spoke for all of us when he declared; 'John, why should we be surprised, you possess a fundamental lack of reality at times and it is a measure of your determination that you have enhanced this characteristic over the years.'

John poured scorn on this assassination of his character and continued; 'Well I managed the eyesight challenge and I do not need specs, but the optician did give me a handwritten note.'

'What was on it?' asked Tom.

'It read, Mr B. N. Busby-Hyde. MBE. DCM. Psychiatrist,' replied John.

'Enough said,' added Stan.

Laughter ensued for a short while and then it was our esteemed literary genius Norman's turn to regal us with a medical story. Norman had to inject some philosophical content into the occasion and began with an oration on the wellbeing of one's mind. He went on; 'Is it not the case dear friends that our perception of good health is reflected in our physical wellbeing? We assume that because we feel fit and healthy, we then deduce that we are in peak condition. But are we? I now give you a salutary lesson in the misconceptions of good health. My uncle

Bob fought in World War Two. He was a tank commander and served in North Africa and Italy. He survived some close shaves during his service and managed to escape from a burning Valentine tank at Tobruk.'

'Where's Tobruk?' Tom asked.

'Just north of Consett,' replied Geordie.

Norman gave Tom a look of disgust and carried on. 'Tobruk is in North Africa, Libya to be exact. Anyway, he left the army after the war and returned to his civilian job as a civil servant in London.'

John could not resist another pearl of wisdom and asked; 'Does that mean he was a very well-mannered waiter?'

'God, you are a fool,' replied Norman.

Geordie then stated; 'I'm enjoying this so shut the hell up the lot of you.'

Norman continued; 'After a number of years working in the Foreign Office, he began to relive some of the trauma he had experienced during the war. At first, he started to relive the various events he encountered as a tank commander. These momentary lapses first began at home, generally at night when he was asleep. My aunt Martha would have to calm him and bring him back to reality. It was often called shellshock, a term used during World War One.

As time went on these apparitions increased in regularity and began to occur during the day. My uncle Bob was a big man and not easily dissuaded, when in a determined mood. One day he arrived at work and completely lost it. He ran into the building and began shouting;

> *Get clear of the tank, we are getting pounded with incoming mortars, we have a full fuel tank on board.*

Then he dived under a colleague's desk and using an imaginary walkie-talkie asked for air cover. His boss had him removed from the building and this resulted in him being sectioned under the mental health act. He never recovered and spent the rest of his life in a Veterans Mental Hospital in Folkestone. I only ever saw him once, when my aunt took me to see him at the hospital in 1968. He had no recollection of who anybody was and during my brief visit he called one of the nurses, Fritz the Twat. So, there we have it gentlemen, a man who served king and country, who returned home to the bosom of his loving wife, only to be institutionalised for the remainder of his life.'

We all sat trying to imagine what that was like and then Geordie spoke; 'I bet the grub was good in that hospital though.'

Stan looked at Geordie; 'You brainless goon, you will have to be careful or you will be locked up under the mental health act if you don't improve that impersonation of a hippopotamus.'

At which point Geordie duly repeated his earlier performance with renewed vigour, only to upset the barmaid who responded by saying; 'Hey you, shut your trap you are frightening customers.'

Norman then suggested to the barmaid that she need be fearful of Geordie's state of mind; 'Take great care my good woman, you are dealing with a man in a state of great turmoil.'

John then added; 'Yes, if brains were made of leather, he would not have enough to make a pair of spats for a canary.'

'What are spats?' replied Geordie.

FAMILY VALUES

It was a damp misty day, one of those days when it could be any time of the day. It was 12.30 pm and meals were being served to expectant customers in the Ship & Royal, in South Shields. This venue was a change from previous hostelries and was in some respects up market for our band of brothers.

This was not lost on Andy when we all walked through the door; 'It's not cheap in here and you can't get Brown Ale.'

Andy's response was not a positive one. 'I'm bloody skint this week, I had to give my mother extra because my old man only managed two days of fishing last week. They couldn't get the boat out because of bad weather.'

'Such is the life of a fisherman Andy, but don't panic the boys will see you alright today mate,' stated Geordie.

'Who is turning out today then?' I asked.

'Well Norman, Tom and John should be here soon and I think Malla is making an appearance,' answered Andy.

Five minutes later Norman came in carrying a number of books. 'Good afternoon and how are you mindless morons today,' he quipped.

'Very well thanks,' responded Geordie.

Norman continued; 'Where are Ying and Yang,' referring to Tom and John.

'Should be here soon and Malla is turning out,' replied Andy.

Geordie tried to shed some light on the possibility of Malla's presence, when he declared; 'I think Malla and his squeeze have split up, a little bird tipped me the wink last night on the bus.'

'Which little bird would that be then?' asked Norman.

'His sister,' revealed Geordie.

Another five minutes went by and then the two absent protagonists duly arrived to a chorus of cheers from their peers. Tom and John collected their drinks and joined their pals. 'We expect Malla to turn out today,' said Norman.

'Is he not out with his bird then?' asked John.

'It appears that is history now, or so we are led to believe,' stated Norman.

Andy changed the focus of the conversation and asked Norman what were the books he had in his possession?

FAMILY VALUES

Norman took a long drink of Guinness from his glass. 'Well gentlemen, as part of my A-level studies, I have to read a selection of books and therefore experience a range of writing styles.'

'Just tell us what the sodden books are called you dweeb,' interrupted John.

'You buggers need some culture and a sense of purpose in your lives. Anyway, the books you enquire about John are, *The Island of Sheep* by John Buchan, *Seven Men at Daybreak* by Alan Burgess and *A Farewell to Arms* by Ernest Hemingway. In addition, I also need to read *Hamlet* by Shakespeare.'

'Didn't John Buchan write *The Thirty-Nine Steps?*' Stan replied.

'Yes, he did Stan, well done. At least someone in this company has some knowledge of the literary world,' answered Norman.

'I saw the film with that fella Robert Doughnut in it,' added Geordie.

'That would be Robert Donat, Geordie,' stated Norman with a shake of his head.

'Now then, don't be so condescending Norman, we are not all as knowledgeable as your good self in this field remember,' quipped Tom.

'Come on then, give us some *Hamlet*,' I suggested.

'Alright, how about this!'

You are welcome masters; welcome, all.
I am glad to see thee well.
Welcome, good friends.
O my old friend!
Why thy face is valanced since I saw thee last.

'What the hell is all that about and what is valanced?' asked Stan.

Norman could not resist another jibe at his peers, 'Albert Einstein once wrote:

The difference between stupidity and genius is that genius has its limits.

The term valanced refers to Shakespeare's reference to your hairy face Stan.'

'I think Norman has just indicated that he thinks that we are all a bunch of pisspots,' added Andy.

Then Malla entered the room and made his way to the table where insults were still being exchanged regarding the general level of intelligence present.

'What's all this about?' he questioned.

'Norman is winding some of us up, but I have not taken the bait. How are you, not seen you for a few weeks mate,' replied Tom.

'What's the script with you?' asked John.

'Well, I'm a single man again John, I got the old 'heave-ho' from Jane last week and I am back on the market,' replied Malla.

'Take a break and save your money, the laughs are better anyway,' I suggested.

'Sounds like a good idea Harry, anyone want a drink?' asked Malla.

'I'll have a pint of lager if you're buying,' answered Geordie as he shot Andy a knowing glance.

Malla made his way to the bar and Andy shouted, 'Anyone for salted peanuts, I'm buying.'

John gave Andy a curious look. 'Have you won the pools then Andy?'

His response was quick and decisive, 'That's a no then John, cheeky sod.'

Malla joined his pals and explained the break up of his relationship with Jane, sighting a difference of opinion on some important issues related to families. Malla had great reservations about the influence of Jane's mother on their courtship. While understanding that her mother had Jane's best interests at heart, being the oldest daughter and without a father on the scene. He still felt that Jane could not let go of the apron strings and accept him in a long-term relationship.

This led to some questions from his little band of chums and Stan asked; 'Where is the father then?'

'He is serving ten years at Durham for GBH, but her mother is not having him back and she has applied for a divorce,' replied Malla.

'Who did he hospitalise then?' asked Tom.

'Some guy in a pub in Camden, London, apparently over an illegal card game' replied Malla.

'How is he in Durham then, instead of Wormwood Scrubs?' probed Tom.

'He asked for special dispensation, to be near his family. However, nobody goes to see him,' added Malla.

'Well, the world's your oyster now mate,' quipped Tom.

John took the opportunity to propose a toast and raising his glass, 'To all of us, to Malla and let's not forget Keith who has joined the boys in khaki in the defence of the realm. Let us stand and toast the future.'

As one we rose and lifted our glasses, to the surprise of a few customers standing at the bar. Norman began to endorse the virtues of a strong family and declared; 'I think we can count ourselves fortunate that each of us have good sound parents and guardians at home, who cocoon us against the dangers and troubles of the world.'

Tom decided to lighten up the proceedings with some humour; 'I knew a lad at school who had a girlfriend, we called him the 'Pilgrim', because every time he took her out, he made a little progress.'

That raised a collective laugh around the table and Norman added his take on love when he spoke; 'Love, is a temporary insanity, curable by marriage.'

John took the opportunity to add his own brand of humour; 'A tramp was caught trying to sneak on board an ocean-going liner, which was about to set sail on a three-day trip to the Bahamas. He was caught by the purser, who threw him off the ship telling him, beggars can't be cruisers.'

'Anyway, I wonder how Keith is doing in Catterick?' asked Andy.

'I heard from his brother that he has joined a special top-secret unit the S.U.A.C.' suggested Tom.

'What the hell does that stand for?' probed Geordie.

'The Special Underwater Archery Corps,' replied Tom, who then burst into laughter.

John then rose and stated; 'Well I need to go and drop the boys off at the pool dear friends, I may be some time.' He then departed to the toilet.

Norman could not resist a comment in relation to John's forthcoming evacuation and added; 'John has this fascination for the long cabin, I wonder if he has a fetish for this primeval abhorrent activity.'

'I think he stockpiles it, so he doesn't inflict the torture on the rest of the household,' suggested Tom.

'Can we change the subject now please? It's turning my beer flat:' I replied.

'Damn right Harry,' and Geordie steered the conversation back onto things romantic and asked; 'Right Stan this new bird, are we going to get to meet her then?'

Stan's reply was somewhat predictable when he reacted; 'You must be joking, can you imagine an economics graduate with so much inherent beauty sitting down with you bunch of insensitive despots and being exposed to nonsensical claptrap.'

'Well, well Stan, these are your soulmates my son. I do think one is being a little vitriolic toward this friendly gathering, you cheeky swine,' replied Tom.

'Here here,' answered Andy.

Then John returned from his visit to the toilet and stated; 'By Christ, that was a ten sticker and it took no persuading, phew it was hell in there.'

Norman looked around the table; 'There you go, I rest my case.'

'Yip, Norman has a point you know,' added Tom.

This time it was Malla that steered the direction of the discussion back onto romance. 'You know a woman is like a piano, if she's not upright she's grand.'

Laughter in abundance now and Andy joined the debate with; 'I guess this new bird Michelle stirs your blood, does she Stan?'

'Yes, you could say that Andy, she ticks all the boxes mate,' replied Stan.

Geordie felt the need to add his own little bit of repartee and sang the praises of an ex-girlfriend and informed all those present that she was well-endowed in the top bollocks department; 'She had nipples like fighter pilot's thumbs.'

This created much hilarity and a call from the barmaid who shouted; 'Keep the noise down you lot; you'll put folks off coming in.'

Just when everyone had settled down and the general mood was one of harmony. John decides to impose a less than pleasing realisation to the proceedings by saying; 'I'm suffering a bit here boys; my arse is putting like a Marmite sandwich.'

Another round of drinks was ordered at the bar and Geordie managed to elicit a pint out of Tom, who had been put in the picture with regards to Andy's financial plight by Geordie.

Malla leaned back in his chair, lit a cigarette and with a look of satisfaction declared; 'This is the life boys, a single man again with the world at my feet.'

'Hang on a minute, you're in the Ship & Royal in Shields on a lousy damp day in December, hardly the Bahamas,' replied Tom.

'Think positive Tom, think positive my son,' he countered.

Then the doors swung open and a particularly good-looking blonde strolled in, closely followed by what can be best described as an abomination. It was in fact a male member of the species, but had it not been for the sharp suit and Italian shoes you would have assumed he had escaped from the *Island of Dr Moreau*. He truly was ugly and had a face that resembled a wedding cake that had been left out in the rain.

Andy was the first to make comment; 'He's got the sort of face that makes you think God had a sense of humour.'

John added his take on this apparition; 'What the hell does she see in him? He's got a face like a pig.'

'That is an insult to bacon John;' I responded.

Norman stated the obvious; 'He will have money my friends and no doubt a big portfolio.'

'I have never heard it called that before;' stated John.

'My cousin Barry knew a bloke that used to jam his portfolio in the door to enhance his dimensions and keep his wife happy,' revealed Malla.

'He did what?' asked Stan.

'Was it the front or the back door?' probed Tom.

'The back door, it was heavier,' replied Malla.

'Get out-of-town, I'm not having that,' said John.

'Oh, yes it's true, he used to go to the doctor for painkillers, but would take nothing for the swelling,' added Malla.

'Well, that pug-ugly specimen has been getting his head jammed in the door as well, judging by the size of his swede,' quipped Norman.

'It's your turn at the bar John, and you can find out what this hideous bloke is doing with that blonde stunner while you're there,' stated Andy.

'I haven't seen you at the bar yet Andy.'

'Yip, I had to give my mother extra this week,' he said in a despondent tone.

'Fish not biting this week then,' suggested Tom.

'Nope, the weather has been shocking, heavy sea and storms all week,' he replied.

'You are good for credit with us, no need to worry, Norman's in the money these days anyway,' I added.

Norman was a little perplexed by my statement that he had

somehow acquired a healthy bank balance; 'What gives you that impression Harry?'

'Well, I heard about your little bit of luck during the week, another little bird told me you won £53 on the horses,' I replied.

'Who gave you that piece of fiction then?' asked Norman.

'Your mother, during our pleasant conversation on the number 32 bus to the Pier Head,' I added.

'Bollocks, you can't even trust your own mother these days. Anyway, I spent it on a night out with Laura,' answered Norman with just a tad too much conviction.

'My word this new chick has expensive tastes,' stated Tom.

'No no no, you can't spend £53 in one night in Shields, I don't care who you are with. That's utter bullshit, come on get us all a whisky chaser you tight sod,' suggested John.

'Alright it's a fair cop, I can't lie and I'll get the whisky in, if you buy the crisps, you nauseating little tick,' replied Norman.

'Make sure they are Tudor,' shouted Andy as John made his way to the bar with Norman. John and Norman stood at the bar and ordered the whisky and crisps. The blonde was only a few feet away and her grotesque male companion was in the process of paying for their drinks, when she turned to John and stated; 'It's not very classy coming out with your brother, is it?'

John's response created a little confusion when he replied; 'Oh, no this is not my brother, he is just a friend; but you are dead right, he is not classy at all.'

Norman shook his head in disbelief at this tactical error and answered; I think this lovely young lady is referring to the gentleman by her side John not us.'

John gave Norman a look of contempt after conceding defeat. The blonde accepted the compliment and said to Norman in what seemed like a south coast accent; 'You are very kind; my name is Caroline and this is my younger brother Derek.'

'Pleased to make your acquaintance, I am Norman and this is John.'

Derek then spoke and said; 'pleathed to meet you' indicating that he had a very pronounced lisp. It also revealed what can be best described as a sight of pure horror. His teeth, if indeed that's what they were; resembled a row of condemned houses and his breath would have stopped the traffic. Norman turned his head to avoid any close contamination as John suggested; 'Why don't you both join us at our table?'

Caroline and Derek walked across to the table, closely followed by Norman and John, who guided Caroline to the chair next to his. Norman took the opportunity to introduce everyone and then sat back in his seat, waiting for the entertainment to begin.

Tom got proceedings started with a classic bit of repartee; 'Now then John, you were telling us about your recent visit to the clinic, did they give you antibiotics then?'

Everyone shot a glance at John, who had a look of a man about to face a firing squad. John's response was to laugh it off and inject a little humour to deflect Tom's derisive comment; 'Well, I went to the doctor last week about a cold I couldn't shake off. The Dr said, if I did nothing, it would last for seven days, but if treated, it will go away in a week.'

Polite laughter followed and John had regained some credibility.

Tom now turned his attention to Derek and Caroline and asked; 'So where are you two from then?'

Caroline spoke; 'We live in Cornwall, but we are here visiting my aunt who lives in Cleadon. We sadly had to attend my uncle's funeral yesterday, he died last week.'

'Sorry for your loss,' replied Tom.

'It's alright, we hadn't seen him for a number of years, and we were closer to my aunt really,' added Caroline.

At this point, Caroline decided to remove her coat, thus revealing a magnificent pair of breasts. Her hair was tied up in a bun and she wore a lace blouse that partly hid her ample bosom, which was in turn held in place by the desired scaffolding. The distraction was overwhelming and Malla tried to navigate the conversation to other things, asking Caroline; 'What do you both do for a living then?'

'I am training to be a nurse and Derek works in my father's business,' she revealed.

'What business would that be Derek?' asked Andy.

'Heeth an undertaker and I work in the offith dealing with cuthtomerths,' replied Derek.

'As you can see Derek has quite a speech impediment and he also has a heavy cold at the moment,' added Caroline.

John couldn't resist a comment; 'Sounds like a dead-end job to me.'

Nobody laughed and Derek replied; 'Yeth it ith John.'

At this point, Caroline rose and went to the ladies room, leaving Derek at the mercy of the remaining agent provocateurs. Geordie chose to clarify Derek and Caroline's length of stay in the North East; 'Are you and your sister here for long Derek?'

Those present were wondering how many words beginning with S; Derek could fit in to his answer. They were not disappointed as he went onto say; 'Yeth, me and my thithter are here for another two weekth in Thouth Thieldz.'

Then Derek produced what could be described as a cross between a cough, a sneeze and a burp that in turn resulted in him firing a ball of phlegm that stuck to the side of Malla's pint glass. Laughter ensued, but Malla failed to see the hilarity of the situation; 'Jesus Christ Derek that's shocking mate, have you not heard of covering your gob.'

Derek was most apologetic and said; 'Thorry, tho thorry.'

More uncontrollable laughter as Caroline rejoined the party; 'Have I missed something?'

Discretion meant that Derek was not subjected to any further ridicule and Andy tried to rectify the impasse with a joke; 'I used to sell deck chairs for a living you know Derek, then the business folded.' Derek found this particularly funny and again began to cough. Only for all those present to shield their glasses from any further obnoxious substance that might be propelled in their direction. Caroline then asked everyone what their professions were and when John responded to the question he replied; 'I am a horticulturist for the local council.'

'This raised a few eyebrows and Stan added; 'Don't you a mean a gardener John?'

John gave Stan a look of derision and gave him a terse reply; 'Stan, what you know about horticulture you could write on the back of a postage stamp. I have an extraordinary skill and my knowledge of flora and fauna is legendary.'

Geordie then had a moment of inspiration; 'Listen, I have had a thought; what about if Derek and John went into business, they could have an advertising slogan of; *From the Death Bed to The Flower Bed.*'

Norman felt the need to intervene at this juncture and rebuked Geordie by saying; 'Geordie, that's a bit insensitive as Derek and Caroline just attended their uncle's funeral yesterday.'

'Oh, yes sorry,' replied Geordie.

As the afternoon progressed it became very evident that Caroline had taken a shine to Malla. This prompted Malla to get to his feet; 'It's my round, the same again boys and can I buy our guests a drink, what would you both like?'

'I'll have a half of lager pleath,' replied Derek.

Caroline was a little unsure what to have and Malla laying on the charm suggested; 'Why don't you come to the bar and make your choice.'

John could see his chances with Caroline diminishing rapidly and turned his attention to Derek the Phlegm Hurler and asked; 'Was it a church service, then a burial yesterday, Derek?'

'It wath a burial but we had a thervith at the thynagogue, our family are Jewith.'

'Oh well, no pork scratchings for you then,' replied John.

Tom gave John a look of disgust and sought to move the conversation on by asking; 'Do you go to the temple regularly back home then Derek?'

'Not really, we are not orthodox in that regard, but my parenth go quite often,' he stated.

Malla and Caroline returned with a tray of drinks, she had chosen a vodka and tonic for her libation. Andy asked Caroline about her family's history and had they always lived in Cornwall.

She informed those present that her parents had fled Germany in 1939 with her grandparents and arrived in England to start a new life in Bethnal Green, London. Her grandfather started his undertaker's business and her father inherited the firm and moved to Cornwall in 1951. She was born in 1953 and Derek a year later.

General chit-chat continued for another half an hour then Caroline suggested; 'Well Derek I think we should leave these fine young men to enjoy the rest of the day and go back to our aunt's house.'

Norman took the opportunity to express his thanks for an interesting afternoon; 'On behalf of all of us I would like to wish you both well for the future and I am sure I can speak for my good friends when I say, it has been a pleasure to be in your company this afternoon. I would like to finish with something from William Blake.'

'Norman, do you have to,' I asked.

'Oh yes Harry' he replied and continued;

When the green woods laugh with the voice of joy,
And the dimpling stream runs laughing by;
When the air does laugh with merry wit,
And the green hill laughs with noise of it;

Caroline was impressed; 'That was lovely, thank you Norman,' and as she rose to leave, she looked and smiled at Malla; 'I'll see you tonight then, around 8 pm.'

'You certainly will,' replied Malla.

As Derek and Caroline left, John turned to Malla and shouted; 'You bastard, you have just ditched one bird, does anyone else get a chance?'

Tom suspected that Malla had put the squeeze on Caroline when they were at the bar; 'You are a crafty sod, Malla; poor John had visions of burying his head in those fulsome knockers. But I suspect you will have to work hard to woo her my good friend and she's not here for long.'

'What can I say, when you are blessed with good looks and charm it is recognised by the fairer sex,' answered Malla.

'And farmyard animals,' added a downcast John.

Geordie then began to analyse the enigma that was Derek and said; 'He was a strange one; you could see him in a funeral parlour though, with all those stiffs. Imagine when he gets lonely and feels the stirrings down below. Then he wonders what it would be like!'

'Don't go there Geordie, there is a name for them fellas who perform on the dead,' Tom responded.

'Yes, it's necrophilia I think,' suggested Stan.

Andy then joined in the debate; 'Christ, I think I have performed that, it was a bird from Leam Lane and she hardly had a pulse, god she was hard work.'

More laughter as Stan said; 'Well good luck tonight, Malla, you will need it and plenty money as well.'

'You will be better off with a Cornish pastie and a jar of worms,' said John.

A MEETING OF MINDS

Another Saturday and our band of intrepid young men had arranged to meet at The Britannia Hotel, which sat opposite the town hall in Shields. It was a cold but dry January day in 1972 and I arrived at 12 noon to find Tom, Stan, Andy, Geordie, Norman and John at the bar ordering their beers.

'What you having Harry?' asked Tom.

'Very kind Tom, I will have a Guinness for a change. It's a meal in a glass my friend.'

'Where is Malla?' I asked.

'Out with his bird, hen-pecked,' joked Norman.

'Very funny Norman, is that the best you can do?' stated Stan.

Andy took the opportunity to say; 'Well, what have we here, none other than Harry Wainwright. This is indeed an auspicious occasion. This small gathering has been blessed with his appearance today fellow playmates. It is a pleasure to have this metalworker and unhinged halfwit in our midst?'

'Alright, less of the sarcasm Andy,' I responded.

'So, Harry, I guess your absence is due to your current squeeze, is that not the case?' asked Tom.

'Yes, you could say that Tom,' I replied.

'By the way, I want to thank you Andy,' I said.

'What for?'

'For introducing me to a totally new experience,' I answered.

Andy was confused and took the bait; 'What do you mean you arse?'

'Being pleased to see you,' I replied.

Cheers and laughter engulfed the bar and Andy reacted, 'Very funny, clever shite.'

'Can you watch your language please?' asked the barman.

'Sorry chief, just a bit of high jinks,' said Geordie.

Tables were selected and chairs gathered next to the dartboard. The pub was fairly busy with a healthy attendance of the opposite sex. The reason for this; a wedding had just taken place at St Bede's Church, just along the road. This was not lost on Stan, Tom and John who were scanning the room with expectant eyes.

Geordie cut straight to the chase in relation to my romantic affair when he asked, 'So Harry, have you given her a good 'seeing to yet'?'

'God help any female that gets involved with you Geordie. You certainly have the gift of the gab,' added Norman with a sarcastic twist.

'Needless to say, Geordie, that information is not for your ears. I would not want to encourage any subsequent action on your part that might result in any unpleasantness with any farmyard animal,' I replied.

More laughter at Geordie's expense this time. John returned from the bar with drinks for me and Tom, Norman then returned to the topic of romance when he joked; 'It seems there is an air of incrimination in relation to those of us who are in a state of adulation with regard to the fairer sex. I myself have an infatuation with the lovely Laura and I hope those present will understand the chemical imbalance that occurs. Even when those of us, who are of a superior intelligence are captivated by desire and covet the infatuation of love.'

'Norman, you don't half talk verbal diarrhoea,' quipped Stan.

'I am so glad you appreciate it Stan. I am trying give you all a sense of the *joie de vivre* when I offer you unequivocal evidence to emphasize a positive hypothesis,' he replied.

Geordie related to Norman's superior intellect when he added; 'Norman, you are certainly destined for greater things. Your future stands before you and you will look back on these gatherings and think, Christ what a sad lot they were. Just think, you could be lying in a dark stinking ship's hold grinding out a bulkhead in preparation for a hairy arsed welder to turn up and burn holes in your boiler suit.'

'That is the voice of experience,' added Stan.

'It's all down to a grammar school education,' stated Norman.

'Wait a minute, I remember you were bloody hopeless at maths Norman. In case you forget, I was in the same maths class as you, arsehole,' added Tom.

'Thanks for that reminder Tom, but we can't all be brilliant at everything.'

'What is your opinion on all this Harry?' asked John.

Before I could reply, Andy jumped in; 'He doesn't count.'

'He can't read or write either,' joked Stan.

More laughter, this time at my expense and I countered with, 'Listen here, you brainless set of barmpots, I have a degree in lethargy from the University of Marley Potts, I'll have you know!'

'Where the hell is Marley Potts?' asked John.

'Why Sunderland of course,' replied Andy.

A MEETING OF MINDS

Norman offered us all an insight into those who hesitate in the face of adversity. 'I will give you a passage from *Invictus* by William Henley when he said;'

In the fell clutch of circumstance
I have not winced nor cried aloud
Under the bludgeoning's of chance
My head is bloody, but unbowed.

The discussion continued to consider our respective careers and Norman maintained the theme adding; 'Now then, let us analyse the world of work! What does it mean to perform a skill or provide a service gentleman? My own experience is very limited of course and therefore I will bow to your superior knowledge in this regard.'

'That's because you are a lazy bastard student,' added Geordie.

'I am destined for greater things Geordie, as you have already alluded to, my good man,' he replied.

Tom then spoke of his job as an electrician and his lack of enthusiasm for the work. 'I am bored with this job and the money isn't great either.'

'Had any shocks yet Tom?' asked John.

'Oh yes, my first pay packet,' he quipped.

'Never mind Tom, this will cheer you up,' said Stan and continued; 'I know a lad called Steve, he was looking for odd jobs in and around Westoe Village two weeks ago.'

'A very affluent part of the town,' added Norman.

'Yes, indeed it is; well Steve knocked on the first door and asked the owner if he had any work for him. Yes, you can paint my porch. How much are you going to charge? asked the bloke. £50 replied Steve.

The bloke agreed and told Steve the paint and paint brushes were in the garage. When he finished Steve knocked on the door to claim his money. You are finished already? asked the bloke. Yep, Steve replied; There was plenty of paint, so I gave it two coats. The owner was impressed and reached into his wallet to pay the £50, then Steve said; By the way, it's not a Porsche it's a Ferrari.'

Howls of laughter all round and Andy asked, 'That's not a true story, is it?'

'Of course not, you stupid sod,' replied Stan.

I ventured into the debate about working for a living; 'Well, we are all young men looking to advance in our respective jobs I'm sure, I reckon John wants to be head gardener, Tom to start his own business and Andy and Geordie will be a double act on the *Val Doonican* show. Norman will be a screenwriter for the Bond films or director of the Royal Shakespeare Company. As for Malla and Stan, not a bloody clue.'

Stan gave us his thoughts about his future, 'I think once I have served my time, I am off to Holland or Germany. That's where the money is in welding these days.'

'I think Malla is considering a change, but what I don't know,' added Andy.

'Anyway, what's the script with Keith?' asked John.

'He is nearly finished his weapons training, according to his mother,' suggested Tom.

Norman then gave us his analysis of the management ladder in organisations saying; 'You often find in large companies that the staff play football; the middle management play tennis and the directors play golf. Now what does that tell us boys?'

'That we will all be kicking lumps out of each other on the footy pitch,' joked Stan.

'Not quite Tom, it means the further that you climb up the corporate ladder, the balls reduce in size,' replied Norman.

'That was very good Norman, and I reckon that is a bloody fact,' added Geordie.

We all charged our glasses as the pub began to fill up, as members of the wedding party returned for drinks. Tom raised the issue about food and a discussion then took place regarding what to eat and where to get it. Fish and chips from Westoe Road was quickly eliminated, due to the fact that the barman was unlikely to allow us to consume on the premises. Dickson's for saveloy dips was also disregarded for the same reason. Pub grub was available, so we settled for toasted sarnies. The choice was limited; you could choose from corned beef and onion, cheese and onion or ham and cheese. We all opted for corned beef except Tom, he selected cheese and onion. When Andy asked him why he chose cheese Tom replied; 'If I have any more corned beef and somebody was to crack a whip, I would be off at a gallop.'

During our consumption of the sarnies, Tom related a tale told to him by his uncle Jack. 'On the first night after moving into his new house Bob went down to the local pub. While at the bar he fell into conversation with the barman, a man of local knowledge and a useful source of information. After a short discussion their conversation was interrupted by the arrival of a well-dressed man, evidently a regular; who greeted the barman, ordered a large glass of sherry, drank it, said goodbye, walked up the wall, across the ceiling, down the opposite wall and then out the door. There was a stunned silence and then Bob said, Wow, that was strange. Yes, mused the barman, he usually drinks whisky.

Not to be outdone John gave us a funny story; 'Listen to this fellas; did you know scientists at Rolls Royce simulate bird strikes by firing dead chickens at their aircraft engines, from a specially designed cannon. American engineers were keen to run such tests and bought a similar cannon from Rolls Royce. When the cannon was fired, the engineers watched in horror as the chicken flew out of the barrel, crashed into their toughest military aircraft and smashed it to smithereens. Each test drew the same result.

The horrified Americans sent Rolls Royce the film of the disastrous results of the experiment and begged the British engineers for suggestions. Rolls Royce responded with a one-line memo. Defrost the fucking chicken.'

As the laughter died down our attention was diverted to the bar where two girls stood waiting for their drinks. Andy recognised one of them saying; 'The one with the ponytail lives round the corner from me and she's called Debbie; she works at John Collier in Shields.'

Geordie then told us about his cousin who had worked in the factory not too long ago, 'It's wall-to-wall women in there, my cousin Sid was there doing maintenance on one of the machines. He said it was a nightmare, he got serious grief from some of the women. He said they were shouting things like get your kit off and let's see what's hanging. One of them had her top bollocks out. He couldn't wait to get out.'

'I am sure they are not all like that,' added Norman.

Tom took the opportunity to warn his comrades; 'Now fellas, here is some very good advice. If you should get yourself into a severe state of intoxication and chance upon a female of, shall we say, questionable morals. If you then embark upon any carnal activity, please follow these simple guidelines. 'Whip it out. Whip it in. Whip it out again.

Wipe it. Then Whip off.'

'Sounds like wise advice to me, and I would give your John Henry a good scrub with a Brillo pad when you get home. Just to be on the safe side,' I joked.

Malla's absence was discussed and Andy asked, 'So, has Malla made progress with the lovely Caroline after he captivated her with his verbal hogwash at the Ship & Royal?'

'Well, I think he has spoken to her on the phone, she lives in Cornwall and I can't see any mileage in it, to be honest Andy.'

John gave us his impression of her brother Derek, I can just picture Derek the phlegm hurler, checking out the stiffs and offering his condolences to the bereaved family members in the funeral parlour. 'I am tho thorry for your loth, would you like to thee the detheethed?'

Geordie changed the theme and mentioned a trip to the races; 'Now here this, why don't we all go to the races boys. The Simonside Club have organised a race day in April.'

'We are not all members of the Sima Club Geordie,' said John.

'That's not a problem, a member can vouch for you as a guest. That will work out because me, Harry, Stan and Andy are all members. What do you say fellas?' replied Geordie.

'Yes why not, it's something different and it will give us time to save enough money between now and April,' agreed Tom.

'How much is it then? asked John.

'I think it's £20 for the return coach trip, but I will find out the exact amount and let you all know,' added Geordie.

'Has anybody been to the races?' I asked.

'I went to Gosforth Park with my old man, but he didn't win a tosser. My mother was not best pleased when we got back,' added Andy.

'Get your cash on Lester Piggott,' quipped John.

'Who the hell is Lester Piggott,' asked Stan.

'Christ Stan, have you never heard of Lester Piggott, he is the champion jockey over the flat,' said Tom.

'Hey, he has a speech impediment just like Derek the phlegm hurler,' joked John.

The barman shouted last orders and we finished our drinks. 'Well, it's time to *Garn Yem* again playmates, anyone in Shields tonight,' asked Norman. 'Eldon Arms at 6.30 pm tonight,' replied John.

DARE TO DREAM

It was two weeks since our last conflab in The Britannia and we agreed to meet in The Simonside Arms on a Saturday in late January. The pub was an out-of-town hostelry not far from home for me, Stan and Geordie it was only a ten-minute walk. I bought the drinks at the bar, a lager for Stan and Geordie opted for a pint of Guinness and I had a black velvet. Two tables were put together and the three of us waited for our friends arrival. A couple of locals were playing darts and other than a couple of bar flies the place was empty. I asked one of the dart players if he fancied a game of arrows later, but he said; 'Sorry mate, we are off in a minute.'

'Going shopping with the wives.'

Stan leaned over and said; 'That's marriage for you, no bloody life and no bastard money.'

'Hang on, I'm getting married in August and you are my best man you swine. You should be extolling the virtues of wedded bliss, not condemning it.'

'Why, I am not going to perjure myself, you might hold it against me Harry and seek compensation in the future,'

Geordie laughed and added; 'The girl that gets me, is going to be one lucky lady.'

'Oh yes, and I bet she has a white stick,' I joked.

'Shite off Harry, she will be a cross between Elizabeth Taylor and Sophia Loren,' replied Geordie.

'Good luck with that Geordie,' added Stan.

As the two dart players left, in walked our soulmates; John, Andy and Tom. One of the bar flies was at the dart board and on seeing this, John shouted; 'One hundred and eighty, get my name on the board, I will take on anybody.'

'Had a drink already then John?' asked Stan.

'Yes indeed, I have had a couple of pints in the Eldon Arms before I boarded the bus. I also managed to enjoy the trip without paying. What do think about that?' he replied.

'Please explain that fraudulent activity then John, you have still got your first halfpenny,' said Stan.

John sat down with his pint of lager; 'Well, the bus was packed and if you are smart like me, you go upstairs and sit at the back. It's only a short distance from Eldon Street and the conductor had not even made it upstairs by the time I was getting off the bus.'

'Oh yes, me and Andy were downstairs when the tight sod jumped on the bus. I knew what he was up to,' added Tom.

John justified his actions; 'There is nothing wrong with being frugal my good man. The money saved will go towards my brother's operation fund. I fly out to La Paz next week with our personal physician and he is not cheap.'

'La Paz my arse, you're not talking to Bucknut Bob now,' quipped Andy.

'Where are Malla and Norman then?' I asked.

'Norman should be here soon, he is getting a lift off Laura's old man,' suggested Tom.

'What about Malla?' asked Geordie.

'Listen to this' said Andy and continued; 'Malla is in Cornwall visiting Caroline. I do not know how he has wangled that. But I suspect Caroline's parents have coughed up for the cost of the rail fare.'

'I hope he is wearing protective clothing, because he will be in close contact with guess who? Yes, Derek the phlegm hurler of Ye Olde Cornish Town,' quipped John.

Norman arrived ten minutes later and joined the quorum. He had to endure a relentless inquisition on his relationship with Laura. The general consensus of opinion was that he had his feet well and truly under the table with regard to her parents. Most of this ridicule was down to jealousy of course; Laura was quite a catch.

Norman's response was predictable and he somehow managed to deflect the criticism and admonish his peers with great subtlety saying; 'I fear that green God of envy has raised it's head and sadly my friends have fallen to their knees in submission. Now fellas, let us examine the situation. Laura has realised that she has fallen in love with the man of her dreams and it is my task to stimulate that infatuation with a guile that is way beyond your comprehension. This ability is something that you have not yet acquired and I suspect you never will. However, I am willing to provide you all with a didactic pedagogy of the intricate expertise needed to create just such a persona.'

Geordie turned to me and asked; 'What the fuck did he just say?'

'I think he means that we are not blessed with the knowledge required to sustain a relationship with the opposite sex Geordie,' I replied.

Norman continued with his retort adding; 'Let us not forget your feeble attempt a few weeks ago in The Grey Hen Andy, when you failed miserably with Iris. Is that not, correct?'

'Well, Laura is still too classy for you Norman. You will get the bullet mate, mark my words,' stated Andy.

In order to change the subject Tom decided to concentrate on Geordie's lack of hair; 'That is one hell of a haircut Geordie, it's right down to the wood.'

'Yes well, I thought I should smarten myself up in order to attract the chicks' he replied.

John then joked; 'You know what Geordie, your barber either hates your guts or he is blind.'

Laughter now erupted at Geordie's expense and he departed to the bar to acquire the drinks. He thought he would escape any further comments until the barman said; 'That's a close one son, are you joining the army then?'

Geordie thought better than to upset the barman so he left him a little puzzled when he replied; 'No, I had to have it cut short because I had a serious infestation of head lice.' He then calmly walked away from the bar after receiving the drinks. As he returned to his buddies, Norman decided to inflict one more derogatory elucidation; 'Geordie, I want the name, address and telephone number of the person or persons responsible for inflicting such barbaric suffering on a very fine friend of mine. It borders on criminal activity and those guilty of this abomination, should be brought before the authorities toot sweet.'

More laughter was generated and I advised Norman that he was sailing close to the wind; 'Norman, I am sure Laura would not be too pleased to see you with a broken nose.'

'Geordie would not inflict such violence on a devoted friend, am I correct Geordie?'

Geordie grinned at Norman; 'Well Norman, you are getting fucking close to a punch in the gob.'

Geordie enlightened us with the reasoning behind his haircut; 'You may laugh boys, but be warned; this fresh look is just the start of a new chapter in the life of Geordie Stevens, also known as the walking sex machine. Look out ladies, this guy is hotter than hell on a holiday and he is on the lookout for a bawdy bird without inhibitions.'

Might I suggest a trip to the Old Fold in Gateshead, you will find plenty of bawdy birds there, one or two of them have teeth,' joked Stan.

The conversation then moved onto the forthcoming trip to York Races and Geordie supplied all those present with an update on the information and logistics regarding the day in question; 'The cost of the coach is £12, that includes the return journey and a packed lunch. You need to be on the bus at the Sima Club, at 9.30 am. You receive a race card when you get on the bus and the time of arrival at the racecourse is around midday. You can bring drink for the trip, but it must be cans only.'

'When is it again Geordie?' asked John.

'Saturday, April 10, and on the way back the driver will be stopping in Thirsk for a few beers,' he replied.

'Where the hell is Thirsk?' asked Andy.

'It's not far from York and it has a few decent boozers according to Davy,' replied Geordie.

Tom touched on the subject of club committee men; 'I heard that the club are looking for a new treasurer.'

'Yep, they are indeed,' replied Geordie.

'I thought they hired a new treasurer only a month ago,' added John.

'Yes, that's the bastard they are looking for,' quipped Geordie.

More alcohol was ordered and the barman very kindly brought them to the table. Stan could not resist a comment; 'This is a most generous gesture my man, my friend Andy here would like to buy you a drink. Is that correct Andy?'

Andy just growled at Stan; 'Of course, no problem; Geordie would you buy our barman a drink out of what you owe me please.'

'The barman saved everyone's blushes when he added; 'It's fine I don't drink, never have.'

Norman then asked the barman; 'Do you smoke my friend?'

'Yes,'

'Well take a cigar,' and Norman produced a pack of cigars from his jacket pocket and asked the barman to take one which he did.

'Very kind, thanks.' The barman walked back to the bar.

Everyone except the non-smokers who were me and Stan, took a cigar and John asked; 'Where did you acquire these from Norman?'

'From Laura's old man. He has a mate in the merchant navy,' he replied.

Stan then threatened Andy with physical violence for blowing smoke into his pint; 'Do that again and I will put you in wards 2, 3 and 4 of Harton Hospital you arsehole.'

Andy recognised that Stan wasn't joking and apologised for his lack of etiquette. He was mindful of the fact that Stan was one of two hard hitters in our little band, Tom was the other one. When you were punched by either of these two, you felt it for a long time.

We sat and chewed the cud on various topics including the progress of our two local football teams. Stan, Geordie, John, Norman and Malla were supporters of Newcastle United, Tom, Keith and Andy followed Sunderland. I myself was a bit of a rarity, I tried to watch both teams. One week at Sunderland and Newcastle a week later. Although I visited Roker Park more than St James Park because of financial constraints.

Tom raised the fact that the two teams have never played each other in a cup final. Andy poured scorn on the possibility and retorted; 'There's not much chance of that happening anytime soon, the way they are both playing. Sunderland have been shite lately and it is purgatory to watch. They couldn't score in a brothel. They do a lap of honour if they win the toss.'

'Yes, one can but only dream. It may be that one day we will be walking down Wembley Way to cheer our teams on,' I added.

'I wouldn't bank on it Harry, it will be a long time coming,' added Tom.

Norman diverted the conversation from football to dreams and asked; 'Who has had a dream lately and what was it about. Before you relate these strange and terrifying illusions take care, there may be sensitive Scots Guardsmen in the pub.'

'I have them all the time,' said Andy.

'Yes we know Andy, not those sorts of dreams. I mean strange dreams that have no apparent reasoning behind them,' replied Norman.

'I have them as well,' added Andy.

Norman was beginning to regret this hypothetical odyssey into the unknown; 'I can't help but think this is a serious error of judgement, but go on Andy enlighten us on your most recent journey into the bizarre world of your subconscious.'

Andy continued; 'Well, listen to this; it will blow your mind fellas. Last Tuesday I was in a deep sleep; you know when you are dead to the world. I'd supped a few beers with a couple of workmates in the County Hotel. On the way home I washed my face with fish and chips. I had eaten them before I put the key in the door and I climbed the stairs to bed.

'You skip the next bit and move onto the dream,' joked Stan.

'Well, the dream was very strange; I dreamt that I married a giant egg.'

We all looked at each other very puzzled, but no one offered a comment and Andy continued saying; 'Yes, it was an egg with a woman's face painted on it. The really strange thing was the face was that of Elizabeth Montgomery. The bird out of *Bewitched* on the telly. The ceremony would be taking place in St Hilda's Church and the egg had to be wheeled down the aisle in a portable egg cup. The best man was Joseph Stalin and the vicar was George Best.'

'Right, I will stop you there Andy, what medication are you on at the moment?' asked Tom.

'Honest, this is true boys, George Best said; Do you take this egg to be your lawful wedded wife? You daft sod.'

Then I replied; 'There is no need for that, you haven't seen her on the nest. This resulted in Joseph Stalin howling with laughter and I answered I do.'

Then Besty asked Elizabeth the same question.

No answer, and Besty then said; 'Does the egg speak?'

Then Joseph Stalin said; 'Nyet'

Well, guess who walked into the church? It was Stan Laurel and he stated; 'I will speak for the egg reverend; she said I do.'

George Best then asked; 'Can the best man provide the ring?'

'So, I looked at Joseph Stalin and he replied; Nyet'

Besty then joked; 'This is no yoke,' and then he pointed to Stan Laurel and added; 'He has egg on his chin.'

I then turned to Besty and said; 'Here, I shelled out a fortune for that ring, you have no idea how much trouble it was to find a ring that fits.'

'Finally, we were pronounced man and egg. Everyone had eggplant and eggnog for the buffet at the reception. When it came to the wedding night in the hotel, I had to ring for the night porter to bring a block and tackle to lift her off me; she was hard-boiled.'

At this stage we were all in hysterics at this lunacy and Tom spoke for everyone when he said; 'Andy, you really must stop smoking the happy backy and when you go to bed; don't forget to put the boxing gloves on. You will sleep much better.'

After composing ourselves, Norman asked; 'If any of us could reproduce anything to match Andy's worrying dissertation.'

'I regularly have a dream where I am being chased by lions buck-naked,' I replied.

'But lions don't wear clothes Harry, you idiot,' stated Geordie.

Everyone looked at Geordie in disbelief and Stan said; 'Geordie I despair of you sometimes; if I had a dog half as daft as you, I would have it put to sleep.'

Andy then suggested that we should be looking to finish our drinks off, as it was approaching 3 pm and closing time. John ended our little soiree with a joke; 'A boxer went to his doctor; I have trouble sleeping at night. I can lay for hours without dropping off. The doctor asked; Have you tried counting sheep? Yes, but every time I get to nine, I stand up.

'On that note, it's time to *Garn Yem* and dream of eggs,' added Tom.

FOOD FOR THOUGHT

Winter had a firm grip in South Shields, it was late February and the snow was hard packed on the pavements, after six days of freezing temperatures. Our venue for this week was the Eldon Arms and we mustered for 6 pm. Keith would be joining us as he had some leave to take from his regiment in Northern Ireland and a special celebration was called for. I arrived with Stan just as Jacky the landlord was opening the door. Jacky was a real character; he was disabled due to having lost his left leg during the war. He had a metal prosthetic leg. The original leg was blown off in Italy in 1944. It was a little strange that he chose to have such a heavy replacement constructed from metal rather than plastic or wood; considering the noise it made when he moved about. He argued that it was not a fire risk and so the logic could be accepted, as he often smoked in bed. However, when you analyse this; you could counteract his reasoning because the bed will still burn with him in it.

The advantage of selecting the Eldon Arms as a venue was down to the pub having a 'snug,' a room separate from the rest of the hostelry that afforded us a certain degree of privacy. Another major benefit was that we didn't even have to go to the bar. There was a bell in the snug that alerted Jacky that further refreshments were required.

Within five minutes, Malla, Keith, Tom, John and Geordie had joined Stan and I. Norman as yet had not appeared, something that Andy commented on. 'That bastard is always late; he just avoids the first round of drinks.'

'Tom sprang to Norman's defence,' and shouted: 'No, that's not fair Andy, remember he is a student and we are all working. He just doesn't have as much money as us.'

'Well keep your gob shut about money Andy or I will lamp you,' added Malla.

'What are you all drinking then?' asked John.

After deliberation the decision was made to opt for Scottish & Newcastle Best Scotch. Although Geordie was a little dubious saying, he always got the 'skitters' when he drank too much of the dark elixir.

'There is nothing wrong with being regular, just don't fart after 9 pm,' added Keith.

At 6.15 pm, the last member of our intrepid socialites arrived to a chorus of jeers, abuse and ridicule. Norman revelled in all this adulation and as usual he was ready with a rehearsed riposte. 'Good evening and a very special welcome to our very own freedom fighter Keith, nice to see you my son. Your presence will empower this band of primeval braindead simpletons to appreciate intellect and create an air of *bonhomie* to the proceedings.'

'*Bonhomie*, that's in Czechoslovakia isn't' it?' suggested Andy.

Norman took the opportunity to correct Andy. 'Give me strength Lord, I am in the midst of intellectual ineptitude. *Bonhomie* is French for good nature, you retard.'

Tom asked Keith for a resumé of his latest posting in Northern Ireland; 'Right then soldier, let's have it; what's it like on the emerald isle?'

'Well remember I have signed the Official Secrets Act boys, so there are a lot of things I can't tell you.'

'Just give us the important stuff then, like chicks, grub, drink etc,' asked John.

Keith then continued with his evaluation of his first posting in the province saying; 'The thing is that it is advised to tread carefully about getting into relationships with local girls, because of security concerns. There are plenty of lovely lasses, but we don't get out that much, unless we have a weekend pass. A number of the lads have gone to Dublin on a weekend pass, it is pretty safe there anyway. The grub is standard army rations. Loads of beef and chicken dinners, pasta and stews. The local grub is nice, I like 'champ'. This is mashed potato with shredded scallions. 'Ulster Fry' is also popular, it's just a big fried breakfast really; with bacon, sausage, egg, mushrooms and served up with soda bread, potato farl or toast. 'Boxty' is another traditional meal, this is basically potato cake.'

'What about the drink then?' asked Malla.

'Guinness is popular, but Smithwick's is a bitter that is pretty good. Others are stouts like Beamish and Murphy's,' stated Keith.

'How did your weapons training go then; did you shoot the sergeant?' joked Stan.

Keith laughed and went on: 'No, but it took me bloody ages to get my eye in. I was missing the target completely. The master-at-arms was doing his nut. At one point he told our sergeant to give me a catapult and keep me away from any combat. I eventually acquired the knack and I can now knock the eye out of a bird flying a mile away,' he joked.

'Well, you are back now among friends and it's only fair that you should buy the next round. Would you ring the bell again John, there's a fine chap?' added Andy.

'You haven't changed then Andy, still have your first penny,' added Keith.

'Like hell he will, I will buy four pints and Keith can get five pints,' stated Geordie.

'Here here, a splendid idea,' added John.

Within five minutes the sound of Jacky's leg was heard and he arrived with refreshments. Money was exchanged, including a tip for our resident war veteran. Keith was brought up to speed with our recent conclaves and the various incidents that had occurred. He was intrigued by Malla's romantic adventures with Caroline and asked for a full account of his progress. He was not alone in this regard, we all sat in silence as Malla eluded to this new chapter of his life saying; 'I wondered when someone would bring it up. Well, I went down to Cornwall a few weeks ago.'

'Who paid for that then?' asked Norman.

'Her old man paid for the return journey on the train and they put me up at their place for four days. I got on really well with her family. They have a huge, terraced house with seven bedrooms and three bathrooms. They even have a snooker room with a full-size table.'

'You didn't do her on the snooker table, did you?' asked Andy.

'Don't be a pervert all your life Andy,' added Tom.

'Just thought I would ask that's all, a number of blokes I know would have tried it,' replied Andy.

'Yes well, let's not bring your father into this conversation,' quipped John.

'Cheeky swine,' replied Andy.

Malla continued with his symposium; 'Tell you what though, her mother is a good looker. She is about forty, I reckon, but she doesn't look it at all.

'You didn't?' asked Norman.

Malla just looked around the table at all of us and with a glint in his eye, said; 'I am not that lucky fellas.'

Norman touched on religion when he asked; 'Are they orthodox Jews then?'

'Well, we never had pork if that's what you mean, but the food was lush. Lots of fish and chicken with chick peas; this is a popular meal in Jewish cuisine.'

'Did you get out on the lash with Derek then?' I asked.

'No Harry, it never happened. He has his own little bachelor pad in the centre of town. He did appear at the house a few times. On one occasion he turned up and he was subjected to a real bollocking from his old man. Apparently, he was in the chapel of rest with a woman whose husband had recently died. She asked to see her late husband, daft Derek directed her to an open coffin. Sadly, the bloke in the box was not her husband, he was in the back getting embalmed.'

'I can just picture the daft sod saying; *tho thorry mithith, thall* I go and find out if *heeth* ready to *thee* you,' joked John.

Much laughter around the table and Tom asked; 'So, how goes it with you and Caroline then Malla. Will there be wedding bells?'

'Too early for any thoughts of marriage yet Tom. The distance is a major problem, but she did say she would like to finish her training up here. She does like the North East.'

'There could be a problem in relation to any marriage though Malla,' I added.

'What would that be then Harry?'

'Well, you are a gentile are you not and she is Jewish. You may require surgery in order to marry her,' I suggested.

'I know where you are going with this Harry, don't even go there.'

John added his take on this subject saying; 'You will have to have your scarf removed, maybe Derek could perform the procedure on the cheap.'

'Do they charge for that surgery? That's a bit of a rip off,' joked Geordie.

'Oh yes and the more foreskin you have, the more you pay. I think it's £5 for every two millimetres,' added John.

'So, that will cost him £10 then,' quipped Stan.

'Alright you have had your fun, there will be no surgery on my member, I can assure you of that,' added Malla.

Tom revisited Keith's tour of duty in Ulster; 'So, what was that all about on Bloody Sunday, where you in Londonderry Keith?'

Keith was mindful of what he could divulge; 'I can't really go into details Tom, but my company weren't there anyway. What I can say is that the DYH are creating major problems in Londonderry at the moment. They are getting soldiers shot by pulling them out of position by hurling bricks and bottles, then snipers can then pick them off. That Sunday the CO in charge ordered live rounds to be used to protect his men.'

'What is the DYH? asked Andy.

'The Derry Young Hooligans,' replied Keith.

'You need to keep your head down then mate,' added Malla.

'Oh, I will, don't worry on that score, I have another eighteen months; then I hope to have a better posting. It might be Belize, Germany or Cyprus,' stated Keith.

Norman lifted his glass and stood up saying; 'Let's raise a toast to postcards from Cyprus.'

We all rose to our feet and as one said; 'Postcards from Cyprus.'

After twenty minutes another round of beers were ordered and Tom and me duly paid. Andy related an incident that occurred at the Bridge Hotel the previous Sunday involving a well-known character in Shields. He was renowned for creating mayhem should the occasion warrant it.

Andy said; 'I was having a pint with Eric, a mate from work. We were stood at the bar and there were a few people in the room. Angry John walked in, he was well-oiled and when he arrived at the bar, he slammed his hand on the counter and shouted; 'A bastard pint of Carling barman.'

The barman was less than impressed by this. 'I am not serving you mate, so you can just turn around and walk out, and don't cause any aggro.'

'Angry John picked up an empty pint glass that was on the counter and threw it at the barman. Luckily, he saw it coming and managed to avoid contact, only for the glass to smash into the big mirror behind the bar. Angry John then leaned over the bar: 'Next time I won't fucking miss, now serve me up the Carling.'

'The barman anticipated Angry John's next move and produced a baseball bat. Which he quickly administered to Angry John's cranium. The big swine fell to the floor sparked out. Within minutes two burly coppers were on the scene. As one of them raised Angry John to his feet, he threw a punch at the other copper. He was then dealt a hefty blow to his midriff and unceremoniously dragged out of the bar.'

'*Ira furor brevis est,*' added Norman.

'Which means what exactly Norman?' asked Geordie.

'Anger is a brief madness,' replied Norman.

'Well, he is as mad as a ship's cat that swine,' added Stan.

'His sister is just as bad, she used to go to Dean Road school. She was a real nutter and she was always picking fights with the lads. God she was ugly, just like her brother. You wouldn't tell her that though, she had a face like a welder's bench,' joked John.

Norman then decided to engage in a philosophical expose: 'As Raymond Chandler once observed;

Alcohol is like love, the first kiss is magic, the second kiss intimate and the third kiss is routine. After that you just take the girl's clothes off.'

'Not much has changed in these little get-togethers then, we talk of life and Norman talks bollocks,' joked Keith.

'Correct, good point; you win a prize,' replied Andy.

The merriment continued until around 9 pm when a decision was made to hit the town centre. A few taxis were ordered thanks to our host Jacky. The Criterion was selected as our first port of call. Stan and Andy bought the beers and to Andy's annoyance the beers were a tad more expensive than the Eldon Arms. Although well populated, we managed to secure a couple of tables with chairs to sit on and enjoy our beers. John voiced the opinion that a curry after last orders, would be appropriate. There was general agreement about the food, although not a great curry connoisseur I reluctantly agreed; 'Well, I suppose I will have my usual omelette and chips, as I am not too keen on washing my boat race with a curry.'

'You will have to try a curry Harry, they are lush,' suggested Malla.

'One day maybe.'

Norman expressed his concerns regarding this proposed late-night dining; 'Oh yes, my friends, let us not forget our last late-night culinary convention at the Shah Jan, when our esteemed halfwit Andy decided to do a runner without paying. I gather you vacated the restaurant via the toilets is that correct you lamebrain?'

'I was not well at all, it was that chicken madras that did it,' alleged Andy.

'Bollocks, you have deep pockets and short arms Andy. You are as tight as a submarine's torpedo doors,' added Stan.

'Don't worry Norman, he will be paying his share this time, if he values his teeth,' quipped Tom.

'Gentlemen, it seems you are very misguided in your appraisal of me, I always pay my debts,' declared Andy.

'You have been warned,' added Geordie.

Stan asked how Geordie was feeling after his consumption of Best Scotch. 'I am fine thanks Stan.'

'You won't be after you have scoffed your curry. Your arse will be like a blood orange,' joked John.

Tom felt the need to add a touch of humour to the occasion: 'A customer in a restaurant said to the waiter, would you please get your knob out of my soup? The waiter replied; So sorry sir, but I have a boil on my foreskin and my doctor told me I have to keep it warm.'

'You just made that up Tom,' joked Malla.

'Never mind that bull rot,' added Keith; 'A man walked into a bar, ordered twelve shots of whisky and started to drink them as fast as he could. The barman asked him, why are you drinking so fast? The man added, you would be drinking fast too, if you had what I have. The barman asked, what do you have? The man replied, fifty pence.'

As the night wore on the pub thinned out a bit, we were considering which curry house to choose for our sustenance, when Tom suggested; 'There is a new Indian restaurant just opened next door to the Pier pub.'

'What's it called then?' asked Geordie.

'The Khaki Starfish, I think.'

Geordie failed to see the humour. 'It sounds like a Chinese to me.'

It was left to Norman to explain the humour of Tom's quip. 'You have had such a sheltered upbringing Geordie. It is refreshing to know that you still possess a degree of innocence in this ever-changing world. However, a word of caution my friend. Whatever you do, you must never say I like the 'Khaki Starfish'. This may result in unwanted attention or severe retribution, depending who you are addressing at the time.'

The penny finally dropped, amid much laughter from the rest of us. John maintained the comedy theme. 'Did you hear about the restaurant on the moon? Great food, but no atmosphere.'

FOOD FOR THOUGHT

It was now 10.30 pm and we had consumed eight pints of beer. The decision was made to eat at The Star of India on Ocean Road. Before entering the restaurant, agreement was reached relating to the seating arrangements, to split up into smaller groups, rather than go in en masse. Restaurants were reluctant to take large groups of blokes who had been on the lash. So, we split into groups of three and entered at intervals. Tom, John and I were sat at a table opposite Norman, Andy and Malla, with Geordie, Stan and Keith in the window table. Despite having drank eight pints; John, Stan, Andy and Malla chose to have pints of lager. The rest of us opted for water. I chose the omelette, chips and mushy peas, my associates selected various dishes including; madras, korma, rogan josh, masala, dhansak, two biryanis and surprisingly Geordie opted for a phaal. He was warned about the high chilli content of phaal but alcohol fuelled bravado got the better of him. Rice and the obligatory naan breads were also ordered. Tom took the opportunity to remind Geordie about his delicate bowels saying; 'You could be making a serious error of judgement here Geordie, phaal is bloody dynamite. It is used by the secret police in India to torture prisoners.'

'Now I know you are talking shite Tom,' he shouted.

Having ordered our food, the manager appeared and asked who had selected the phaal? Geordie spoke up confidently; 'Yes, I have ordered that wonderful dish.'

The manager gave him a worried stare; 'Have you had this dish before sir? It is very spicy and made with a lot of chillies.'

Geordie realised that he may have chosen a dish beyond his limitations, but he did want to be seen as weak and joked; 'I will be fine, anyway I have had them Vesta beef curries and I was fine.'

The manager looked at Geordie, then looked at the rest of us with a sense of foreboding, he put his hands in the air; 'Alright sir, but I have warned you in the company of your friends. Are you sure you want to have this phaal?'

'Oh yes, I am looking forward to it,' he answered with an unconvincing grin on his face.

My omelette and chips arrived first, closely followed by the rest of the meals, Geordie's phaal was the last to arrive.

The feeding frenzy began and Geordie jammed a spoonful of chicken phaal in his gob. We waited for the result and at first the reaction was somewhat muted; but once he had swallowed the 'spicy Semtex' he was subjected to the full extent of the inferno. At first, he could not speak, his eyes were like organ stoppers and it looked like he was going to have a seizure. Beads of sweat appeared on his forehead and his next move was to grab the jug of water and take a giant swig, drenching his shirt in the process. At this point, most of us were in hysterics and even the waiters were laughing. After about three minutes he finally spoke saying; 'Christ all fucking mighty, remind me never to go to India as an MI5 spy. I can't eat this stuff, I will die.'

'Well, you were told you stupid sod, even the manager warned you,' I said.

The rest of us enjoyed our banquet, much to Geordie's irritation. As a mark of sympathy, he was given portions of curry by Tom and John, which he mopped up with his naan bread. Having eaten our fill, we asked the manager to book us taxis to take us home.

'I will do that certainly, after the bill has been paid,' he replied.

John put the whole thing in perspective when he looked at Geordie and said; 'That was an expensive mouthful mate.'

'That's what Doris Day said to Errol Flynn,' joked Stan.

MAKE FAST AND AVOID THE BEER GOGGLES

Our troop of intellectual primates gathered once again on a cloudy Saturday in March 1972, to indulge in one another's lives and pass comment on relevant issues. Today's chosen watering hole was The North Eastern, a town centre pub with a decent jukebox. My associates assembled at 1 pm and I arrived some five minutes later.

'This is a surprise Norman, I thought you would still have your head in a book,' I said.

'I have exhausted my capacity to extend my knowledge of all things literary Harry and I was ready for a libation.'

'Who bought the beers then?' I asked.

'Andy and Malla purchased the drinks, but what troubles me is that Andy actually volunteered to get them in. I think he should be under the doctor because this is abnormal behaviour. There are strange forces at work here,' declared Tom.

Andy's response was nothing unexpected when he countered; 'You bastards have this ridiculous opinion that I am tight, well I am not. I just do not like getting ripped off.'

Stan gave his own view on the matter and added; 'Andy it has not gone unnoticed that you have a tendency to negate your financial responsibilities, when it comes to sharing your wealth.'

'Bollocks, I am putting some sounds on the jukebox, any requests?' he replied.

'Put *Crossroads* on, tight arse,' said John.

'How about *Black Dog* by Zeppelin,' suggested Geordie.

Tom bought me a bottle of Brown Ale and I joined him, Stan and Norman sat at a table. John, Andy, Malla and Geordie were seated at an adjacent table. Having primed the jukebox Andy asked; 'Well, what's the script men?'

Norman started the conversation and concentrated on the limited number of films showing on the TV; 'I am shocked at the lack of quality cinematic entertainment available on the TV at the present. If you're not a John Wayne fan, you are struggling.'

Tom agreed and stated; There is a lot of shite on the box now, I mean *Bless This House* it's about as funny as a broken leg and *Budgie* with Adam Faith, what bull rot is that?'

John joined the debate and added; 'Have you ever watched *Cannon* with William Conrad? I mean this guy is about 5 ft 3 in, and the shape of a beer barrel and he is throwing blokes 6 ft 3 in, and half his age all over the place.'

Malla decided to put a positive slant on the discussion saying; 'Let's not forget *The Two Ronnies, The Persuaders, The Old Grey Whistle Test* and *Match of the Day*, what do you think Harry?'

'Yes, they are decent, along with *The High Chaparral* and *The Comedians*,' I suggested.

Geordie found the conversation tiresome and said; 'Enough of this TV bullshit. I have a ticket to see Rory Gallagher at *The* Mayfair next month.'

'I thought the concert was sold out two weeks ago,' added John.

'Nope, I managed to buy one at the box office yesterday, somebody had returned a ticket. I bought his latest album *Deuce* last week. I can't wait to see him; I hope he plays *Sugar Mama*. I bet you are jealous as hell,' he answered gleefully.

Norman raised his glass; 'A toast to our absent friend, currently serving Queen and country in Northern Ireland, to Keith Harper.'

We all raised our glasses and Tom added; 'I heard another soldier was shot last night in Belfast, while on patrol. He was seriously wounded and undergoing surgery. All this has nothing to do with religion you know, they are just using it as an excuse to maim and murder innocent people. There is nothing brave about blowing up men, women and children with car bombs. It really pisses me off.'

'I am in no doubt that your view is shared by all of us, but the IRA look at it as a fight for independence. I am not making excuses for them, I am just saying that is their political view, albeit a pathetic one,' added Malla.

'Let's just hope Keith gets through his tour of duty safe and sound,' I added.

'Here here to that, and I heard he should be back for the trip to the races next month,' declared Andy.

It was my turn to feed the jukebox and I selected *Maybe I'm Amazed* by Paul McCartney and *Won't Get Fooled Again* by The Who. The mood had become a little sombre after the comments about Northern Ireland. However, a couple of one liners from John created a more jovial ethos when he joked; 'A woman with a £50 note stuck in each ear walked into her bank. Oh yes, shouted the manager she is £100 in arrears.'

MAKE FAST AND AVOID THE BEER GOGGLES

'Dear me John, that was poor,' quipped Stan.

'Listen to this,' and he continued; 'A young lad gets home from school and says, Dad I have a part in the school play as a man who has been married for twenty-five years. His dad replies, never mind son maybe next time you will get a speaking part.'

'Very funny John, it's my turn for drinks. How about me, Harry, Stan and Tom staying in a round and the rest of you cretins do likewise,' suggested Norman.

Having availed ourselves of further refreshment Geordie gave us his latest bulletin in his search for romance; 'I was with my cousin Ray last Saturday night at the ABC Cinema to see *The French Connection*. It finished about 8 pm and we nipped into The Pier for a pint. From there I suggested that a trip into town would be a good idea and The Scotia became our next port of call. Then The Criterion and the Ship & Royal were visited for more beer. At about 11 pm a decision was made to go to the La Strada. After half an hour Ray disappeared and I ended up chatting to this bird. By now I had the beer goggles on and my memory is somewhat unclear after that. However, I ended up back at her place, she had a downstairs flat in John Clay Street.'

'What was she like, blonde, brunette, tall, short, skinny and how old was she?' asked Stan.

'I think she was blonde, short and I seem to recall she had a slight limp,' replied Geordie.

He continued; 'Well, it was the ultimate nightmare. I must have keeled over and fell asleep in her bed. I woke up next morning in a state of high anxiety. I turned over and there she was. My first reaction was to try and remember if I performed any carnal activity. I could not be sure, so I carefully examined my genitals without disturbing her and I formulated the opinion that I would have to have had a gun at my head to undertake such an act. She had more chins than a Hong Kong phone book. To carry out any sexual intercourse, health and safety would be a major priority and with that in mind, I would have needed a plank tied to my arse.'

We were all in fits of laughter now, but Geordie pressed on; 'I couldn't even remember her name. Anyway, as I lay there contemplating my next move, it awoke. She turned to me and whispered; 'You were well-oiled last night Brian.'

My first thought was who the hell is Brian. But that could be a bonus in any subsequent police investigation, so I went along with it and answered; 'Yes I guess I was, sorry about that.'

Then she suggested; 'We can make love if you like, but first I need to go for a slash and you will have to help me out of bed.'

'This confused me, but I got up and walked around to her side of the bed. She pulled back the sheet and what lay before me can only be described as a giant seed potato; and to my horror, she only had one leg. My first reaction was to scan the room for a parrot. She sat up and said; Pass my leg please, it's leaning up against the wardrobe door. True enough there it was, a wooden leg and it still had a shoe on. I was now in a state of shock and I handed the prosthetic leg to her. After fixing her leg into place, she rose to her feet and spoke; 'Not be long, then we can have a good hump. Not bloody likely I thought and as she limped to the toilet, I made my escape. I was dressed and out the door before she returned.'

Our little band of revellers were in hysterics now and John managed to control his laughter and say; 'It's just as well you didn't slip her a length; you could have suffered serious damage. You could have trapped your nob in the hinges or lacerated yours nuts on the screws.'

Having recovered our composure, Norman voiced his concern in relation to the temptation of the fairer sex and suggested; 'Geordie, we are often propelled into a precarious position when imbibing in the demon drink. As the night moves on, the ladies begin a transformation. What happens is this; the beer goggles start to play games with your sight and the girls start to look like Raquel Welch or Rita Hayworth. This is an illusion of course because the realisation is all too apparent when you wake up alongside a mutation of Groucho Marx and a pot-bellied pig, the next morning.'

'Rita Hayworth, what a stunner she is. I would love to show her my collection of World War Two hessian underpants,' joked Tom.

The hilarity subsided and Malla moved the discourse onto literature; 'What are people reading today Norman?'

Norman always liked to stimulate the conversation with his knowledge of the written word and provide us with literary examples that he thought might empower our desire for learning and said; 'It gives me great pleasure to enlighten this distinguished audience on what I consider to be fine examples of current literature. I would suggest the following reading that will both engross and energise your lust for learning. I would recommend the following publications gentlemen.

'*The Exorcist* by William Peter Blatty, *The Day of the Jackal* by Frederick Forsyth, *A Life Navigated* by Haydn Watson, *August 1914* by Aleksandr Solzhenitsyn and finally *Hitler, My Part in His Downfall* by Spike Milligan. These are a few of the books gaining notoriety at the moment. Of course, you do not need to buy these books. Just pop down to the public library; if they are not available, they will order them for you. Have any of you dunderheads ever visited the library?'

'Now that is a bit below the belt Norman, I am often in the library reading the papers,' replied John.

'They are making a film called *The Exorcist* and I think *The Day of the Jackal* is going into celluloid as well,' added Andy.

'I heard they are going to ban *A Clockwork Orange*; it was only released three months ago. Apparently, the film censors have reviewed it and deemed it too violent,' added Stan.

'It's time for humour,' suggested Tom; 'A talking sheepdog got all the sheep in the pen for his farmer. He returned to the farmer and revealed that: All forty sheep are accounted for. The farmer exclaimed; I only have thirty-six. The sheepdog responded; I know, but I just rounded them up.'

Stan had a conundrum for us; 'Which was the first film to show a flushing toilet on screen? You have four choices, they are: *Psycho, A Clockwork Orange, The Dam Busters* or *The Good, the Bad and the Ugly*.'

'Well, it wasn't *The Dam Busters*, that's just bastard stupid,' replied Malla.

'I have seen all these films and I think it is *Psycho*, it's the shower scene if I am correct,' answered Norman.

'Well, he is correct, clever shite,' said Stan.

'It's time for another pint fellas, it's my shout this time and who is feeding the jukebox?' I asked.

'I will select the music for us, I do hope they have some Val Doonican or Perry Como,' joked Norman.

'Get the blues on you dog molester, B. B. King or Willie Dixon,' shouted John.

'Hey ginger, you are not paying for this? I will decide what music to entertain us with. So, go and boil your head,' replied Norman.

Having selected the tunes Norman gave us all another one of his monologues; 'Now boys, it's time you behaved like men and abandon this malodorous insensitive abuse. We are here as bosom pals enjoying a fine ale and as a result, are free to extoll the virtues of our destiny. So, to end this short monologue it would be prudent to remember this simple thought; the grown man knows the world he lives in.'

Geordie changed the direction of the conversation when he asked Malla; 'How is the romance with Caroline. Have you not invited her up here again to enjoy our hospitality and those scrumptious saveloy dips?'

Malla sensed a tinge of jealousy in Geordie's question in relation to his *affaire d'amour* and went on the defensive replying; 'Nothing organised at the moment, but we keep in touch via the telephone.'

'Oh yes, you have a telephone, so rich,' countered Andy sarcastically.

Malla fired up the conversation when he added; 'She wants me to go to Tenerife with her in August for two weeks. I don't know if I will get the time off, but her old man is going to pay for it.'

'You dirty lucky swine, never mind the time off. Just go on the sick you idiot and can I carry your cases?' joked John.

Andy was looking a little downcast at this revelation. No doubt he was still smarting from Malla's efforts to woo Caroline in the Ship & Royal a few months ago and added; 'Me and John were ready to make a move on Caroline in the Ship & Royal, but you were like a dog at broth and impressed her with your verbal diarrhoea remember.'

Before Malla could reply Stan intervened and uttered; 'Andy, were you going to share the affection for this girl with John, because from where I was sitting, there was no bloody way she was going to let either of you anywhere near her. Anyway, neither of you have a bastard phone.'

'That might be true Stan, but my uncle Jim has pigeons and they fly all over the shop,' joked John.

Geordie felt the desire to change the theme and asked Andy; 'How is your old man doing Andy, has he been fishing lately?'

'Yes, the boat was out for five consecutive days, fishing off Seahouses and Blyth. We have caught a lot of cod, ling and a decent haul of mackerel. The old man had to take the boat to Harrison's the boat builder on Thursday though.'

'Why was that? asked Tom.

'When the boat returned just after 7 am, we unloaded our catch at North Shields. Having birthed at the jetty in Shields around 10.30 am, we cleaned and wrapped the gear up. My old man asked my uncle Bob to make fast. I returned home for a kip and then my dad and uncle Bob walked up to the Turks Head for a pint at 11 am.'

'Explain what *make fast* means Andy?' asked Malla.

'It means tie the boat up alongside the jetty,' replied Andy and continued. 'But uncle Bob hadn't tied off at the stern. He was sitting in the Turks Head when he realised. My old man rushed out of the pub to see the boat drifting across the Tyne. Luckily, the Tyne Pilot spotted it and managed to throw a line on board to tow it to the fish quay jetty on the north side. It suffered a little below water damage, but my old man will be fined £200 for not securing a maritime vessel. It's at Harrison's at Bill quay for repair at the minute and out of commission.'

'That was a costly mistake,' added John.

'The cost doesn't mean whale shit; it could have been a lot worse. If it had struck another vessel, it could have cost my old man his licence. The problem is my uncle Bob, he is my old man's brother. He is as daft as a brush; he would chase paper in a gale force wind. He can't read or write and my old man takes pity on him. Working for my dad, is the only job he could be paid for,' declared Andy.

'Is there just the three of you on the boat then,' I asked.

'No, there is Billy as well, he has worked for my old man for years. Sometimes if the weather is fair, we go out on a Friday night, answered Andy.

'I bet that bird I was with last Saturday often gets tied up at the jetty and I would wager she has a summer job, swimming up and down Loch Ness. God she was a monster. Wide birth, she was that alright,' quipped Geordie.

More alcoholic beverages were ordered and the banter gravitated onto our forthcoming trip to York races and Andy produced a piece of paper; 'As Neville Chamberlain once said; with this piece of paper, I bring peace.'

'Yes, and what a plonker he was,' declared Tom.

'Anyway, I have the important details regarding our trip to the races. So, please pay attention or I will instruct John to drop his member in your pint. We have to be on the bus for 9.45 am at the Sima Club, it will leave at 10.00 am prompt, do not be late. You can bring alcohol, but only cans. Food will be provided on the bus; in the form of sarnies, pies and crisps. There will be a toilet stop at the services on the A19. You are required to be smartly dressed; remember you are representing the club. The cost of the trip is £20, which includes your entry to the course. This must be paid to Davy Bullock prior to the bus departing. There must be no gambling on the bus and no bad language, there will be ladies and sensitive Scots Guardsmen on the bus.'

'What soldiers as well?' quipped Stan.

'I think Andy was trying to be funny,' suggested Norman.

Andy carried on; 'The bus will leave the racecourse at 5.30 pm, then we will travel to Thirsk, where our party will spend the evening. The bus will leave for Shields around 11 pm and should return at approximately 1 am in the morning. Are there any questions men?'

'What happens if you miss the bus?' added Geordie.

We all looked at Geordie in disbelief and I answered; 'You won't go to the races you idiot.'

'Ladies on the bus, no one mentioned that and no swearing,' added Malla.

'I think it's just Davy Bullock's missus, she is going to keep an eye on him,' added Andy.

'How much spending money should one take then?' asked John.

'I reckon you will need about £50,' declared Stan.

'Sounds about right,' added Andy.

'Will Keith be given all this information?' asked Tom.

'Yes, I have given his mother a copy of this sheet,' replied Andy.

Norman added his final thoughts; 'I would suggest that we stick together on our arrival in Thirsk, to ensure we all get on the bus home. Finally, I would like to make you all aware of my sense of apprehension with regard to this forthcoming enterprise. There are many paths to happiness dear friends. I feel our trail is littered with diversions of both romantic and monetary contradictions. However, it should be remembered that a sense of bonhomie will propel us to our destiny and fulfil our ambitions in this unforgiving world of mediocrity.'

EVERYONE A WINNER

The day had arrived, a warm Saturday in April and our group of performing animal impersonators were about to inflict a brand of lunacy on the innocent racegoers of York. The history of York Races is long and distinguished. The first ever race meeting was in 1730 on the sight known as the Knavesmire. I arrived at the Simonside Club at 9.30 am along with Stan, Tom and Malla, who had earlier called at my house for a cuppa, prior to walking to the club. When we arrived Geordie, Andy and Keith were already present, they were chatting to a few other lads waiting for the bus.

'Where are the rest of our team then Andy?' asked Malla.

'Norman rang the club ten minutes ago and told me they were just getting on the bus. They should be here soon,' replied Andy.

'Well Norman is on his way, he is our expert tipster,' added Tom.

'Not sure about that, I have a few tips of my own,' I replied.

'Right then, I hope you are going to share them Harry,' said Geordie.

'I might, if you behave yourself and buy the beers when it's your bleeding round.'

'Here we go again, I have told you lot that I am more than happy to get my round in. As long as it is very late on when you are all pissed,' joked Geordie.

'You know what Geordie, I have drank more green paint,' added Tom.

'Settle down Tom, if you were a fish, you would never be in the water, you bite every time,' said Malla.

'Yes, and watch your language, there are women on this trip as well,' added Stan.

The women that Stan spoke of were Davy Bullock's missus and the driver's wife Doreen. On boarding the coach, we were introduced to Ronnie the driver, his wife Doreen and Davy and his missus Sandra. Having selected our seats at the back of the coach, John and Norman arrived to a crescendo of cheers and a quip from Malla; 'Here they are, Lester Pigshit and Scabby Beasley.'

The coach began to fill up and the food and refreshments were loaded on board, thanks to the generosity of the club. This included two complimentary cans of Norseman lager and a pack of two ham and pease pudding sarnies, along with a packet of Tudor beefy crisps.

This of course was a 'lining on' in readiness for the copious amounts of beer that would no doubt be consumed as the day progressed. In addition to the complimentary refreshments, our band of tipsters had all arrived with our own selection of beer in the requisite carrier bags.

As the coach moved off, the sound of ring-pulls being pulled back permeated the coach and Tom leaned over to me and whispered; 'That Sandra is a bit of alright Harry.'

'Now listen here Tom, she is married to Davy, let's not forget that and therefore he must not be upset in any way, is that clear? After all he has organised this little event.'

Tom just winked and added; 'Well, it's going to be a long day Harry and I am sure she will need help with her selections on the course.'

As the coach left Simonside John shouted; 'Ok Wavy Davy, let's get this show on the road and 'book em Danno.'

What relevance this *Hawaii Five-O* catchphrase had to do with the trip, only John knew.

'Are you a mate of Davy then John? asked Geordie.

'Nope, never seen him before, but he has wavy hair and he is called Davy, so he is now Wavy Davy.'

Davy just smiled at the outburst, but the salacious Sandra did not see the funny side and turned and gave John a look of contempt. Davy then moved down the coach collecting £20 from everyone except Geordie, which did not go unnoticed by his pals and Malla asked; 'You not paying then Geordie?'

Before Geordie could respond Davy said; 'Oh no, he gets a free trip and entry to the course, that is his commission for getting you lot to go.'

Geordie's face was a picture as he shot Davy a look of poison. As a result, Geordie was subjected to a tirade of abuse from his peers. Andy was the first to admonish Geordie; 'You bastard, you weren't going to tell us, were you?'

'You have more faces than the town hall clock Geordie,' added Stan.

Norman took a different take on it and offered Geordie an olive branch; 'Dear friend Geordie, you may have been less than transparent relating to your renumeration in this venture, but I for one do not begrudge you this small reward for your efforts. Furthermore, we are all in your debt for your contribution.'

Any further ridicule was curtailed as the food was dished out. Most just collected their sustenance and put it aside. John wasted no time and said; 'I am starving, I could eat a raggy mat.'

'Christ, you are a hungry swine John, the bus has only just left Shields,' said Keith.

'Anyway, who made the sarnies?' John shouted down the coach.

Sandra, was sitting four rows from the front, and heard the question; 'That would be me love, any complaints?'

'Oh no, none at all, I love ham and pease pudding, is the ham slow roasted then?'

Sandra's reply was definitive in its pungency; 'Be careful ginger or you might just receive a beer shampoo.'

Tom could not resist a comment and with Davy talking to the driver at the front of the coach he said; 'I love a dominant woman; you can beat me with a hot saveloy anytime love.'

Instead of a rebuke Sandra just turned to Tom and smiled; 'I like a man that goes like a steam hammer.'

We all looked at Tom, who just grinned and started to rub his hands in glee. I turned to him and said; 'What did I say? You have been warned. If you throw a spanner in the works, you will be on the end of a punch.'

Norman veered off on a tangent and added; 'I have their LP.'

'What the hell are you talking about you moron?' queried Stan.

'Steam Hammer, they are a rock band you ignoramus.'

Norman took the opportunity to subtly ridicule Stan; 'I have shared this information with you and by sharing it, I have somehow dispelled the myth that your knowledge of the rock scene is accurate. In a similar way it also relates to Andy's reluctance to spend money when he is with loyal friends. This casts a shadow on both his uncommonly reluctance to share and a mistaken philosophy on friendship. I am without doubt the genius in this youthful rabble and I will continue to evoke a sense of unequivocal meticulousness with zeal and candour.'

'What a load of verbal diarrhoea Norman. However, you are surely bound for a career in the House of Commons and politics. You have this ability to avoid saying yes or no to any direct question,' added Keith.

Malla completely changed the subject; 'Hey, I thought we were getting pies as well as sarnies.'

'Yes, that's right, pies are to be provided,' added Geordie.

Before Geordie could make representation to Davy, John shouted down the coach; 'Hey Wavy Davy, who has eaten all the pies then? This is a rip off.'

Wavy Davy's missus, the voluptuous Sandra responded with; 'You cannot want them already, Jesus, you are a load of gannets down there.'

'I remember meat, my mother once bought a tin of PEK chopped pork,' joked Tom.

The journey from then on was quite uneventful, having eaten most of the pies; we played dominoes and cards. Norman and Keith read the newspapers looking for inspiration from the racing pages and exchanged tips. Tom continued to flirt with Sandra, despite my threat of castration. The coach stopped at the designated services on the A19 and all present opted for a toilet break. The coach pulled up at the Knavesmire around midday. Having gained entry to the course we made our way to the bar to refuel.

Andy surprised us all when he suggested he would be the first to buy the drinks. A collective decision was agreed to stay in teams of three when buying drinks, this was to ensure prompt service at the bar. I was teamed up with Tom and Stan, John, Norman and Andy made up another group with Geordie, Keith and Malla making up the other drinking trio. The remainder of the coach party decided to have some lunch, it was now 12.30 pm. Having had lunch Wavy Davy and Sandra joined us in the bar along with Ronnie the driver and Doreen. The rest of the party avoided us like the plague, probably a wise decision.

The weather was sunny and warm with a pleasant breeze, as we took tables on the balcony overlooking the parade ring. The first race of the day was at 1.30 pm a handicap with twelve runners.

Andy asked Tom what horse he was betting on. 'That information will cost you Andy, I have the winner and I just can't divulge that information to all and sundry. It will create a stampede, with punters throwing hard cash on it and therefore the price will drop dramatically.'

'Tom that is a load of shite. When you put the bet on you get the price there and then and it doesn't alter. He is just winding you up Andy,' stated Malla.

Norman pressed Tom on the identity of this nag; 'How certain are you about this horse then Tom?'

'Well, put it this way, I was in the toilet having a run off, when two jockeys walked in and one said to the other; I hear you're on the winner of the first.'

'That's bollock's Tom, how do you know what horse that jockey is on? asked Geordie.

'Listen stupid, think about it, I know what he looks like you cretin. So, I only have to look at which horse he plonks his arse on in the parade ring,'

'Oh yes, smart thinking Tom,' replied Geordie.

'I think it would be very gracious if you shared this information with all of us Tom,' added Keith.

'Nope, you are on your own fellas, maybe I will share my selections after this one wins.'

Andy had given this some serious consideration and he came up with a plan to identify the jockey in question. 'I know how to find out who the jockey is boys; as the jockeys enter the parade ring just ask them one at a time if they were in the toilets at 12.45 pm?'

'This I must see Andy, you will be dragged off for trying to proposition a jockey,' joked Stan.

Andy and Geordie tried to pick Tom's horse by looking at their race cards. The rest of us chose our selections and looked to ascertain the best prices before placing our bets. Geordie continued to pester Tom for his tip and finally Tom relented saying; 'You have never put a bet on before have you Geordie?'

'No never, I don't know a thing about horse racing.'

'Alright, but just this once I will help you out my son.' As they made their way to a bookmakers stand Tom whispered to Geordie. 'The horses name is Bar, it's a great price at 20/1.'

Geordie looked at the prices available and the horses listed on the bookie's board and sure enough there it was at the bottom, Bar at 20/1. Tom sloped off and put his bet on with another bookie. Tom met up with Geordie as they joined the rest of us in the stand and he asked Geordie how much he had bet on the horse?

'I have put £2 on to win Tom and thanks for the tip.'

'That means you will be £40 up after the first race, if it wins Geordie.'

Geordie smiled and said; 'Champion the wonder horse, I can't wait to see it pelt over that finishing line first. Let's make our way up into the stand.'

What Geordie did not know was that Tom had set him up and he had asked the bookie to take his £2, but to just go along with it. After the race Geordie would get his £2 back. Having all gathered and waiting for the race to start Malla asked Geordie which horse, he had chosen.

'Oh no, I am not going to tell you until it flies past the winning post first Malla.'

'Alright then, how much did you put on it? asked Stan.

'I put £2 on to win Stan at 20/1,' he replied.

'Christ Geordie, each way bet would have given you a better chance of winning money,' added Norman.

'No, I have a good feeling about this one Norman.'

A decision to go down to the track and find a position near the finish line was agreed. We all had selected different horses, so surely one of us would have the winner. It was an eight-furlong race and they were evenly matched two furlongs from home. Then a horse called Never Again hit the front and drove on unchallenged to win four lengths in front of the second horse called Mister Bojangles. Malla had the winner and was jumping around like a demented chimp as Norman asked Geordie. 'Well, where did your horse finish?'

'The bastard was never mentioned Norman.'

'What was it called then? he asked.

'Bar and it was 20/1, I wasted £2 on that sodden nag. This was Tom's tip, well, he has lost as well,' he shouted; 'Hey Tom, so much for your tip mate.'

Tom laughed; 'Mine was second Mister Bojangles at 10/1. I had £2 each way on it, I win a fiver.'

'What, your tip was Bar at 20/1,' added Geordie.

Then Tom revealed all, much to the amusement of his peers. Geordie was fuming. 'You bastard, what a trick to play on a friend.'

Tom then apologised and accompanied Geordie to claim his £2 back from the bookie. I couldn't resist another jibe at Geordie's non-runner and as they returned, I said; 'Now Geordie, never back on the last horse on the list, it never wins.'

'Piss off Harry, at least I got my money back. How much did you win then?'

'Sweet bugger all and I am £2 down,' I replied.

Our team of intrepid punters all trooped back to the bar for another libation and to scan the horses for the next race at 2 pm. It had twenty runners over a mile and a half. Norman decided to offer Geordie a sympathetic riposte to his earlier embarrassment. Geordie, you have the mental agility of a yard brush, but you are a bosom friend and we will never desert you. You bring your own sense of humour to this unwashed band of sardonic miscreants and it is not undervalued. As Nathanial Hawthorne once said;

> *We can be but partially acquainted even with the events which actually influence our course through life, and our final destiny.*

'What the hell are you spouting about now Norman?' asked John.

'Well John, basically what I am saying is this. Events in our lives make us stronger and more adept in dealing with situations that present themselves to us.'

'A bit like the garbage Tom gave us about his hot tip from the toilet,' joked Malla.

'Correct Malla,' added Stan.

The afternoon brought luck for some of our punters, notably John, Keith, Stan and ironically Geordie, they all made a profit on the day. The rest of us ended up a little poorer after our odyssey into the world of horse racing. We all boarded the coach at 5.30 pm in a state of merriment, an agreement was reached to limit the consumption of beer. Sadly, Wavy Davy was in an intoxicated state, much to the annoyance of Sandra, who chose to sit some distance from her husband on the coach. This was not lost on Tom; he took the opportunity to get acquainted with Sandra. My advice and threats of GBH were ignored by Tom, he gave me a wry smile as he sat next to Sandra, while Wavy Davy slept like a baby.

Stan brought up the subject of my impending marriage and suggested that serious thought should be given to my stag night: 'Look dear cousin, I am your best man. It is important that a discussion should take place as to where and when this auspicious event takes place.'

'I reckon the Quayside, Newcastle,' suggested John.

'If it is a Friday, there might be a band on at the Locarno in Sunderland,' added Keith.

Malla decided to send Tom a broadside while he was chatting up Sandra and shouted; 'What's your wife's name Tom?'

Tom turned in his seat and flashed two fingers in our direction. Then Geordie joined in the denunciation, 'Tom, did you manage to see about getting those genital warts sorted out at the clinic?'

A chorus of laughter rang out among our little band of brothers, which resulted in another insulting gesture from Tom. Returning to the topic of my stag night, Malla added; 'Well, don't forget, I am in Tenerife in August.'

'Oh yes, you have an invite from the lovely Caroline,' quipped Andy sarcastically.

'I am to be married on Saturday August 12. So, a week before would be a more convenient plan,' I replied.

'That's fine by me, I don't go to Tenerife until the August 15. So, I will be available for the stag and the wedding,' added Malla.

'Is it a church wedding then Harry?' asked Norman.

'No, the registry office in Chapter Row, then Careme House for the reception.'

'Would you like me to write your best man speech Stan? asked Norman.

'Not bloody likely, it won't take me long to tell all those present what an idiot the bridegroom is. If you write it, the guests will lose the will to live.'

'A man of a lesser fortitude than me would take offence at that slur Stan.'

'Please Norman, take offence and shut the fuck up,' added Geordie.

John chose the opportunity to relate a funny story and went on; 'Paddy walked into the Crown Posada on the Quayside and ordered a pint. As he paid for his drink, he recognised a bloke standing at the end of the bar and asked; It's Sean is it not? The bloke turned and replied; Bloody hell Paddy, I haven't seen you in twenty years. Not since we worked at Swan Hunters in Wallsend, how the hell are you doing? Oh, I am fine; I am a postman now Sean, replied Paddy. I am still at Swan Hunters and married now, what about you, have you a missus then?' Yes, I have been married for eleven years now and I have eight ankle biters as well.

Bloody hell Paddy eight kids, have you not got a TV then? joked Sean. Paddy laughed; I put all this breeding down to the wife Doris and her homemade stew.

They continued to chat about old times, family and the future. Then

Paddy invited Sean back to his place saying; When we get home Doris will have a pan of her stew on the hob, she made it this morning, you will have to have some. Sean agreed and after a few more pints they set off for Paddy's place. On arrival the house was a hive of activity with children everywhere. Sure enough, Doris had a huge pan of stew that covered three rings on the cooker. As they sat down to enjoy this baby making elixir, Sean noticed the pet Labrador lying in front of the fire and said; Bloody hell Paddy, look at the size of that dog's bollocks.

Doris quickly responded with; Oh yes and he only licks the plates.' Much laughter and then Geordie asked; What's the dogs bollocks got to do with it?

Norman raised his hands and said; 'Do not even try to explain boys, this one is lost in translation. The penny might drop within the next few hours.'

'Alright cheeky swine, we are not all as sharp as you Norman,' moaned Geordie.

'Geordie you have the IQ of a sherbet fountain,' added Keith.

'Malla turned to me and said; 'Looks like Tom and Sandra are getting on like a house on fire.'

'If Wavy Davy wakes up, Tom will be getting burnt,' I replied.

Our coach was about fifteen minutes from Thirsk, Wavy Davy was still snoring like a horse with sinusitis as John shouted down the bus; 'Is there any more grub on the go?'

'There are a couple of mince pies left, if anyone wants them, but they are cold,' Doreen shouted.

'If you want them warmed up John, I would just slide them between Tom and Sandra. They are generating a lot of heat at the moment. However, if you choose to carry out this exercise, would you kindly ask Tom if he needs to change his incontinence underpants?' I joked.

More laughter from the back of the coach as John answered; 'Will do, but I think I might get a punch in the gob.'

'Well, you are on your holidays, treat yourself,' I added.

John duly collected the pies from Doreen and suggested the heating of the culinary items might benefit from my suggestion. Tom declared; 'Go forth and multiply John.'

So, John asked if anyone would like a pie, no such interest was forthcoming and he ate both pies with a fervour reminiscent of a lion tearing at the carcase of a cape buffalo on the Serengeti. We arrived in

Thirsk at 6.30 pm, this destination had been chosen by Ronnie the driver as a watering hole before our return to South Shields. He parked up in the Market Square. Wavy Davy was still sleeping soundly and Sandra resisted the temptation to wake him. She had spent the last hour in the close company of Tom, who was working overtime with his repartee, despite our constant barracking. She had planned for the evening and she had brought a change of clothes, which she carried into the first pub, the Black Bull. To avoid overcrowding at the bar the coach party chose to populate various hostelries and drifted off to the Red Lion, The Three Tuns and the Blacksmiths Arms.

Ronnie, Doreen and Sandra remained with the nine retarded Sundancer's. Wavy Davy was left alone on the bus in deep slumber. Sandra emerged from the ladies toilet in a figure-hugging black velvet dress that left nothing to the imagination and this only served to enhance Tom's carnal aspirations.

Having acquired our drinks, Keith noticed that the dart board was free and suggested that we have a competition to ascertain the best player in our group of unhinged disciples and he said; 'I reckon £1 from everyone and the winner takes all. It would be better with eight players though.'

'I am not bothered Keith,' replied Norman.

'No count me out as well,' added Stan.

'That means we only have seven now,' added Keith.

'I will play, I like a game of arrows,' said Sandra.

A draw was made and I had to play Andy, Malla would play Keith, Geordie would be up against Tom and vivacious Sandra would play John. After the draw John, informed all present that he could not go first as he had to go to the bog to 'pinch a loaf'.

'Charmed, I am sure, he is such a romantic and the girls must just flock around you John,' replied Sandra sarcastically.

'Well, you're not wrong there love. Don't worry though, I always wash my paws after an evacuation,' and off he went.

'Let's be thankful for that,' she added.

The competition got under way and Keith beat Malla with a dart on double 20. Malla still had 200 on the board. The other games favoured Andy, who easily defeated me, Tom was victorious over Geordie and to our surprise Sandra emerged the winner over John. As the draw was carried out for the next round, the rest of us decided to move onto another boozer and the Blacksmiths Arms was selected. Once seated, a round of toasted sarnies were ordered to ensure that the volatile mixture currently lying in our stomachs could be stabilised.

Malla felt the need to crack a joke; 'A man walked into a pub and bet the landlord a drink that he could fart the Beatles, *Ticket To Ride*, the landlord said; There is no chance you will do it, I'll take the bet. The man stood at the bar, dropped his trousers strained and shit all over the bar. What the hell are you doing? You have shit all over my bar screamed the landlord! Relax, replied the man; even Frank Sinatra had to clear his throat before he sang.

'I'll have to try that,' joked John.

'Not tonight, you bloody won't,' replied Stan.

At 9.15 pm we returned to the Black Bull to find Keith and Andy in the final of the darts competition. Tom and Sandra were missing in action and I suspected that they had moved onto another venue that afforded them a little privacy. As the final began, in walked Wavy Davy after his lengthy snooze on the coach and asked; 'Have you seen Sandra?'

Andy as tactless as usual declared; 'Oh yes, she has been here playing darts and she easily beat John, she looks great in that black dress by the way.'

Wavy Davy looked a little confused and before Andy dropped Tom in the mire, I added; 'I think she is with Doreen and Ronnie; they might be in the Red Lion.'

'Well, I will have a beer in here and then I'll go and find them,' he replied.

I had my doubts about Davy finding his spouse and so I pressganged John and Malla in joining me to look for Tom and Sandra. First, we tried the Red Lion, but no luck there. Then the Blacksmiths Arms, again no luck. So, a decision was made to have a pint and then move onto The Three Tuns, still no sign of them. It was now 10.15 pm and I said to my comrades; 'I have an idea gentleman, I think I know where we might find them, follow me.'

The three of us found the coach parked up behind the market square. It was parked in a dimly lit far corner of a public car park. We quietly strolled up to the coach and having got within 30 yards, the moans and groans emanating from inside the vehicle generated a sense of restrained laughter and John whispered; 'Let's burst onto the bus and catch them at it and give them an almighty shock.'

'No, let's just see if we can find a better vantage point. It looks like they are on the back seat, judging by the movement of the coach,' added Malla.

Slowly moving silently and within a few yards of the back of the coach, voices could be now heard. They were in full flow and then Sandra said; 'Come on big boy, drive me home.'

Holding back the laughter, we managed to keep our composure. That was until a big hairy arse illuminated by a security light appeared.

John said quietly; 'That's not Tom's arse.'

I turned to Malla and whispered; 'How the hell does he know that, is there something John needs to tell us?'

Malla exploded into laughter, this startled the two lovebirds and Sandra whispered; 'Shit, who is that? Someone is out there.'

This was our cue to storm the coach. Having done so, it revealed Sandra hastily pulling her knickers up. However, it was not Tom who had been servicing the lovely Sandra, but Ronnie the coach driver, he stood buck-naked from the waist down. He was far from impressed by our ill-timed intrusion and said; 'What the hell do you want, and how long have you been watching you perverts?'

John took the opportunity to respond and added; 'Well now Mr bus driver or 'Big Boy' if you prefer, although that is a bit of a contradiction from where I am standing. You are a major disappointment really, this woman deserves a better performance, she hasn't even broken sweat yet.' 'Basically, I have seen *more life in a tramp's vest.*'

Sandra seemed a tad concerned, probably wondering if her darling husband would find out what had occurred; 'You're not going to tell my husband are you boys?'

Malla brought the scenario to a close; 'My dear lady, you have a very low opinion of us. Our lips are sealed.'

We then left them and as we walked away, we gave a rousing rendition of; 'Come on big boy drive me home.'

On our return to the Black Bull, we bumped into Wavy Davy, who had been searching for his missus.

'Have you found her yet?' asked Malla.

'No, have you seen her boys?'

'Sorry mate, never seen her for some time,' added John.

'It is nice to see you again fellas, had a pleasant evening, have you?' asked Norman.

'Just pub-crawling Norman,' replied John.

Five minutes later Tom appeared and asked; 'Who won the darts then?'

'Keith won and where the hell have you been?' asked Stan.

'I have spent a wonderful night chatting up a lush blonde in The Three Tuns.'

'Hang on a minute, we were in The Three Tuns, never saw you in there you arse,' I replied.

'Well Harry, you didn't look in the snug, did you?'

'What a story we have for you Tom,' quipped Malla.

Having bought our last pint in the Black Bull, the evenings matinee performance was relayed to the rest of our team. Andy, Keith, Norman, Stan and Geordie were somewhat peeved that we did not invite them along for the sexual proclivities on the coach. Tom seemed unfazed by our revelations relating to Sandra's exploits with Ronnie the driver and added; 'Boys, I have a telephone number that I will be ringing tomorrow to organise a rendezvous with this very pretty blonde.'

'Well, what's her name and I must say that Thirsk is a long way for a romantic liaison,' added Norman.

'No names at this juncture and no, she is not from Thirsk boys. She is actually from the North East, she is in Thirsk visiting relatives,' replied Tom.

As we all boarded the coach, Sandra was sitting in the front seats of the coach next to her hubby Wavy Davy. She looked a little pensive, but our lips were sealed and her late-night sexual activities were never mentioned.

However, Stan could not help himself; 'I thought you two would be on the back seat.'

Wavy Davy was a little perplexed by this; 'I could do with the rest mate.'

Having consumed copious amounts of alcohol, the banter on the bus was limited. After ten minutes the silence was broken by John and Malla singing;

Come on big boy, can't you drive any faster?

Before drifting off to sleep for a couple of hours Andy decided to indulge in a little humour and said; 'Kev and Bob were taking a shower after a game of football, when Kev noticed that Bob had a huge cork stuck up his arse. Kev said; Bob that cork looks uncomfortable. Why don't you have it removed? I can't, it's permanently up there, he responded. What, how the hell did it happen? Bob explained; I was walking along the beach and I tripped over an oil lamp. There was a puff of smoke and then a genie came floating out. He said; I am a genie and I can grant you just one wish. I replied, no shit!'

We were roused from our slumber at 12.45 am as the coach arrived back at the Simonside Club. Sandra and Wavy Davy were first to leave the coach.

John and Tom serenaded them as they walked from the coach with; *Love is a many splendid thing.*

BEER, BIRDS AND BEDOUINS

It had been two weeks since our trip to York Races and our next seminar was scheduled for the May bank holiday. The Harbour Lights was selected as a venue, this boozer is situated on the Lawe Top overlooking the mighty River Tyne. There was a good reason for this choice, on occasion a 'lock-in' might occur. Several pubs were well-known for lock-ins, including the Mechanics Arms, the Lambton Arms and the Douglas Vaults. These boozers were in the town centre, but the Harbour Lights provided a more relaxed atmosphere.

Keith had returned to Belfast to rejoin his regiment and Malla was spending a long weekend in Cornwall with Caroline. Stan, Geordie and yours truly arrived at the designated hour of 7 pm. John and Andy were already in the pub, having just bought their beer.

'Who's turning out tonight then?' asked Andy.

'We are just waiting for Tom and Norman,' I answered.

Andy related to the current situation in Northern Ireland; 'I see there was more death and mayhem in Belfast last night, I hope Keith keeps his head down. It must be a nightmare living there at the moment.'

'Keith knows the script, he is a sandancer, he will want to return home for Harry's stag night and wedding in August anyway,' stated John.

Tom and Norman arrived to complete the full complement, they bought their beers and joined us at a table in the window. The pub was well-populated and Tom said; 'I am surprised there are so many in here at this time, must be payday.'

'They have a great jukebox in here, I am off to put a few sounds on,' replied Stan and he duly fed the machine.

'Anyone bought any LPs lately?' asked Geordie.

'I just bought *Parachute* by the Pretty Things the other day and no you can't borrow it, Andy. Not until you return my *Blues Alone* by Mayall,' I added.

Andy reacted; 'Don't worry you will get it back Harry, I've only had it a month.'

'If it's scratched, I will banjo you. I bought that LP new remember.'

'Yes, yes you told me,' answered Andy.

The topic of romance was introduced when Geordie asked; 'So, how you getting on with Laura then Norman, is there another marriage on the cards then?'

'Well, I am fully aware of your aims Geordie, but I am not going to give you any personal details of our relationship, suffice to say that all is well and the lovemaking is out of this world,' replied Norman.

'I need some new binoculars, mine only have a range of 500 yards,' joked John.

Stan sarcastically embellished John's comment; 'Now there is romance for you, how better to become acquainted with someone. All you have to do is wait until it's dark and sit in your bedroom window. Then using high resolution binoculars scan the neighbourhood for scantily clad females. Why didn't I think of that?'

Norman then produced a handful of cigars, a gift from Laura's dad; 'Here you are, you band of degenerates, have a cigar and enhance the atmosphere with a little sophistication.'

'Have you bumped into Long John Silver's daughter lately Geordie?' asked Andy.

'No, thankfully and I hope I never do,' he answered.

'Let's hope she is not up the duff, otherwise, she will have a search party out looking for you mate. Then your life will change forever,' added Andy.

'Oh, it will change forever alright, I will join the fucking foreign legion,' he added.

I then asked Tom about the mysterious blonde he met in Thirsk two weeks ago and I asked him if he had made contact with her.

'Well Harry, it so happens that I rang her the other day and we agreed to go to the cinema next week,' he replied.

'Where does she live Tom?' asked Stan.

'She lives in Murton and she is studying at Sunderland Polytechnic,' Tom responded.

'Where the hell is Murton, I've never heard of it?' asked Geordie.

'Well, that's no real surprise Geordie, you don't know where your own house is,' joked John.

'Kiss my arse John.'

'What film are you going to see then Tom?' I asked.

'We're going to see that new Clint Eastwood film *Dirty Harry*. It has excellent reviews apparently.'

'Alright then Tom, it is vital that you provide the details of this new girlfriend. I want a name, age, height, chest measurement my son,' added Stan.

'Just to arouse your *idée fixe*, her name is Jane, she is eighteen and I would say she is about 5 ft 6 in. As I have only met her once, I have as yet not ascertained her chest measurement. However, I would hazard a guess she measures around a 36, offered Tom.

'Steady Andy, wipe your mouth, you are salivating again,' joked Norman.

It was now 7.50 pm and Norman fed the jukebox and another round of beers were ordered to the sound of Joni Mitchell's *Big Yellow Taxi*. As we sat and badgered Tom on the new love in his life, a guy came in looking somewhat inebriated. He made it to the bar and ordered a brown ale and he poured half into his schooner. Having completed this task, he scanned the pub in all directions and shouted; 'Who put that shite on?'

This was a reference to the dulcet tones of Joni Mitchell. Norman decided to stay silent and didn't claim responsibility for the choice of music. The well-oiled new customer repeated his question with an enhanced level of vitriol saying; 'I asked, which idiot put this shite on?'

'Is there a problem mate?' asked the barman.

'No, I was just asking what wanker has just gone to the jukebox and put that crap on? Oh, and by the way I'm not your mate sunshine.'

The barman tried to ease the tension; 'It does not matter who put it on and when you say it is not to your liking, well, you are all entitled to an opinion. But remember opinions are like arseholes, everyone has one sunshine,' added the barman.

Tom had heard enough and decided to speak up; 'It was me that put Joni Mitchell on mate, what's the problem?'

The barman did not want an incident on his hands and quickly tried to diffuse the situation; 'Let's not be unpleasant about this, you are here for an enjoyable night,' and he tried to appease the guy by saying; 'You are quite welcome to put what you want on if you wish.'

This had little impact on the guy and he turned to Tom and shouted; 'You must be bent to put this shite on.'

Tom rose to his feet and as he did the barman added; 'I want no trouble in here, if you want to continue this discussion, will you go outside please?'

Tom did his best to placate the guy and suggested that he was a tad disrespectful. His advice fell on deaf ears and the guy seemed to be spoiling for a fight. Unfortunately, he had picked on the wrong man. Tom, along with Stan, were the two hard hitters in our little band of friends. The barman was getting nervous and he repeated his request that the matter be settled outside. It was becoming a sideshow for the rest of the clientele in the pub. Tom suggested that the problem must be addressed and said to the guy; 'Why don't you and I go outside and I am sure we can sort this out.'

The response was predictable when the guy said; 'Oh yes, I will sort you out alright mate, let's go.'

Stan turned to me; 'One of them is going to be knocked out and it won't be Tom.'

As Tom followed the guy out of the door, he passed our table lifted his thumb and winked. This was an indication that this would not take long chaps. Our table afforded a grand view of the proceedings. Tom managed to manoeuvre the guy away from the pub doorway and close to a high hedgerow 20 yards away. We sat and observed, along with the rest of the pub's customers, who were stood at another window to the left of the door.

The guy continued to berate Tom and then swung a punch. Tom easily fended off the blow and landed a right hander on his opponent's right eye. The punch sent him falling back into the hedgerow, there he was, prostrate at an angle of forty-five degrees sparked out. Tom examined his opponent and turned to his audience and shouted; 'What do I do now?'

The barman came to the door and asked; 'Is he breathing?'

'Yes, he is just sparked out,' said Tom.

'Just leave him there, he will come around shortly. I can keep an eye on the fool from here,' he replied.

Tom returned to our table and Stan said; 'If you didn't deal with that arse, I was going to. What an obnoxious git he was.'

The barman showed his gratitude and provided us all with a drink and a packet of crisps. After around five minutes the 'Hedgerow Halfwit' awoke to a chorus of cheers from the pub and stumbled away, nursing one hell of a shiner. A customer at the bar thought that he had seen this guy before and said he was from North Shields. He had seen his face in The Porthole and The Chain Locker near the ferry landing on the north side.

'Well, he will know better than to criticise the music of Joni Mitchell from now on,' added John. He then decided to inject a little humour into the proceedings; 'It was on the news today that there was a fire at the regional tax office, but it was put out before any serious good could be achieved.'

Our band of revellers were joined by a friend of Tom's. Abdi Hussain worked with Tom and lived on the Lawe Top, in Vespasian Street. Abdi was always full of fun and asked; 'Who was that sad git in the hedge then?'

'That would be the bloke Tom has just lamped,' replied Stan.

Norman returned to the subject of Geordie's one-night stand with the peg leg lady; 'If the worst happens Geordie, at least you will attain a splendid suntan in a warmer climate. The French foreign legion has bases all over the world, but especially in North Africa. Of course, contact with the opposite sex is very rare, but that's the way it is remember, you go to forget.'

Abdi introduced a new dimension to the conversation when he brought up the plight of the Bedouin tribesmen of North Africa and the Middle East and said; 'Those Bedouins are a queer lot, they just trek around the most inhospitable parts of the world on camels. A number of tribes don't even have women with them, camels become a source of revenue and they are highly valued. I was reading about it in one of my old man's *National Geographic* magazines.'

'Not your sort of reading material Abdi, it has words in it,' joked Tom.

'Very funny Tom, I do have other interests and the world in which we live in has a wealth of knowledge in which to accumulate,' replied Abdi.

Stan returned to the Bedouin topic and added; 'I have heard about these Bedouin fellas. Pin back your lugholes and listen to this. These camels that the Bedouins have, carry gallons of water you know. They store it in their humps and they can go without water for hundreds of miles. The Bedouins make them fill up at every oasis, but sometimes the male camels need a little persuasion. So, when the male camels are drinking from the oasis the tribesmen creep up behind them and slam their bollocks together with two heavy rocks. This causes the camel to go ooooooooooohhhh, therefore causing it to suck up copious amounts of water.

Tom was in mid-swallow having just taken a drink from his pint and he nearly choked as he tried to subdue his laugh, raucous laughter followed.

'That was very funny Stan, but what happens to the female camels then?' asked Geordie.

'They just eat them buggers,' he replied.

'That's a load of bollocks that is, camels are not daft. They would soon wise up to that caper, they would walk into the oasis backwards, so the tribesmen couldn't creep up on them,' joked Andy.

'Any more jokes then?' I asked.

'Yes, I have a cracker,' revealed Norman; 'An old man went to the doctor to see what treatment he could have for his constipation. It's terrible he said. I haven't moved my bowels in a week. Have you done anything about it? asked the doctor. Of course, he replied, I sit in the bathroom for an hour in the morning and again at night. No, the doctor answered; I mean do you take anything? Of course, you daft sod, he answered I take a book.'

It was now 9.30 pm and the pub was well occupied with an even smattering of both sexes. We had now consumed around five pints each and were all in a state of high merriment. Tom was regaling us with his thoughts about his recently acquired LP *Live at Cook County Jail* by B. B. King, when in walked Geoff, an acquaintance of ours who had been living and working in Canterbury. Having bought his pint, he joined us and we shared our respective stories.

He was working with a squad on building a new school and his next contract was in Derby, starting in three days time. He informed us how much money he was making and it raised a few eyebrows when he revealed he made £70 per week after tax.

Geordie was shocked; 'It would take me three weeks to make that.'

To add insult to injury Geoff told us he also had a car, a Triumph Stag.

'I bet you pull the birds in that Geoff,' suggested Abdi.

'Well, I do have a girlfriend Abdi, she lives in York,' he replied.

'We were just in York two weeks ago, at the races,' I added.

'Never mind that bollocks Harry, what does she do for a living then Geoff?' asked Norman.

'She works in a solicitor's office,' he added.

'That will be handy if you end up in jail Geoff,' said Geordie.

Norman chose to join in the conversation; 'Trust you to see the negative aspect of a relationship Geordie. I am sure Geoff has no intention of being locked up and no doubt his fine lady would not be too happy about it either.'

Andy's attention was drawn to two young ladies at the bar and he asked Stan; 'Do you fancy trying it on with those two at the bar?'

Stan looked at the girls and after weighing up the possibilities; 'Why not Andy, but try and think before you open your gob alright.'

Andy gave him a look of derision as they rose from their seats and made there way to the bar. The shorter of the two girls had long blonde hair, blue eyes, bright red lipstick and matching nails. The other girl was a little taller with short, cropped brown hair and brown eyes. She had limited make-up on, save for a little pale blue eye shadow. They were both wearing jeans and the blonde had a tight-fitting jumper that left nothing to the imagination and her friend wore a floral blouse.

Stan opened with; 'Hello girls, how are we today then?'

The blonde girl responded with; 'Hi, fine thanks, but our glasses are nearly empty.'

'Well, I am sure that can be rectified,' said Stan.

No response from Andy and Stan turned to see Andy transfixed by the other girl and Stan repeated his last comment. Andy realised he had perhaps lingered too long in his detached concentration; 'Oh yes sorry, can we buy you a drink then. What would you ladies like?'

The blonde answered; 'I will have a Martini and Sylvia will have a Campari.'

Stan turned to Andy with a smile that stretched from ear to ear; 'There you go Andy; would you buy these lovely ladies their drinks please?'

Andy slid along the bar and ordered the drinks. Stan asked the blonde her name and she replied saying her name was Fiona and her friend Sylvia was French and her English was not great. Stan thought that any progress with Sylvia might be too much like hard work, he therefore concentrated on Fiona. Andy returned with the drinks and waited for an opportunity to join in the conversation. Stan then introduced himself; 'Sylvia is French Andy, which is a coincidence is it not, you are fluent in French is that not so?'

Andy's panic-stricken face spoke volumes. 'Well, I know a little French,' he suggested.

'Go on then, gives us a little French,' replied Stan with a wide grin on his face.

Andy was now hoping for some divine intervention. It didn't happen, so he took the plunge; 'Ciao, arrivederci femme fatale, non compos mentis.'

Sylvia burst out laughing and Fiona responded; 'That was a real mouthful.'

'You're not the first girl to say that love,' Andy joked, in the hope that would deflect his ignorance of the French language.

Stan just looked at Andy in amazement and Fiona said; 'I think it would be wise to stick to your native tongue and as they say in France, *fermez la bouche*. Which in English translates into shut your gob.'

The conversation became somewhat strained after this and Andy became a little impatient to return to his buddies, having decided that his chances with Sylvia were virtually non-existent. Stan spared any further embarrassment; '*Tempus fugit*, we must rejoin our friends. It has been very pleasant to meet you both and I hope we meet again soon.'

They both made their way back to our table and suffered the torment and ridicule that was meted out with glee.

Tom then introduced a little humour with a joke; 'Waiter, waiter! This soup tastes funny. The waiter answered with; Then why are you not laughing, you stupid bastard?'

Geordie continued the comic theme and added; 'Mr Wilson, I have reviewed this case very carefully said the divorce court judge and I've decided to give your wife £900 per week. That is very fair of you, your honour, replied the husband and every now and then I will try to send her a few quid myself.'

'Now then brothers, what are we going to do to cheer up our pal Andy. It seems that he has not acquired the panache to woo the ladies?' I added.

'Well Harry, I would give him a jar of worms and a nude picture of Raquel Welch, that should do it. Failing that, he should go down to The Ferry Tavern or The Mermaids Tail and spend £20 on a boiler for the night,' added Abdi.

'Sounds like you are speaking from experience,' suggested John.

The evening meandered on without any further incident and as we didn't manage to attain a lock-in, the night ended with us heading home at 11.30 pm.

IT WILL NEVER HAPPEN TO ME

Our next gathering took place at The Criterion Hotel on the corner of Fowler Street and Ocean Road. It was a warm Saturday in May 1972. It was 1 pm and I sat with Andy and Stan, we were all enjoying a cool bottle of Newcastle Brown Ale.

'Where's Geordie?' asked Andy.

'Out with his new girlfriend,' I uttered.

'What's she like?' said Stan.

'She is from Jarra,' I declared.

'Wo, behold the wrath of God,' added Andy.

'Now then chaps, let us not be too critical at this stage, she might be a very nice young lady,' I suggested.

'What the hell is she doing with Geordie then,' joked Stan.

Before any further comment could be made, John and Norman arrived and John stated; 'I am choking for a drink, I could drink a pint of lukewarm badger's piss.'

Having overheard this comment, the barmaid exclaimed; 'We don't serve that here and keep the foul language down please.'

'That's you told,' added Norman.

They bought their drinks and joined us. Stan informed John and Norman of Geordie's new femme fatale and John stated; 'Oh yes, I have met her. She is a looker and far too good for Geordie. She has long black hair, beautiful green eyes and a great figure. Her name is Amanda and she works in the offices at the town hall.'

'Well, he has no doubt charmed her enough to be interested in him,' added Norman.

'He will be here around 2.30 pm, so we can give him the third degree when he gets here,' added Andy.

'What about Malla and Tom, where are those two knaves?' I asked.

'They said they were coming Harry, I am sure they will be here,' revealed Norman.

As with most young men of our era, the issues of girlfriends and their impact on our lives was always a contentious subject. The thought of being hen-pecked and under the thumb of a girlfriend would send shockwaves through our little band. We all had girlfriends and, in my case, I would be married in August. What my pals did not know was that I would also be a father in December. I would be divulging this information as soon as all of my companions were present. At 2.35 pm

Geordie arrived to a chorus of jeers and insults, some of which even questioned his parentage. John was the first to admonish Geordie; 'Where have you been, you dirty little sod?'

Andy then added his own verbal chastisement when he added; 'You will get a nasty rash on your genitalia, if you over indulge Geordie.'

Geordie stood and took all the flak, once the insults had subsided, he answered; 'It appears that my so-called good friends are jealous of my new romance.'

After the dust had settled and he had furnished himself with a drink, he enlightened those gathered of his new girlfriend and provided a pen picture of Amanda. Having completed his expose, Stan suggested; 'Well Geordie, don't forget to use seagull's wellies, if you don't want ankle biters.'

'A wise policy indeed Stan,' added Norman.

The conversation had given Norman an opportunity to regale us with his thoughts on love and he launched into another one of his monologues saying; 'Is it not a wonderful obsession gentleman, this thing called love? It consumes one to the point of singular independence. We are the messengers of emotion and the innkeepers of desire, as we journey through this love affair. Is it not so, that we, as mere mortals have an inbuilt passion for failure, in that we are consumed by love and yet we cannot control it? As men we stand on the precipice of greatness and it forsakes us, as we prostitute ourselves to these sirens of temptation. Brothers in arms, let us not despair, for I have a cunning plan that will avail us of all our needs with regard to the opposite sex.'

Having sat and digested this rhetoric, John asked; 'So, what is this plan, then Norman?'

'Well John, to enhance your nocturnal activities. I have it on good authority, that there are three strippers on at the Vets Club tonight starting at 7.30 pm.'

John's response was to crack a joke; 'I spent two days in hospital last week and I took a turn for the nurse.'

At 2.45 pm in walked Tom and Malla, again they had to endure serious grief from their peers. Tom was the first to respond; 'Never mind all that bullshit, I need a drink. Get me a Guinness will you Malla?'

'I have drank more green paint,' added Stan.

Tom just gave Stan a look of contempt; 'Now Stan, shut your gob. My grandmother can shift more drink than you mate.'

The conversation continued on the theme of girlfriends and Malla provided all those present with a tale of horror; 'A lad called Tony Welford, who lives on our estate, went to the doctor with a sore knob. Guess what? He had the pox.'

'And how do you know this?' asked Andy.

'My sister knows his sister,' stated Malla.

'So much for family loyalty,' added Norman.

Malla continued; 'He had to have the umbrella down.'

'Why did it stop raining,' joked John.

Laughter in abundance, although there was a level of ignorance relating to the topic, which Norman had picked up on and in order to enhance our understanding of this medical curse, he once again gave us his considered appreciation of the subject; 'My good friends, I will seek to educate you all with regard to any over-indulgence in the ways of flesh. The pox as we affectionately call it, has been with us since time began. It is a consequence of engaging in sexual intercourse with numerous partners.'

'Can you get it off a horse?' asked Andy.

This brought a cacophony of laughter from those gathered and Norman offered; 'Well Andy, I am not sure on that but don't let it stop you my son. The important element to remember is that treatment is somewhat barbaric. If the pox is in an advanced state and penicillin will not cure it, then the umbrella comes into play. The pox comes in two flavours, syphilis and gonorrhoea and it is not particular who it chooses to infect. Some notable people have suffered its curse including Al Capone, Adolf Hitler and Elmer Fudd.'

'Hang on a minute, Elmer Fudd is a cartoon character you idiot,' shouted Geordie.

'Well that just tells you that this disease does not differentiate,' stated Norman.

John joined in the debate and added; 'This bird I was seeing from Whiteleas will be buried in a Y-shaped coffin.'

'You better book an appointment with the doc then John,' added Tom.

Norman continued with his oratory saying; 'What I am about to tell you will send shivers down your spine and it's not for the squeamish.

So, if any of you would like to depart to another room, now is the time to do so.'

'Get on with it you pisspot,' replied Andy.

'Very well, you have been warned. The umbrella is a device that the doctor will use as a last resort in the treatment of the disease. It looks like a fountain pen, but this is not for writing your memoirs. It has a small lever at the end. The implement is slowly inserted into the hole in your penis up to the point where the lever is just visible. Then the lever is activated, this results in the implement to open up like an umbrella in the upside-down position. It is then slowly pulled from the penis and on doing so it removes the infected smegma. All of this procedure is carried out without any anaesthetic.'

'What, you are joking,' quipped a startled Tom.

'I fear not,' declared Norman and he went on; 'Do not despair my good fellows, this procedure is very rarely undertaken unless the disease is in an advanced state of infection.'

Unknown to us our conversation had attracted the attention of two blokes seated at a table in the bay window. One of them spoke up: 'Hey, when I was in the merchant navy, my mate had to have that done in Malta. When the doctor had finished my mate belted him and broke his nose. We used to call it 'Snotty Cock'.

'That is a lovely term,' whispered Stan.

'Christ, can you imagine going through that boys?' added Malla

'No bloody way,' I said.

John decided to inject some humour into the state of affairs; 'I used to go out with a lass from Marsden and she had a face like a bucket of angry frogs. I once went around to her house and as I went in, her mother said; she is upstairs filing her teeth. This lass could eat a banana underwater. She was so ugly; she had a summer job swimming up and down Loch Ness. Her father was into animal husbandry, until they caught him. He was a small bloke, so small he had turn-ups in his undercrackers. Anyway, here is a question for you. How can you stop a fish smelling?'

'Come on then, let's have it,' answered Tom

'Cut off its nose.'

'Did you have any sexual relations with this vision of loveliness then John,' I asked.

'Oh yes Harry, but her dog used to sit and watch. I am sure the dog told her mother, because she started to get a little too friendly with me,' he quipped.

'Was that the dog or the mother then John? asked Geordie.

'You are nuts John, you really are mate,' suggested Malla.

It was now time for me to break the news about my impending marriage and fatherhood; 'Gentlemen of Shields, I have some earth-shattering news that may come as a surprise. I am to be married in August, and a father in December.'

Before I could continue, Geordie stated; 'Well, you are the first Harry and it's time to celebrate men. Let's raise our glasses.'

John insisted that we all have a whisky to celebrate and sent Norman to the bar to acquire the required spirit. 'Who is paying for this lot,' asked Norman.

'Harry of course,' suggested Malla.

'Not sodden likely, you will all chip in. I am exempt from this purchase,' I shouted.

Norman could not resist one more oration; 'Well dear Harry, you steaming son of the sands. Your life is about to enter a new chapter and I am sure that I speak for all your contemporaries when I say, it is with a glad heart that I speaketh now and I implore you to heed these words of wisdom and solidarity. Women like silent men, they think we are listening. This of course does not apply to your good self and I therefore advise you to hear my cry when I say; I am a lone voice in the wilderness, but you must open your eyes and embrace this thing called marriage. It is your destiny and as your good friends we will give you unanimous support in this venture, but behold you enter a land where you must equip yourself thoughtfully. You must resist temptation or face the turmoil of many offspring and then there will be a day of atonement. That is when you will be called upon to answer for your sins.'

'I will look forward to that,' quipped Stan.

John felt the need to inject more humour; 'My uncle Bob is so tall; he has to stand on a ladder to shave himself.'

'You really need a check up from the neck up John,' joked Tom.

Stan provided more humour; 'All this drinking will be the urination of me.'

'Good point Stan, whose round is it anyway?' added John.

THE STAG NIGHT

In eighteen days time, I would be a married man and today I would be the object of celebration, it was my stag night. In 1972 exotic trips to foreign climbs were very rare. My associates had suggested a number of possibilities including a day in York or Durham. In the end my final hurrah was to be called the Two Rivers Drinking Extravaganza. Proceedings would begin at 11 am in Sunderland and at around 5 pm we would depart for Newcastle. Various hostelries were chosen and the first venue was The Saltgrass, down near the banks of the River Wear. Then our band of halfwits would enjoy some food at the Ling Hong Chinese restaurant in Vine Street, in order to provide a *'lining on'*. The tour party would then move onto the Boilermakers Arms, then The Londonderry and finally The Ivy House.

Then the expedition would move north via public transport to Newcastle, the watering holes chosen were the Adelaide, the Blackie Boy, Redhouse, The Cooperage, Crown Posada and the Duke of Wellington. Norman appointed himself as tour guide and he made the reservation for the meal at the Ling Hong, for 1 pm. I was given prior warning from both my mother and my betrothed not to end up tied to a lamppost in Gateshead devoid of any clothing or handcuffed to a toilet on the last train to Kings Cross. I reassured them that nothing in that regard would happen, as my friends were of sound character and deportment. However, just to reinforce any such notions my friends had in this regard; I suggested that any such behaviour on their part, would result in serious facial disfigurement.

We all met at Dickson's in South Shields and consumed the initial *'lining on'* with saveloy dips and all the trimmings and boarded the bus to Sunderland at 10.20 am. Stan insisted that I would not be paying for anything on this auspicious day and he bought my saveloy dip, complete with pease pudding and stuffing. Having arrived at The Saltgrass at 11.05 am, the barman bid us good morning with; 'Well, you fellas are early, special occasion, is it?'

'Oh yes, our friend Harry will soon be married and to emphasize this sacrifice, his brothers in arms are giving him a send off that will go down in the annals of history as a time-honoured epilogue for the single man,' announced Norman.

I insisted that I should buy the first round of drinks, my pals were very reluctant to agree, but succumbed to my threats of violence and sanctioned my decision. Having acquired our libations of Double Maxim we selected tables in the bay window. Geordie opened the conversation with his recent viewing of a wildlife programme on the TV and said; 'I was watching this David Attenborough show on the BBC on Tuesday night and it got me thinking.'

'Now we have warned you about this 'thinking' have we not Geordie. It could lead to over stimulation of your brain,' joked Keith.

'You are a sarcastic swine Keith,' he replied and went on; 'Anyway, it was about them grizzly bears in Canada and it was filming them catching salmon in a fast-flowing river.'

'I am worried where this conversation is going,' added Norman.

'Shite off Norman, just listen, will you? Those bears obviously eat loads of fish, along with berries, deer and thick Canadians who go wandering in the woods. So, what I was thinking was; how do all those bears get the scraps of food out from between their teeth.'

Blank looks around the table suggested that an air of bewilderment had descended after this revelation. Regardless of our obvious cynicism Geordie continued saying; 'Look, I know you think I am bonkers.'

'Yep, I am sure we are all in agreement with that,' quipped Malla.

'Yes whatever, but I think there is a business opportunity here,' he suggested.

'A what, you have been on the Bob Hope again Geordie,' shouted John.

'It's a chance to develop a money-making venture,' added Geordie.

Laughter was in abundance now and Andy quipped; 'You need a check up from the neck up Geordie.'

'Undaunted Geordie pressed on saying; 'Listen, what if you get all them bears together and sat them down, you could hire a marquee or a big log cabin.'

'Right, that's enough Geordie, you are talking bollocks now,' added Tom.

Geordie chuckled; 'Bear with me, you could convince the bears that by using specially designed toothpicks, it can enhance their chances with the female bears in the mating season. Just picture the scene, a male grizzly with an enchanting smile and a gob full of gleaming white teeth. This will surely attract the females.'

Keith did not share Geordie's business proposition and added; 'Geordie, can I just take a minute to explain a few things about grizzly bears. First of all, they do not talk; secondly, they don't understand the English language. In addition, they very rarely attend gatherings in marquees. One would anticipate absolute mayhem and probable mutilation of any human life that may be present.'

In order to give Geordie some support with his theory Malla said; 'Now then, I would reckon you could make your own TV documentary Geordie. If you get twenty grizzly bears into a marquee somewhere in the Canadian Rockies and avoid getting your arms and legs torn off, it could make for great TV. You could even show them a film demonstrating the toothpicks using scantily clad female grizzlies as models.'

More laughter and Tom added; 'Malla, you're as daft as him.'

John joined the hilarity; 'What film would you show them Geordie? I would suggest *Grizzly Adams* or *The Barefoot Contesa*.'

Norman brought the discussion to a predictable end when he responded with; 'Geordie, the brain of a grizzly bear is not sufficiently advanced to formulate sensory activities such as; speech, formulating opinion or comprehending tactile information whether verbal or visual. The North American grizzly bear has four main functions in life: To eat, generally by dismembering other animals, to hump, to shite in the woods and finally to hibernate in the winter.'

Geordie brought the conversation to a close with a disturbing admission; 'Well, I do three of them.'

'Let us hope he has taken up hibernating in the winter,' joked John.

Geordie was subjected to further ridicule and had to endure various bear jokes before another round of drinks were ordered. Stan reminded us that we were booked in at the Chinese saying; 'I think it would be prudent to take it easy at this stage partners, not too much ale until our meal is consumed at the Ling Hong at 1 pm.'

'I have drunk more red oxide,' I joked.

'Yes, whatever Harry,' added Stan.

Andy took the opportunity to relay a tale about someone he knew from work who had recently experienced his stag night; 'Two weeks ago Bob Johnston was on his stag night in Shields. They did all the boozers; The Scotia, The North Eastern, Station, Ship & Royal and The Criterion. By 10.30 pm they were all in The Ferry Tavern and Bob was well-oiled. His mates put him on the last ferry to North Shields. When he got off the ferry, he wandered into The Chain Locker for

THE STAG NIGHT

another pint. While he was there, he became acquainted with a prostitute. She very kindly took Bob back to her place and subsequently rolled him. She took all his cash, his watch, his engagement ring and his Levi jacket.

He was then bundled into a taxi and returned to the ferry landing around midnight. Needless to say, the last ferry to South Shields had long gone. He spent the rest of the night in the doorway of The Chain Locker. He managed to borrow 10p from a tug boatman at five in the morning and rang his old man.'

John brought up the issue of thirst and his early morning trips for a drink to quench it; 'I keep waking up thirsty, it's like a Bedouin tribesman who has been abandoned in the Sahara Desert for five days without water. Then he comes across a broken-down truck and he decides to open the rear doors, what does he find? Boxes stacked high filled with Jacob's cream crackers.'

'Why don't you have a glass of water next to your bed, you idiot,' asked Keith.

'Mmm well you know what, I never thought of that,' he replied.

Another libation was downed and at 12.40 pm the nine of us ventured on to our oriental eatery. As we walked from The Saltgrass, Malla returned to Geordie's theory about grizzly bears; 'I am just getting a mental image of twenty grizzly bears sitting in a marquee somewhere in the Canadian Rockies, listening to Geordie pontificate about the advantage of using toothpicks. Geordie you really need psychiatric help.'

'I don't know who needs it more you or Geordie,' added Stan.

We arrived at our destination five minutes early and sat and waited until our table was ready. The Ling Hong was busy with most tables taken. Our table ran down the middle of the restaurant with nine places set. Once we were all seated Norman felt the need to set some ground rules while scoffing our grub; 'Now listen, no jokes or impersonations of our Chinese brethren and Andy; chopsticks are for eating with, not for jamming up your snout. It is vital that we enjoy the food and then be on our way, without any unpleasantness.'

The decision was made to have the banquet and share the various dishes presented.

The dishes included were sweetcorn soup, Chinese curry, duck and pancakes, sweet and sour pork and chicken chow mein. Copious amounts of rice and prawn crackers were also served. The cost of this cornucopia of oriental cuisine was £5 per head. As we sat and piled into the food, Norman set us a challenge; 'Gentlemen, I have a question for you all to ponder. It might indeed create an air of doubt in your minds and cause you to reflect on your outlook of the world around you. Picture the scene, a tree falls in the forest. However, there is nobody there to hear it, therefore does it make a noise?'

Most of us just glared at Norman in disbelief and Tom said; 'Of course it makes a noise you pisspot.'

'Yes, but how do we know that? There is nobody there to hear it,' added Norman.

'Norman are you on the same drugs as Geordie? asked Keith.

'Look you nugget, it's irrelevant that there was no one there to hear it. It will still make a noise when it hits the ground,' added Stan.

Norman had a knowing grin on his face; 'Well, I thought I might catch one or two of you out on that one.'

As if prompted, Geordie could not resist a query; 'What kind of tree was it?'

'Geordie, shut the hell up. This has gone far enough,' added Andy.

Alcohol was not available in the Ling Hong and so we had tap water to quench our burgeoning thirst. Andy found the Chinese curry somewhat spicy saying; 'I am as hot as hell on a holiday.'

'Now that is complete nonsense Andy,' quipped John.

'Very interesting, should I analyse that conundrum then boys?' asked Norman.

The general feeling around the table suggested that perhaps it would not be a good idea. Having finished our meal, the bill was paid and we made haste to the Boilermakers Arms for more alcoholic consumption. A few bar flies were present and we cobbled some tables and chairs together. The barman again asked if this was a special occasion?

'Yes, indeed it is my fine fellow, our bosom pal Harry Wainwright, bachelor of the parish of Simonside, is soon to be wed,' answered Tom.

'So, which one of you would that be then?' he asked.

'Well, who looks the most miserable?' replied Geordie.

The barman scanned those before him and pointed to Andy; 'Him, he looks suicidal.'

Cheers and laughter broke out and I raised my hand; 'It is me; my future may take many turns, but today I am embracing the prospect of married life.'

'Good luck son, you will need it,' suggested the barman.

Having collected our drinks, we returned to our chairs and Tom guided the banter onto heroes; 'Alright then, who are your heroes?'

Geordie opened the debate; 'John Wayne, he rides tall in the saddle.'

'Yes, that's because he has haemorrhoids, they keep piling up on him,' joked John.

Norman was less than impressed with Geordie's choice and added; 'Well, John Wayne was instrumental in getting a lot of his peers in the film industry put on the black list in the fifties, for their so-called anti-American views. Writers, directors and actors were singled out and ostracised for their left-wing political opinions, let us not forget.'

Geordie would not be swayed; 'What about *True Grit*, he won an Oscar for that remember.'

'Again, that is irrelevant you idiot, his actions caused decent hard-working people to be professionally ruined,' added Norman.

'Come on Harry, who are your heroes then?' asked Stan.

'OK, my heroes are Laurel and Hardy, the Marx Brothers, Pele, Eric Clapton, Frank Zappa, Robert Louis Stevenson and H. G. Wells,' I replied.

'That is a very interesting short list Harry,' said Keith.

Andy took the opportunity to drop himself in it; 'Stevenson, that's him who invented the rocket.'

'Christ, I wish you were on the next rocket into space Andy. Robert Louis Stevenson was a writer, George Stevenson built the first steam train, you daft swine,' quipped Malla.

'Come on then Andy, who are your heroes then? asked Stan

'Elvis, The Flintstones and Top Cat,' he offered.

'You really need to get out more Andy,' quipped Tom.

Norman then gave us his personal choices; 'Now gentlemen, some of these characters will be unknown to you uneducated morons. But nevertheless, I will proceed with my selection of the people whom I hold in high esteem, they are; William Shakespeare, Karl Marx, Fidel Castro, B. B. King, Elizabeth Taylor and Charles Dickens.'

'Well then Norman, give us a quote from Karl Marx,' asked Stan.

'I will be glad to Stan;

Religion is the feeling of a heartless world. It is the opium of the people.

'I am all against drugs in church,' joked John.

'That was very good John, very entertaining,' added Keith.

'Hang on, some of your heroes are dead Norman,' suggested Andy.

'Yes, but which ones Andy?' he asked.

This gave Andy a moment of reflection and much to the delight of all those present, he dropped himself in it yet again; 'Karl Marx is still alive; I saw him on the telly last week, in the Marx Brothers film, *Duck Soup*.'

This resulted in raucous laughter, even the barman could not help but join in the hilarity. Tom took it upon himself to admonish Andy and clarify a few facts; 'Andy, you never fail, Karl Marx is buried in Highgate cemetery in London. He was the founder of communism you arsehole.'

'Yes, but did all his brothers know this?' joked Malla.

'Enough of this inane banter, it's time for a cigar,' suggested Stan.

He then produced a pack of cigars and passed them around and even the non-smokers were obliged to accept a cigar and light up. This we all did and I took a couple of draws before admitting defeat after a coughing fit. Tom being another non-smoker said as he looked at his Havana cigar; 'It's big, I don't think I will manage this.'

'Yes, that's what your girlfriend said last week when she tore my underpants off with her teeth,' Geordie joked.

Tom was just as astute with his retort; 'Geordie, you have been turned down more times than the beds in the Holiday Inn.'

The theme of death was raised by Malla; 'Has anyone wondered what happens when you die?'

'You stop breathing,' quipped Keith.

'No, I think what Malla refers to is the afterlife Keith, and therefore are we reincarnated,' added Norman.

'And before you drop yourself in it again, the theme is not about Carnation Milk Andy,' joked John.

'Very funny, kiss my arse John,' was Andy's terse response.

'I love Carnation Milk on them Mr Kipling apple pies,' said Stan.

'Now then men, we are getting a little bogged down with non-sensical claptrap. Can I develop this debate on the afterlife?' suggested Norman.

Despite ridicule and sarcasm from the rest of us he continued with his hypothetical ramble; 'The thing is, do we have a soul? If so, is it transformed into another being? Do we pass on elements of our personality; or is there an invisible transfer of our soul to our children?'

'Well, if we are reincarnated into something else, I am coming back as a mirror in Lulu's bathroom,' stated Geordie.

'Right then, I am coming back as the toilet seat in the ladies toilets in Newcastle Central Station,' added Andy.

'I know this is a really stupid question Andy and I am regretting asking it, but why the Central Station?' asked Stan.

'I like the sound of trains,' he answered.

'There it is men, that would baffle some of the greatest minds in mental health. I am proud that we have a true enigma in our midst. Andy, you never fail to astound us with your thought-provoking infirmity and how you manage to portray your affliction with so much guile and incisive repartee,' stated Norman.

'What did he just say? asked Andy.

'He is paying you a compliment,' added Keith.

'Well, I will change my reincarnation to Muhammed Ali then,' said Andy.

'Look Andy, you have not grasped it have you? You cannot be reincarnated as Muhammed Ali, because he is not fucking dead yet. As far as coming back as a mirror or a toilet seat. Well, that's bollocks. How the hell can you come back as an inanimate object, beats the shit out of me,' argued Tom.

'Alright, I will return as a spider and hide behind Lulu's mirror.'

'What happens if Lulu is frightened of spiders, then Andy. You will get your head smashed in, you plonker,' I added.

'What about you Keith?' asked Geordie.

'I think it's a load of crap and it's time to change the subject,' he replied.

'Damn right, this is getting stupid,' agreed John.

Norman did his best to keep the topic alive; 'What if we have no say with life or death? It's like that film starring David Niven called, *A Matter of Life and Death*. In the film, the decision was made by a celestial court.'

'Is that like a magistrate court then?' asked Andy.

'No, you moron, it's a heavenly court,' sighed Norman.

'Alright this is getting bastard stupid now. It will be a matter of life and death if I don't get another drink down my neck. Whose round is it anyway?' asked John.

'I think we need to have a kitty. Let's start with a fiver each and see how far that goes,' suggested Tom.

'Splendid idea, I will be able to contribute to that,' I replied.

'Oh no you're not Harry, but the rest of you can get your hands in your pockets and cough up,' added Tom.

The funds were collected and another round of drinks were ordered at the bar. We were behind schedule and a collective decision was made to quicken the pace somewhat. The party arrived at The Ivy House at 2.20 pm. A couple of tables were positioned and the required chairs, then Malla brought up a recent news item; 'Did you see that on the news, where a herd of stampeding elephants had killed twenty-four people in India.'

'John decided to paint a picture of the incident occurring closer to home; 'Can you imagine, a herd of bloody elephants pelting down King Street. They couldn't all get in the Ship & Royal. They would have to split up and seek refreshment in The Scotia and The Criterion.'

'Stan returned from the toilet; 'There is a bloke in trap 2 and he is having some trouble curling one out. He is straining like the anchor man in a tug of war competition.'

'If and when that blind eel hits the water, it will be a job for Dyno-Rod.'

'Hold that lovely thought, I can feel that Chinese travelling north as I speak,' moaned Tom.

As we were just finishing our beers, John took the opportunity to provide us with a little humour; 'How do you drive a Scotsman mad? Put him in a circular room and tell him there is a fiver in the corner.'

Another forty minutes was all the time remaining in which to enjoy another pint before we all made our way to Park Lane to get the bus to Newcastle. A state of high merriment was present within our band of revellers and the benefactor of this condition was the bus driver who collected a tidy sum after he was told to keep the ticket. This was a gesture that would give us a little freedom with regard to our raucous behaviour on the journey. We sat upstairs to avoid any old ladies, children or sensitive hod carriers who may be offended by our conversation, it was now 3.25 pm.

Having taken our seats, Andy decided to give us an update on the mental health of his grandad. At eighty-three years of age, he was sadly

THE STAG NIGHT

in a severe state of dementia. As was the case in many such circumstances, the immediate family took up the challenge of caring for him. He was allocated a spare bedroom and the family received some assistance from both a visiting nurse and a home help. Because of the dementia, he was generally unaware of his surroundings; who people were and where he was. He was also prone to use profanities of a sexual nature when in the company of the fairer sex. It got so bad that the local health service was threatening to withdraw their support.

Andy gave us the latest developments; 'My grandad doesn't give a shit about what he says or does. My mother heard him calling from his bedroom; she went up to see what he wanted. When she got there, he was sitting having a dump on the bed with his underpants on his head shouting, 'I am Tonto and I am leaving a message for the lone ranger.'

'He has lost his marbles, it's really sad.'

'Does he not use the toilet then?' asked John.

'He has got a commode in his bedroom, but he never uses it these days. He is like a baby; he wears nappies most of the time.'

'It must smell like the Westoe Netty in your house,' added Keith.

'It has my mother round the twist, she thinks that he will not get proper care if he goes into a home. He gives the nurse real grief at times and he regularly gets his todger out when she is in the house. He never keeps his clothes on and he is always feeling the weight of himself,' sighed Andy.

'Bloody hell, I hope I don't get in that state,' said Geordie.

'Hang on, I seem to recall an incident on the bus to work Geordie,' added Tom.

'Trust you to bring that up you swine,' said Geordie.

'Your flair for the obtuse knows no limitations Geordie. I would recommend a lobotomy, but I fear the surgeon may have difficulty in establishing where your brain resides,' added Norman.

'Now then boys, this is my night and I will not tolerate any malevolence on this special occasion. We will soon be arriving at Worswick Street and then onto our next destination for more of the Broon Dog,' I suggested.

Our tour party arrived at Worswick Street at 4.15 pm and we made our way to the Blackie Boy. Fortunately, it had just opened its doors. As the first customers we positioned ourselves near the bar. Newcastle Brown Ale was the desired libation for all except Tom who decided that a Guinness would yield some relief from a touch of heartburn he was suffering from. The manager of the pub greeted us with; 'You boys are early; I gather you are all eighteen years old.'

All present nodded in agreement and Malla said; 'Yes, we are seasoned alcoholics and are here to celebrate the forthcoming marriage of our good friend Harry, it is his stag night.'

'Well enjoy yourselves boys, but don't give me any trouble. It will be busy in here as the night wears on,' he added.

'Yes, captain sir, will do,' quipped Andy.

The manager just gave Andy a look of disdain and returned to the bar, then Stan asked; 'Andy, do you want a fat lip? Keep that gob shut if you can't think of something intelligent to say.'

The manager accompanied the barmaid to our tables with the drinks and asked; 'So, who is the bridegroom to be then?'

'That would be me sir,' I announced.

'And this is a special occasion. It is my stag night and therefore my last night of freedom. I might also add that my friends and I will be the epitome of etiquette and I assure you that we will endeavour to create an atmosphere of jubilation and laughter never before witnessed in this hostelry. As it is written in Matthew, chapter 18 verse 20;'

For where two or three meet in my name, I shall be there with them.

'Just ignore him good sir, he has had a few sherbets,' chimed Norman.

'Who has the kitty then?' asked Keith.

'That would be me and we are still solvent,' replied Tom.

The pub began to fill up and Malla suggested that further orders would have to be done at the bar for the next round. Here write down what you want, it will be easier at the bar. Norman gave Tom a pen and paper; Right, what we having then?'

'I fancy a Carlsberg Special and a Barley Wine,' said Tom.

'Hell's teeth, you will die drinking that stuff Tom,' added John.

'Oh yes, but what a way to go,' he answered.

'It must be brown ale all round,' quipped Geordie.

'Nope, I am having a gin and tonic,' I said.

'I want a lager,' added Malla.

'Good job I am writing this down,' stated Tom.

'Do you want a beer chaser with your gin and tonic Lord Harry of Simonside,' joked Norman.

THE STAG NIGHT

'Go on then, spoil me,' I replied.

Just as Tom made his way to the bar accompanied by Andy and Keith, a party of girls entered the boozer. It was very evident that it was a hen party; the bride-to-be was festooned with a plethora of appendages, including condoms, L-plates and an assortment of badges. We rose to our feet and offered our seats to the ladies, some chose to stand, but four of them including the bride-to-be, accepted our offer. Tom, Keith and Andy returned with our drinks. Five of us were still seated alongside our female guests and Andy lent over to me and quietly whispered; 'I have done the sums and there are only seven of them, looks like you will be missing out Harry.'

'Well, fill your boots Andy,' I suggested.

'I fancy that one in the green dress,' he added.

'Right then, a word of warning; the woman in the boob tube looks like the mother of the bride-to-be. You don't want to get them mixed up later on. She is a horror, she has a face like a pile of bricks,' I said.

'John was listening to our chat; 'I bet she is a very nice girl under all that creosote and yacht varnish.'

During the conversation with the bride-to-be, she revealed that she was from Gosforth and her wedding was set for the same day as mine, August 12. This date was also the start of the grouse season.

She told us that her fiancé was in the Royal Navy. This brought various comical quips from our band of idiots and Stan was the first to indulge in the hilarity; 'Geordie, that's ironic, your father was a sailor on HMS *Repulse* was he not?'

'Cheeky swine, go and play with the traffic Stan. I will have you know that my old man was torpedoed three times on the Atlantic convoys during the war, fighting for King and country,' he added.

John suggested that was a similar scenario to what was happening back home; 'Yes, but I imagine your mother was torpedoed more than three times, when your old man was away.'

Even Geordie had to laugh at that one. The jollity continued until Norman suggested it was time to move on to our next port of call, the Redhouse. Keith felt the need to question the geographical logistics of the pub crawl; 'Who planned this fucking pub crawl? We are now going to the Redhouse, then The Cooperage and then the Crown Posada. What happened to the Adelaide? We have to walk all the way back up to the Duke of Wellie from the Quayside.'

Tom rebuked Keith; 'The walk will do us good; it will give us a second wind my good friend, therefore, I suggest that you shut your gob or I will slacken your teeth.'

'Now then ladies, let us not get tetchy and fall out. We still have a long night ahead of us and the shadows lengthen. Let us make haste to the Redhouse forthwith, where further refreshment will be consumed and much merriment made,' added Norman.

We all trudged off to Dean Street and rolled into the Redhouse at 7.30 pm. John and Geordie had washed their faces with mince pies to facilitate an extra lining to their stomachs. Some of us were reaching capacity in this regard with half-pints and whisky chasers becoming prevalent. The Redhouse was well populated, but we managed to arrange some seats and a table near the bar. Stan continued to mix his libations, on this occasion he and Tom ordered brown ale snakebites; the combination of cider and brown ale was indeed rocket fuel.

Keith then regaled us about his current tour of duty in Belfast; 'I will be glad to get out of Northern Ireland, don't get me wrong, the people are very friendly. We don't have a lot of contact though, for security reasons. I was told my next posting has been cancelled because more troops are needed on the ground in the province. I was hoping to go to Cyprus or Belize, but I will just have to wait a little longer, I guess.'

'Where the hell is Belize?' asked Andy.

'It's in Central America, it borders Guatemala and Mexico. It is a British protectorate and there are great beaches there,' replied Keith.

'So, why are our troops there Keith?' added Geordie.

'Belize is part of the British Empire and therefore, we have an obligation to serve and protect, just like the Falkland Islands and the British Virgin Islands.'

'Well, let's hope things improve and you go to warmer climes and get the sun on your back. When you do, you will have to organize a little holiday for us and we will join you and enjoy the hospitality of the locals,' declared Tom.

Malla felt the need to add some humour to the conversation; 'Did you hear about the bloke who was charged with murder for killing a man with sandpaper. When he was questioned by the police he said; I only intended to rough him up a bit.'

John added another comical interlude; 'Paddy kept going to the optician, because his left eye hurt so much. The optician said; you say your eye only hurts when you drink tea, is that correct? Yes, that's true. Well, I suggest you stop drinking tea then. Yes, but I love drinking tea replied Paddy. OK then, just make sure you remove the fucking spoon.'

Laughter followed and Stan joined in the fun; 'Listen to this it's a gem. One dark night, a burglar broke into what he thought was an empty house. He was creeping through the living room when he heard a loud voice say; Jesus is watching you. The burglar froze in his tracks, but silence returned so he carried on. Jesus is watching you came the voice again. The burglar stopped dead, frightened. Frantically he looked around. In a dark corner he spotted a bird cage. In the bird cage, was a parrot. He asked the parrot; Was that you who said Jesus is watching you. Yes, replied the parrot.

The burglar breathed a sigh of relief and asked the parrot. What's your name? Clarence said the bird. That's a silly name for a parrot, sneered the burglar. What idiot named you Clarence?

The parrot shouted; The same fucking idiot who named the Rottweiler Jesus.'

Geordie felt the need to circulate; 'Anyone fancy a bit of a wander around?'

No great enthusiasm from his pals until Andy agreed; 'Alright then Geordie, let's see what the chicks are like. I feel lucky tonight.'

'Can't see any blind women in here tonight Andy, looks like you are out of luck mate,' joked Malla.

Andy just raised his middle finger as he and Geordie wandered off. The rest of us discussed the issue of transport home. The last bus to Shields was the number 6, which left Worswick Street at 11 pm.

Norman was more inclined to maintain the status quo and carry on celebrating my stag night; 'We must sustain this evening of celebration gentlemen and indulge Harry. It is his night and we must not fail him.'

'This is our duty and I personally believe one and all should accompany him to that den of iniquity, the Tuxedo Princess. Let us all enjoy the delights of that nightspot with uncommon zeal, and embrace the atmosphere of carnality that is available. Let us all revel in that sticky carpet and revolving dance floor with great exuberance in the presence of a plethora of fine young ladies.'

'Now, who could not be tempted by that description. I say we should embark on this odyssey,' suggested Tom.

'I gather I don't have a say on this proposal then,' I asked.

'No, you do not Harry,' added Keith.

'As the best man, I have a duty to make sure Harry gets home safe and sound. If I don't my uncle Harold will hospitalise me,' said Stan.

John added his own take on the proposal; 'Look, we have enough money in the kitty to go to the Tuxedo Princess and taxis home. We can come back in the morning to unlock Harry from the anchor chain.'

'Very funny John, but I warned you all about any devious activities in that regard. The threat of plastic surgery is still viable remember,' I added.

'Yes alright, we will go to the Tux and dance the night away.'

Geordie and Andy returned from their crumpet search and they were informed of the plan and Andy said; 'We haven't been to the Duke of Wellie yet and it's 9.30 pm now.'

A unanimous decision was made not to go to the Duke of Wellie. Instead, we would venture to the Crown Posada and then The Cooperage, before finally making for the floating nightclub. Andy seemed to appreciate that time was on our side when he suggested; 'We have oodles of time fellas, the birds need to get more drink down them before they become more amenable.'

'They will have to be fucking unconscious before you get anywhere near them Andy,' joked Malla.

Norman chose the moment to give us all his thoughts and proclamations in relation to the circumstances we were about to encounter; 'My good friends, it is my considered opinion that we have generated an ethos of unconditional licentiousness. The fair ladies of this city deserve better, I of course am spoken for. I have the lovely Laura to return to and Malla has Caroline to share his nocturnal activities. Harry will soon join the ranks of married men. That leaves the rest of you scrambling about like bees around the honeypot.'

'Please take care young men of Shields, your rapacious impiety may well suffer the slings and arrows of outrageous fortune and as a consequence you will be left despondent and devoid of virtue.'

'And you may well acquire nasty puss-ridden eruptions on your genitals,' added Tom.

It was now 9.45 pm and we made our way to the Crown Posada. Needless to say, getting a seat proved to be problematic. The Posada

THE STAG NIGHT

was probably the smallest pub in town. It had a snug near the main door, but that was full and the passageway was heavily populated. However, we got served and rather than beer, we all had a short of whisky or gin. Norman chose to have a brandy, much to the annoyance of Geordie who said; 'Norman, that's a damn sight dearer than a whisky or gin.'

'Relax my son, our kitty will stand the cost; fear not, thee of little faith,' he answered.

One or two of us were a little hungry and thankfully there were a few sandwiches available on a tray next to the ever-present record player. We bought what was left and shared them out. The LP playing on the turntable was *Live at The Regal* by B. B. King and John said; 'This is great stuff boys; I would love to see B. B. King.'

'You will one day John, he tours all the time,' I suggested.

We were out of the Crown Posada within fifteen minutes and heading for The Cooperage. It was a warm night and when we arrived at The Cooperage, some of the ladies were already making their way across the Swing Bridge to the Tuxedo Princess. This was not lost on Andy and he said; 'I think we should go straight to the Tux now fellas.'

'Keep your powder dry Andy, you have of plenty of time my son,' replied Keith.

The Cooperage was surprisingly quiet with only a few punters enjoying a drink. We had no trouble putting tables together and a final bottle of brown ale was ordered for all, before hitting the Tux. The conversation was devoted to recent concerts that had taken place and comments as to the quality of bands on record were aired. Keith spoke of a record he had just acquired; 'I bought *Flowers of Evil* by Mountain last week. It's incredible. The B-side is live and Leslie West is dynamite, he starts with *Roll Over Beethoven*.'

'I have a ticket to see them in September at the City Hall and Black Sabbath are the support, I can't wait,' I added.

John joined the conflab; 'Beckett are on at the Londonderry Hall next Friday night. I was talking to their guitarist Arthur Ramm in the Eldon Arms last night. They do a great version of Free's *I'm A Mover*.'

The banter continued with various anecdotes on recent gigs involving the Who, Ten Years After, Iron Butterfly, John Mayall, Deep Purple and John Hiseman's Colosseum. A few guys came in and Tom recognised someone and went across to talk. He returned with a guy and introduced him; 'This here is Dave; he lives on the Leam.'

Dave grabbed a chair and joined us. He spoke of a concert he was at recently; 'I was at the City Hall and saw Emerson, Lake and Palmer, it was tremendous.'

'Hang on, I was there for that, where were you sitting?' I asked.

'On my arse,' he quipped.

'Very good that Dave, you will fit in well here mate,' added Malla.

John announced that time was not our friend and we should be thinking about making our way to the floating disco. We said farewell to Dave and his pals and stumbled out of The Cooperage. Malla was rolling a bit and Keith suggested that he had consumed too much of the Brown Dog; 'You need to stop drinking now Malla. I am not taking you home again, the last time I got a bollocking of your bastard mother.'

'How dare you, my mother was not an illegitimate child,' he replied.

'You know what I mean you daft sod.'

While in The Cooperage, Tom had done his sums and informed us that we had £21 left in the kitty. He suggested that another £2 from each of us would get us into the Tux and we would still have enough for taxis home. Drinks in the Tux would have to be bought separately he declared. It was 10.30 pm when we boarded the Tuxedo Princess and Tom paid us all in, much to the surprise of the girl on the desk. Tom used the scenario to explain to her that this was an act of generosity on his behalf; 'This is my treat love, I have just returned from the South of France. I have a yacht there. It is undergoing a £1 million refit. I would not miss this auspicious occasion for anything, no matter what the cost. The girl looked dumbfounded by this revelation but gave Tom an encouraging smile.

We trooped in to the Tux and found a couple of tables. We just sat and observed the activity without ordering any drinks. Stan introduced some humour; 'Have you heard about the new film called *Constipation*, it hasn't come out yet.'

Not to be outdone John added; 'I can do better than that, two men were sitting at the bar in their local boozer. One starts to insult the other one and screams; I slept with your mother. The rest of the bar goes quiet as everyone listens to see what the other man will do. The first man yells again; I slept with your mother. The other man says, go home Dad you're pissed.'

THE STAG NIGHT

The place was starting to fill up and we decided to split up into groups of three and circulate the surroundings. I joined John and Tom, Norman, Keith and Andy made up a trio and Stan, Geordie and Malla combined to make up the last threesome. During the tour we each had a half of lager and observed the plethora of ladies advertising their wares. Tom decided to make a move on the girl that had been on the desk. She had vacated that responsibility and she was dancing on the revolving floor with a female friend. He waited for the song to finish and he made his move, the friend of the girl got the message pretty quickly and left her friend chatting to Tom, who then escorted her to the bar.

'He is like a dog at broth that Tom,' suggested John.

We stood taking in the atmosphere then Geordie appeared; 'I can't find Malla.'

'I bet the bastard has gone overboard,' added John.

'Well, if he has, I hope it's on the port side, because he can't fucking swim,' I replied.

We found the rest of the team and John went to tell Tom of this worrying development. Having all gathered Stan suggested; 'Let's try the obvious place, the netty.'

'Why didn't I think of that?' asked Geordie.

'Because you have the mental aptitude of a cobblers last Geordie,' answered Norman.

'Never mind that crap, let's hit the bog,' I suggested.

We entered the toilet to find only one trap engaged. Malla are you in there?' shouted Stan.

No response. 'Bollocks to this,' shouted Andy and he kicked the door in.

There he was on the pot, pants around his ankles, sleeping like a baby. 'I will go and get an empty glass and fill it with water,' said Norman.

'I told him that he had drank too much beer,' replied Keith.

Norman came back with the glass and filled it at a sink. Tom grabbed it and poured it over Malla's head. He sprang into life and crashed his head off the cistern. This brought laughter and cheers from his pals and a few bystanders that had gathered round. Thankfully no bouncers had presented themselves and Malla got himself cleaned up and we all found a table not too far away.

As we sat, I noticed the mother of the Gosforth bride-to-be, who was in the Blackie Boy. She now looked a little worse for wear and resembled a hippo in a boob tube. I took the opportunity to inform Andy of my sighting; 'Wow, she is a stunner,' he agreed sarcastically.

'You could do a lot worse,' joked John.

'You would be better off with a jar of worms,' added Stan.

Raucous laughter again and Keith nearly choked on his drink. 'Where is Tom? He is not in the bog, is he?' asked Andy.

'Take a look at the end of the bar, he is chatting to that bird from the reception desk again,' said Norman.

'Oh yes, the bird he impressed with his verbal diarrhoea about his yacht in the South of France,' added Keith.

'It is strange you should mention shite Keith, it appears that I need to go to the toilet or I will likely soil myself,' replied John.

After some fifteen minutes Tom returned to the bosom of his friends and said he would be ringing this girl tomorrow, with a view to a date. 'Lucky sod Tom, she must have swallowed your story about the yacht,' asked Geordie.

'Well Geordie she is not thick and she found the story very funny. She basically thinks I am gorgeous and wants to make mad passionate love to me,' answered Tom.

'So, you have been blown out then Tom,' added Norman.

'Yep, got it in one,' he agreed.

John returned from his emergency evacuation and we agreed to leave the floating melting pot of lust for home. Agreement was reached about our next reunion, we would muster in the Lord Clyde on Thursday, August 10, at 7 pm. We jumped into three taxis and as Stan, Andy and I sat in the car travelling back to Shields, Stan decided to cheer the driver up with a joke; 'A bloke was talking to his mates in the bar and said; Last night when I was with you in the bar, a burglar broke into my house. Did he get anything? One of his mates asked. Oh yes, a broken jaw, six teeth knocked out and two broken ribs. How did that happen then? Well, it was really late at night and my wife thought it was me coming home pissed.'

I asked the driver; 'Well, I hope that has cheered you up mate.' 'Yes, it rings true, my missus would be tempted to do the same,' he joked.

I got home at 1.15 am, as usual my mother was sitting waiting for me. I hit my bed fully clothed and within seconds I was unconscious.

LIFE

On a warm Saturday in September I was sitting in the lounge of The New Crown Hotel waiting for my partners in crime. At our previous soiree, agreement was reached to convene at this hostelry for 1 pm. I was a little early and I sat and enjoyed the dulcet tones of Bob Dylan permeating from the jukebox. As the last few bars of *Blowing in The Wind* faded out in walked Norman, Tom, John and Geordie.

'Now then Harry, you are early,' said Tom.

'I have only been here 15 minutes. I had a very pleasant walk down from Laygate. I thought I would get some fresh air into my lungs, this in turn gave me the appetite for a pastie at Akins the bakers. This I consumed with gusto on my way here.'

'Who the hell is gusto, a mate of yours then?' asked Geordie.

Norman shook his head, looked at Geordie, and said; 'Does anybody want to explain this to our esteemed cretin?'

'Nope, life is too short,' added Tom.

Geordie just gave us all a blank look and added; 'I was just trying to make conversation.'

'Yes, you were Geordie, it is good that you seek knowledge. The man that hides his enthusiasm for learning is but a servant to ignorance,' replied Norman.

'Where are Malla, Stan and Andy?' asked John.

'They should be here soon, they will be walking from the Pier Head,' said Geordie.

'I wonder how Keith is getting on in Belfast; hope he is keeping his head down, dodging those bullets and car bombs,' said Tom.

Norman maintained the theme of the troubles in Belfast when he added; 'It is becoming senseless this sectarian violence. Yesterday, a postman was sitting having his evening meal with his wife and two daughters, when two men wearing ski masks burst into the house and shot him dead. Why? Because he was a catholic, when is this going to stop?'

'Keith should be on the beach in Belize or Cyprus, instead of trudging around the Falls Road,' stated John.

The three absentees duly arrived at 1.15 pm. They made their way to the bar and bought their respective drinks and joined us. Tom raised the forthcoming FA Cup match at Simonside Hall where South Shields would be up against Scarborough saying; 'Now you loyal Sundancer's, how about we all get tickets for the Shields game against Scarborough in two weeks time.'

'Is it free to attend then?' asked Andy.

'Andy you are watertight, no it's not free, not unless you want to climb the wall at the junior school,' said Stan.

'We have done that a few times, Harry?' added Malla.

'Oh yes, and got caught a few times as well,' I replied.

General agreement was reached and the venue for a pre-match drink was discussed. Simonside Hall will be packed and not being members would guarantee that our presence would not be tolerated.

'How about The Satellite, we could have a few pots and then your mother could make us dinner Harry,' suggested Geordie.

'No bloody way is that going to happen,' I stated.

'Why not just pay at the turnstile, asked John?'

'You have not been paying attention John, it's an all-ticket game,' quipped Norman.

Tom agreed to buy the tickets and he would be reimbursed on the day of the game. Norman did hesitate with his acceptance and said; 'It may be that a few of this exalted company have alternative arrangements for that particular day.'

'Sod off Norman, you have nothing on you turd. Unless you would rather go shopping with the lovely Laura,' queried Geordie.

Norman's response was predictable and he subjected Geordie to another monologue detailing his failings in the appreciation of life; 'Geordie, you will never comprehend the inner workings of the female mind. The next time you are watching Pan's People on *Top of the Pops* and at the same time, playing pocket billiards, consider this: The organisation of the human body is dependent on microscopic cells. Each cell has its own structure. In your case Geordie, the cells that are in your body are in a state of crisis. They constantly change from a rational structure to a moronic structure and this in turn leads to bizarre and unpredictable behaviour.

In other words, you have the IQ of a beer mat. To summarize, I would like to give you a quote from *The Wedding Knell*;

> Beloved of my youth, said he, I have been wild. The despair of my whole lifetime had returned at once, and maddened me.

'Well, there we have it; Norman you speak like a member of parliament and your literary repertoire is boundless. How do you remember all this stuff?' asked Stan.

'Having the missing link in attendance does help Stan,' he joked.

'Alright clever shite, go and boil your nuts,' was Geordie's response.

Now then boys, let's not enter into a witch hunt; what news does anyone have to share with his friends?' asked Tom.

I chose to enlighten those gathered with a review of my presence at the recent concert at the City Hall to see the American Band Mountain saying; 'Well fellas, you missed a great show last Wednesday night. The guitarist Leslie West was incredible, he did a twenty-minute guitar solo that included the *Who's My Generation*, *The Planet's* by Gustav Holtz and *Roll Over Beethoven* by Chuck Berry. He had this Gibson Les Paul Studio sunburst guitar and it looked like a child's toy in his hands.'

'Which piece of the *Planet Suite* did he do then Harry?' asked Norman.

'Trying to catch me out, are you Norman?' I replied.

'Well, the suite has a number of movements,' he added.

'Yes, it has, he did *Jupiter, the Bringer of Jollity*,' I offered.

'Very good, one of my favourites,' added Norman with a wry smile.

The cinema was then brought into the conversation and Tom informed us of a new film doing the rounds. 'I went to see Dennis Weaver in *Dual* at the ABC last night. It was great edge of the seat stuff, loads of tension. It's about a bloke in a car, who is chased by a driver of a petrol tanker. The strange thing is, you never see the driver of the petrol tanker.'

'What happens at the end?' asked Andy.

'No, that will spoil it for everyone, you plonker. But the actor that drove the petrol tanker was called Cary Loftin,' added Tom.

Malla informed all present that a new film called *The Godfather* was due for release; 'Barry Norman reviewed it on *Film Night* and Marlon Brando plays the lead role as a Mafia boss.'

'I hope Brando is better in this film than he was in *Julius Caesar*, he was so wooden in that. Unlike *On the Waterfront* and *A Streetcar Named Desire* in which he was brilliant, 'replied Norman.

We refuelled at the bar and the smokers within our assembled gathering lit up. Geordie decided to relay a story about his father which happened a couple of years ago; 'I was out with a couple of fellow apprentices on a Thursday night. I got completely rat-arsed and stumbled into the house at 11 pm. My mother was in bed, but she made my old man wait up for me coming in. He was not amused and went berserk. He took off his belt and started to lash me with it saying; I'll give you 11 o'clock, that's a crack for every bastard hour. He walloped me eleven times with that leather belt.'

John suggested that Geordie had missed a trick; 'You daft sod, you should have come in at 1 am. He would have only cracked you once with the belt.'

Much laughter followed and Andy suggested; 'Geordie, you really are slow on the uptake my son.'

Malla moved the debate onto decimalisation, which was introduced the previous year; 'I can't get used to this decimalisation, if 10p is two bob, we are getting ripped off.'

'It is all down to the Common Market; Britain has to conform to the metric system. That is why top engineers like us are now working in millimetres instead of imperial measurement,' replied Stan.

Malla was having none of that and quickly admonished Stan; 'I am not accepting that garbage Stan. You are a welder, all you have to do is the following; firstly, some bloke cracks you on the back of your head, then the welding mask covers your face and you start welding. They train chimpanzees to do that in Nigeria.'

More raucous laughter and Stan's riposte was equally funny; 'Malla you are only a plater, this means you are just a binman with learning difficulties.'

John then informed us about a recent visit to his doctor; 'I went to the doctor last Monday and told him I had a problem with my 'John Thomas.' He said drop your trousers, which I did. He looked at my todger and asked; How long has it been like that? I answered, it's always been this long. No, I mean those scratches and abrasions, he replied. Oh them, that is down to the girlfriend doctor. Are you engaging in sexual intercourse? he asked. Yes, I answered. What about contraception? That's fine, I go to the toilet every day doctor, I replied. No no, are you practising safe sex? he asked. We are way beyond practising doctor I stated. Yes yes, but are you taking precautions? he said. Well, we don't do it in the street or on the bus, if that's what you mean?

No, you misunderstand, are you using condoms or are you using the rhythm method? No, she is on the pill I replied. Has your girlfriend tried wearing a Dutch cap?' he asked. Sounds a bit kinky to me doc. I don't think she has got one of them, but I could get her to wear my old man's World War Two tin helmet I suppose. He seemed a bit frustrated and added; Do you mind if I ask a colleague to take a look at your penis? No, I don't mind doc. He went out and came back with a bloke wearing a boiler suit and rubber gloves. This is Dr Brown, don't be alarmed, he has just been working on his car, he said. So, Dr Brown takes a look at my todger and says; How long has it been like that? We have already gone down that road added the doctor.

Has your girlfriend ever had thrush? asked Dr Brown. No, but her mother has got a budgie, I replied. They looked at each other and I had the distinct impression that they were on a different wavelength to me. So, I asked if there was anything they could give me for the pain, but leave the swelling. My doctor then rang for the police and I did a runner.'

We were all in fits of laughter at this point and Andy stated; 'You must have spent a long time on that tale John.'

'Oh no it's a true story,' he joked with a wide smile on his face.

Norman continued with the topic of health; 'We take our health for granted fellas. There is the assumption that we are in good health. However, on occasion a life-changing moment befalls us. I had a cousin who died from a brain haemorrhage at the age of twelve. How can anyone see that coming?'

'Yes, well I remember Steven Wilcoxon at Westoe School, he was sat at his desk on the Monday and dead the next day. He had a serious asthma attack and died, he was only fifteen,' I added.

Geordie then navigated the conversation onto an individual we were all familiar with and went on; 'I heard 'Monkey Smith' has been causing more trouble. The lunatic will end up in the Ingham Infirmary soon. He was up to his usual stupidity of climbing and running along the walls of houses in Dacre Street the other day. I am sure his descendants were baboons. He is a fucking barmstick and he will break his neck one of these days. One day last week he was clambering over a wall in Alice Street, he slipped and fell through the roof of an outside toilet. An old man was sitting having a dump. After crashing through the roof, there were tiles, plaster and shite everywhere.'

'Well, if the old codger was suffering a touch of constipation Monkey Smith soon remedied that,' joked John.

Malla alluded to a recent painful experience he had; 'I had this bloody big boil on my arse a few weeks ago. Of course, I was too embarrassed to tell my mother and hoped it would just go away. Did it hell as like, it got worse and turned septic. I went to the clinic at Stanhope Parade and they sent me to the Ingham Infirmary to have it lanced, Christ it was painful.'

'They are caused by poor personal hygiene Malla; you should wipe your arse properly. Anyway, which hand do you use to wipe your arse with?' added Andy.

'My right hand, what's that got to do with it?' he asked.

'Well, there you have it you dirty swine. I use toilet paper,' joked Andy.

'Speaking of toilet paper, I hate that Izal bog roll. It's like using glasspaper on your casing,' added Tom.

'I think it's time to change the subject,' I suggested.

'I agree entirely Harry, have you found a house yet?' asked Norman.

'Yes, I have a two-roomed upstairs flat in Garwood Street,' I replied.

'Where is Garwood Street?' asked Stan.

'It's in Corstorphine Town,' stated John.

'It will have an outside netty in the yard then,' added Geordie.

'Yep, it has a bloody hole in the roof and we share it with a family in the downstairs flat,' I replied.

'How much is the rent?' asked Norman.

'It's only £2.50p a week, it is a bit of a dump, but I will make it ship shape,' I answered.

'When is the housewarming party then?' quipped Geordie.

'I will let you know when I have finished all the graft.'

'We refuelled our glasses and at 3 pm, Stan, Malla, Geordie, Norman and me decided to go home. John, Tom and Andy chose to have another libation and then make their way to the Corporation Club in Laygate.

AN EMPTY CHAIR

Another Saturday for a gathering of the clans. Today's venue was the Station Hotel. Chosen for its comfortable seating and the lovely voluptuous Hilda, the resident barmaid. The weather was surprisingly good for November, sunny and warm. All but one of us arrived around 12.30 pm.

Andy was the last to arrive. Gliding in at 12.45 washing his face with a Dickson's pork sarnie, with all the trimmings; Pease pudding, mustard and crackling. Tom was quick to admonish Andy; 'I suppose it never occurred to you, to bring a few sarnies for your best mates then Andy.'

'I am not Lord Rothschild Tom? I am not rolling in bastard money,' he answered.

Malla raised the issue of Andy's late arrival; 'Well, the pork sarnie is a get out clause. It meant that Andy would be late and therefore the tight bastard would not have to buy the first round.'

'Shame on you Malla, how dare you cast aspersions on one so delicate and vulnerable,' added Norman, with just a hint of sarcasm.

'Piss off Malla,' was Andy's blunt reply. Andy then made his way to the bar and returned with his beer, joining us at a table in the window.

Geordie provided an observation relating to John's position at the table; 'You always sit facing the door John.'

'Yes, because I like to see who comes in. You never know, someone might be looking for me,' disclosed John.

'You in trouble then John?' asked Tom.

Before John could reply, Norman offered us his observation and added; 'Let's just think about that now. Whoever could be looking for John?'

'How long have you got,' joked Andy.

Norman continued; 'Well, it could be a number of individuals such as; the rent man, coalman, milkman, taxman, police, Salvation Army, Sooty and Sweep, Edward Heath, Elton John, Daft Bob from the Stags Head, Shirley Bassey, Lester Piggott or a crazed husband seeking retribution for John's nocturnal proclivities.'

That brought laughter to the proceedings and John replied with; 'Well, you never know.'

I asked if Keith was due home anytime soon and Geordie revealed; 'He is back for Christmas and he has been informed that his next posting is in Cyprus, starting in January.'

'How did you gain this information,' asked Stan.

'I was chatting to his sister Beverley, in Green Lane fish shop on Wednesday night,' revealed Geordie.

'He will be chuffed about getting out of Northern Ireland,' added Tom.

'Cyprus, it will be hot there,' I suggested.

'Another soldier was killed in Belfast last week; how many is that now?' asked Andy.

'Too many soldiers and too many civilians,' said John.

'Let's change the subject,' I asked.

'Alright, you bunch of morons, anyone want a pint?' asked Andy.

'Thought you would never ask, a full round would be grand,' replied Malla.

'I am not getting you all a fucking drink, I will buy Harry, Tom and Norman a beer. The rest of you can organise yourselves for your own,' added a disgruntled Andy.

John then bought beers for Stan, Malla and Geordie. Having charged our glasses, Tom raised the topic of romance; 'Now then Norman, how goes it with Laura?'

'Very well thank you Tom,' answered Norman.

'Up the spout yet?' asked Geordie.

Norman gave Geordie a look of despair, shook his head; 'Geordie, my dear fellow. Bringing a child into this world requires a great deal of soul-searching and commitment.'

'No, it doesn't, Harry's has one on the way,' added Andy.

I shot Andy a dirty look; 'Where is this conversation going Andy? Because you just might receive a smack in the gob, if you're not careful.'

'No offence Harry, but Andy has a point. You need to look at the world we are living in at the moment. Unemployment, the miners strike, power cuts, war and famine. It makes you think,' uttered Tom.

'And that's just in Horsley Hill,' joked John.

'I know where you are coming from Tom, but life has to go on and if you are happy with your lot, then so be it,' I stated.

'This conversation is getting me down, how about a touch of humour to liven up the atmosphere,' suggested Stan.

'I have a gem, listen to this,' said Malla.

AN EMPTY CHAIR

'I was in the toilet at work 'pinching a loaf,' when a bloke walked into to the trap next to me. He sat down and then he just unleashed this cacophony of explosive farts and subsequent waste material. It lasted for ages, when it all died down, I heard him open a packet of crisps and he started munching. I couldn't believe the dirty sod. I flushed the toilet and washed my hands. I just had to see who it was, I hung around taking time to dry my hands.

He finally flushed and opened the door. As he walked out, he was picking bits of crisp out of his mouth. He just walked out of the toilet without washing his paws. This is the best bit. He is Bob the labourer, he makes the tea for everyone on our work section.'

'You will be making your own tea from now on then,' suggested Tom.

'Just think Malla, he could have syphilis, herpes, green monkey disease, crabs, the plague or dysentery and he is making your tea,' added Stan.

'Thanks for that, but he won't be making me anymore fucking tea, I am taking a flask from now on,' added Malla.

Hilda appeared to collect the empty glasses and remove the ashtray, and she took the opportunity to say; 'It would help me a lot, if you brought your empty glasses back to the bar gentlemen.'

Norman took the opportunity to embark on a monologue extolling the virtues of our resident barmaid; 'My dear wonderful sensual Hilda. Was it not for my allegiance to a beautiful maiden called Laura? I would sweep you up into my arms and whisk you off to a romantic Pacific Island to favour you with trifles and sweetmeats. We would make mad passionate love under an endless moonlit sky. Together we would have a plethora of children in a world far away from this mundane existence. What say you my fair damsel, if the lady Laura spurns my affections, will you join me and leave this purgatory behind?'

Hilda stood and considered the options; 'If your performance between the sheets is anything like your chat-up lines, I will put my coat on now.'

This caused Norman to blush, which we all took full advantage of, much to his disgust. Hilda smiled and gave Norman a wink; 'This Laura must be fond of a treat,' and she returned to the bar.

It was now 2 pm and the issue of food was raised. The Station

Hotel would close at 3 pm, but unlike a number of boozers, it would reopen at 5 pm.

'I have a plan, let's have a hearty meal at Carrick's or Binns, then return here for a few more beers,' said John.

'Sounds like a capital idea young Johnny,' added Norman.

'Are you all up for this or have you other commitments?' I asked.

Andy looked a little pensive; 'Well, I should really go home, my dad wants me to help him lay flags in the back garden.'

This brought a torrent of abuse and scorn from all present and Stan added; 'Are you a man or a mouse? Your mother can help with that surely.'

'Very funny, if I don't go back, he will be laying me out,' replied Andy.

'Now Andy, you can't let the team down,' added Malla.

Andy succumbed to the pressure and we finished our drinks off and walked the short distance to King Street and Carrick's cafe. The culinary delights on offer were; pies, peas and chips, fish and chips, bacon, sausage, egg and chips or a selection of sarnies. Norman asked the female assistant; 'Have you any Larks Tongues in Aspic, my dear.'

She just stood and stared at Norman, not sure what to say, she then asked another somewhat rotund assistant, whose eyes seemed to be moving in different directions; 'Is this dish on the menu?'

The assistant with the wandering eyeballs asked; 'What is it anyway?'

Norman gave up the ridicule; 'It's alright my fair maiden, I will settle for one of those wholesome steak pies, with a generous helping of peas, please.'

She leaned across to her colleague; 'He is a fucking idiot.'

Norman expressed his disappointment at this remark; 'Charmed I'm sure, I will have you know that I passed my 'Cycle Proficiency Test' first time.'

We all ate our fill and had lashings of tea to wash it all down. Geordie suggested a walk across the road to The Garrick's Head, because of its earlier opening time of 4 pm. This was disregarded in order to allow our food to digest.

John suggested a visit to the museum. After all, it was free to get in and it would kill half an hour. 'Splendid idea, let's go and see Lenny the stuffed lion,' added Andy.

Norman expressed a degree of caution and suggested that it would not be prudent to become over excited by the exhibits on display; 'Now Geordie, the animals have recently been stuffed, so please do not try to get too friendly. It is still a crime to molest stuffed animals.'

Geordie's reply was swift and to the point; 'Norman, go and boil your nuts.'

We trooped into the museum and the doorman gave us a timely reminder; 'The museum closes in thirty minutes fellas.' Tom informed the guy that we would be on our best behaviour and act correctly at all times; 'However, there is a member of the party that has a tendency to become excited when he sees anything on four legs. I will monitor his behaviour.'

The doorman, an elderly gentleman just gave Tom a look of total confusion.

As the tour of the museum progressed, a running commentary from Norman was provided on the various exhibits, until Stan decided to call a halt to Norman's didactic input saying; 'Norman will you just shut your gob?'

Norman agreed to this request, as failure to heed to Stan's request, would have resulted in a swift kidney punch. The visit lasted fifteen minutes and we left with Tom chatting with the elderly doorman. If he was confused when we arrived, he was totally bewildered when after Tom stated; 'May I thank you for your patience old soldier. You may need to examine one or two of the exotic animal exhibits. It appears that the zebra has acquired a pair of fishnet tights and the chimpanzee appears to be in a compromising position with the barn owl, farewell to you sir.'

The walk-up Mile End Road brought us to our destination, Malla decided to offer a bloke advice as to the whereabouts of a particular street. He had done this before and we watched in expectation as he approached this bloke and asked; 'Excuse me, could you direct me to Brokenhead Avenue?' The bloke looked baffled, and finally answered; 'Sorry, I am not sure where that is and I have lived here for thirty years.'

Then Malla performed the *coup de gras*; and said; 'Well, what you need to do is follow this road until' .... Malla rambled on for another two minutes explaining a detailed route on how to navigate to this fictious place. The bloke just stood and stared at Malla in disbelief. We all managed to keep our composure and tried to look interested.

When Malla had finished his monologue, the bloke looked at Malla, then at us and said; 'you fucking lot need psychiatric help,' he then walked off shaking his head.

We returned to the Station at 5.10 pm and regained our original seating arrangements. The debate moved onto previous jobs and Tom asked; 'Harry, you used to work in the Co-op butchers on Dean Road, am I right?'

'Yes, I did Tom and I loved it. I used to be paid £4 a week. I worked on Thursday night and Saturday until 2 pm,' I replied.

'Did you receive any free meat?' asked Andy.

'Oh yes, on Saturday the boss Mr McDermott, used to give me any spare pies or pasties that had not sold,' I replied

'Did you have to cut and carve up the meat?' asked Geordie.

'Yip, I used to skin the sheep's heads and pull the eyes out. The boss used to bollock me for belting the eyeballs around the floor with the brush. One day, I stuck two eyeballs on the fridge door, he was not happy.'

'Who the hell eats sheep's head?' asked John.

'You would be surprised; a lot of older people boil them and make sheep head soup. They often leave the brains in when boiling the heads,' I replied.

'My grandad used to do that,' added Norman.

'I have heard of cooking pig's trotters, oxtail and bull's bollocks, but never sheep's heads,' said Tom.

'You will need a big plate for bull's knackers,' joked John.

It was now 6.15 pm and we recharged our glasses. The phone behind the bar starting to ring, Hilda picked it up; 'Is there a Norman Kennedy in here?'

'Yes, that's me,' shouted Norman.

'Well, there is a young lady on the phone for you,' added Hilda.

Norman rose to his feet and strode to the bar. He was subjected to loud applause, wolf whistles and cheers as he picked up the receiver. Within seconds he just raised his hand and turned to face us, with a look of horror on his face, silence descended. As he listened, we could see the tears welling up in his eyes.

'Everything alright,' asked a concerned Hilda.

After a couple of minutes, Norman gave the receiver back to Hilda and put his head in his hands. Tom and I jumped to our feet and

AN EMPTY CHAIR

joined Norman at the bar. 'What's wrong Norman?' asked Tom.

Norman raised his head; 'That was Keith's sister Beverley, Keith has been shot in Belfast, he's dead.'

Andy shouted, 'What's up.'

'Keith is dead,' I replied.

The three of us returned to our seats in shock. The news had left us all stunned and bewildered. Stan stood up and collected another chair and placed it at our table; 'This is for Keith; he will always be here.'

One empty chair
Nobody there
He gave his life
But we were not there

One empty chair
A young man was there
Why was he chosen
A good friend who cared

One empty chair
No laughter to share
He no longer sits in
One empty chair

BESIDE STILL WATERS

Headlines in the *Shields Gazette*, November 27, 1972

Shields Soldier Killed in Belfast

Corporal Keith Harper was killed in the Falls Road, Belfast yesterday morning, along with Private John Humble of Morpeth. Both men were serving with the 9th Field Regiment of the Royal Artillery. We send our sincere condolences to both families at this tragic time.

It was 10.30 am on December 15, we all stood in the grounds of Trinity Church. It was a cold day and a heavy frost lay everywhere. We seemed dumbstruck and conversation was very strained until Malla uttered; 'I still can't believe what has happened, I can't get my head around the fact that I will never ever see Keith again.'

Norman added, 'We all feel the same Malla, it's hard to comprehend.'

Reverend Patrick Johnson strode to the front of the church to greet the mourners and having spotted us, walked across; 'Good morning boys, this is a very sad day for us all. How are you holding up?'

'Well, it's very difficult to get our heads around it,' replied Tom.

'I have prayed daily for Keith's family and you, his close friends. I wish I could have met you all again under different circumstances,' added Reverend Patrick.

He shook all our hands and expressed his condolences saying 'We must all try and take strength from the memories that remind us of Keith. You boys have had many happy times in his presence and you must hold onto the contribution he has made to your lives.' As he spoke, Keith's hearse pulled up at the church; 'I no doubt will see you all after the burial, I must now go and welcome Keith's family.'

As he left us, Keith's commanding officer and eight soldiers poured out of a minibus that was just parked across the road. They would be the pallbearers who would carry the coffin into the church. We would then carry it out of the church at the end of the service. Keith's coffin was draped in the Union Jack and the regimental colours. The church was packed, with many mourners having to stand at the rear of the church.

At the request of Keith's family, TV cameras and representatives of the press were asked not to be in attendance inside the church. The eight of us were sat three rows from the front, as Reverend Patrick climbed the pulpit to begin the service. He began by welcoming everyone to Trinity Church and began his eulogy:

> *Some time ago, I had the pleasure of meeting Keith, along with his good friends for the first time. It took place in the West End Vaults, just across the road from where we are now. I recall being invited to join them as they enjoyed a lunchtime drink. What struck me at that time, was the comradeship that was in good measure that day.*
>
> *We talked of many things that afternoon and I indulged in a couple of pints of Guinness before my attention was diverted in helping a less than fortunate son of South Shields, who had fallen on hard times. What impressed me about that afternoon was the humour and zest for life this group of young men had. I even got them to attend a Sunday service here at Trinity Church, some weeks later.*
>
> *We are here today not to mourn, but to embrace the life and passion of a young man, whose personality shone like a beacon. You may have noticed that I have not mentioned God or Heaven. I am an appointed guardian of Christianity. Now is that not some job!*
>
> *So, my words and proclamations should inform you that Keith has surely found a place at God's right hand. If that is so, how can it be proved. Of course, as mere mortals we cannot prove it. What we can do however, is to remember Keith for what he was and what he believed in. Each of us must look to embellish our lives with his sense of justice, honesty, loyalty and love. We all owe him that. I would now like to ask Keith's sister Beverley to read the 23rd Psalm.*

Beverley ascended the pulpit and read, only pausing once to compose herself. Reverend Patrick returned to his eulogy;

> *Keith chose to join the army and he had the support of his parents, who knew he wanted it so much. I have spoken to his commanding officer and some of his comrades and they talk of a young man who was single-minded in his devotion to his work. I myself, as you can no doubt tell by my accent, hail from the emerald isle. The people of Northern Ireland, as Keith would often say; are a friendly and caring people. They deserve peace in their own land. We must all pray that it will be realised sooner rather than later. I would now like to call upon Keith's commanding officer, Lt. Colonel Kenneth Perkins to say something about Keith.*

Lt. Colonel Perkins alluded to Keith's influence on his peers and how this endeared him to all those who came into contact with him;

> Keith will always be remembered for his excellence as a professional soldier. He commanded the highest respect from all who served with him. His devotion to duty was unrivalled and he was instrumental in maintaining a positive outlook to the duties he undertook. He was given a corporals commission some ten weeks ago and fully deserved the promotion. It is with great sadness that I stand before you all today and I would like to pass on my heartfelt condolences to Keith's family and friends. The regiment has lost a great soldier and a wonderful young man.

He left the pulpit and walked over to Keith's coffin, saluted and said;

> *Corporal Keith Harper of the Royal Artillery we will remember you.*

Keith lay in a closed coffin, a consequence of the fatal injuries he received from two bullet wounds to the head. Even the most skilful of morticians could not disguise the trauma that was inflicted on our close friend.

Reverend Patrick asked us all to stand and sing the hymn, *How Great Thou Art*.

After the hymn, Reverend Patrick asked Norman to say a few words in memory of Keith. We all wanted to say something, but it wasn't feasible. So, Norman spoke for all of us and said;

> Keith never looked back, he always had a positive approach and looked ahead. When we all last gathered, he spoke of his next posting, hoping it would be Belize or Cyprus. He knew the danger he was in, but he felt that he was there to help the genuine people of Northern Ireland. He said many times, that the people he came into contact with were friendly and helpful. He hoped that they would soon be living in a peaceful environment once again.
>
> I am sure that we all hope and pray that the troubles there will end soon and the people of Northern Ireland can live in peace. Our good friend has left us, but his spirit and memory will live on. Every time we all meet, we will set aside a chair for Keith. His presence will be everlasting. Your lifelong friends, Tom, Stan, Harry, John, Geordie, Andy, Malla and Norman.

The Reverend Patrick gave a reading from Matthew, Chapter 16, Verses 21-28.

He then asked us all to stand and sing the hymn *Jerusalem*.

Finally, Reverend Patrick asked us all to recite the Lord's Prayer.

When the prayer was over, Reverend Patrick gave us the nod to position ourselves at the coffin ready to carry Keith out of the church. So, Tom, Stan, Geordie, Andy, John and me moved to the altar and lifted the coffin as Keith's favourite piece of music, Blind Faith's *Presence of The Lord* began to play.

I have finally found a way to live
Just like I never could before
And I know I don't have much to give
But I can open any door
Everybody knows the secret
Everybody knows the score
I have finally found a place to live
In the presence of the Lord

As we left the church, soldiers from Keith's regiment formed a guard of honour. The coffin was placed in the hearse and the funeral cortege made the ten-minute journey to Harton cemetery for the burial. Keith's parents wanted us to join them at the burial and two extra cars were available for us. The burial was traumatic for all of us, but Keith's mother was on the brink of collapse at times and only Keith's dad and Beverley managed to keep her upright. Once the coffin had been placed in the grave, we quietly left the scene to allow the family to say goodbye to Keith.

We left Harton cemetery and walked to the Careme House in Beach Road, where the mourners were invited to attend in memory of Keith. It took twenty minutes to complete the walk, which was done in virtual silence.

On arrival, we were welcomed by Keith's parents and sister Beverley. We made our way to the bar and Tom; Geordie and Stan bought the drinks and selected a quiet corner and gathered enough chairs for all of us and one extra for Keith.

Keith's commanding officer and his comrades were the last to arrive and having noticed that we were seated together, Lt Colonel Perkins joined us. He was about to adjust Keith's chair when Andy stated; 'Sorry, but that is for Keith.'

Realising his mistake, he said; 'My apologies gentlemen.'

He then introduced himself and shook hands with every one of us and pulled up another chair to join us; 'Firstly, can I offer my sincere condolences to you all, I know what a friend Keith was to all of you. I know he held every one of you in high regard. Some weeks ago, I had the privilege to sit down with Keith and discuss his future with the British Army. Three weeks earlier I was in a position to offer him a corporal's commission, which he gladly accepted. At the age of nineteen to be given such a promotion, spoke volumes of his skills and character as a serving soldier.

When he spoke, he spent a great deal of time talking about his hometown and his good friends, he called 'The Nine'. I recall him saying that Norman was the sage and Andy was the frugal member of the crew. He also said that John kept everything in perspective with his tales and jokes.' At this point Andy became very emotional and rose to his feet saying; 'Sorry, but I can't take this, it's just too much.'

Tom then suggested; 'Andy don't, we all feel the same, sit down.'

Andy reluctantly sat back on his chair and the atmosphere was fraught with grief. Lt Colonel Perkins offered some words of comfort; 'This is a difficult time for you and Keith's family. I will do my best to answer any questions you have for me, but please remember that I am limited in the information I can divulge, because of the OSA.'

'What's the OSA?' asked Malla.

'The Official Secrets Act, I am afraid. I can only provide information that does not include any operational or logistical content. I am sure you understand.'

We all nodded in agreement. Tom then posed the question; 'When will all this senseless murder and mayhem end?'

'My God, that's a difficult one, but what I will say is this; it will take years to regain peace in Northern Ireland. As soldiers, we are deployed at the request of the UK government and ours is to serve and protect all British citizens. The people of Northern Ireland must find a solution to the troubles through their elected politicians. Sadly, there is a historical element to the troubles that goes back to the Civil War and the creation of the north/south border. This is not the sole reason, but people have long memories in the province.

The men and women of my regiment have played no part in the creation of the troubles, but we must strive to enforce peace and prevent those bent on death and destruction from gaining a foothold in Ulster.

I will give you an example of the tension and violence we face every day. Six weeks ago, the unit were doing a routine patrol in the Falls Road. I was present, along with my captain and C Company, which included Keith. Depending upon the gravity of the situation, we are given the option of using rubber bullets or live rounds.

Due to the real possibility of sniper fire, I chose live rounds. We were taking too many casualties from the rooftop and drive by shootings, not to. We approached a street corner, when a boy of no more than fifteen years old sprang from a doorway brandishing a Barretta pistol. He was shouting obscenities and waving his pistol.

My first reaction was that this was a distraction and that the IRA had something else planned. Then he took aim and I hesitated and delayed my response. He fired, but his aim was all over the place. Nevertheless, the bullet cut through my sleeve near my elbow and removed a good deal of cloth and skin as it continued into a house wall.

This kid was only twenty feet away. The adrenalin was obviously pumping through his veins now and I could see he was going to get another round away. So, I ordered my captain to send a round into his leg. My captain duly obliged and fired a round into his right leg above the knee. The impact sent him backward some six feet screaming in pain, with a severe loss of flesh and bone to his leg.

The medical orderly got to him pretty quick and administered a tourniquet and morphine, then he was dragged clear. The danger being that we were soldiers in the firing line and prime targets for any shooters at windows or rooftops. Thankfully, the patrol completed the patrol without any further incident. The boy made a recovery, but he will never play competitive sports and will always walk with a severe limp for the rest of his life. This is urban violence and those who are hell bent on this carnage must never succeed.

So, to answer your original question Tom, I think it will take a generation for that wonderful country to rid itself of the hatred and violence that now saturates it. But again, it will be the people who ultimately decide.'

Geordie joined the conversation; 'I feel like joining up and playing my part.'

'That would be wrong because, you would be doing it for all the wrong reasons. We are not in the business of revenge,' replied Lt Colonel Perkins.

'So why are Catholics killing Protestants and vice-versa?' asked Stan.

'Again, it's a means of destabilising the province. It has nothing to do with religion, it's Christians murdering Christians. Look, you remember Keith as a close friend and support his family at this difficult time. It has been a pleasure to talk to you boys, I just wish it was in different circumstances.

He stood, gave us all a salute and shook all our hands, before leaving.

Norman spoke for us all; 'Christ, can you imagine what it must be like in that environment. Not knowing if you will be alive tomorrow.'

A pause descended until Stan stated; 'Well, he did paint a picture of what it must be like over there. Words of wisdom alright.'

When I find myself in times of trouble
Mother Mary comes to me
Speaking words of wisdom
Let it be
Let it be, let it be, let it be, let it be
Whisper words of wisdom
Let it be

IN SEARCH OF LOVE

Two weeks had elapsed since Keith's funeral. Agreement was reached that our next gathering would take place at The Mariner in Mortimer Road. This was an out-of-town boozer where we could meet in a more relaxed atmosphere. I arrived with Andy and Stan at 7 pm. Tom, Norman, Geordie and Malla were already in attendance. It was a cold December night in 1972 and the only absentee being John. Tom had already set aside a chair for Keith and said; 'When John gets here, we will stand and raise a glass to Keith.'

I bought the beers for Stan, Andy and myself. Instead of the usual brown ale we plumped for Lorimers Best Scotch. The atmosphere was still a little subdued after the events of the last few weeks and the conversation was somewhat strained. All that soon changed when John walked through the door five minutes later. He made straight for our tables and was just about to sit on Keith's chair. Then he realised; 'Oh Christ, this is Keith's chair isn't it, sorry lads.'

'It's alright John, buy your beer, it's time to raise a glass for Keith,' said Norman.

The lounge was empty, save for a young couple sitting in the corner at the end of the bar. While at the bar, John took the opportunity to inform the landlord the reason for this gesture and he very kindly offered the next round of drinks on the house. John collected his beer and joined us.

We all stood and left it to Norman to make a speech;

Whenever and wherever we gather, a chair will be set aside in remembrance of our good friend Keith, who was taken from us. He will always be our beacon of hope and we will never forget him.

Our glasses were raised and as one the response was;

To Keith.

Tom suggested a minute's silence would be a good idea and asked the landlord if that was acceptable. 'Yes, that would just fine lads, please carry on,' he replied.

We all regained our seats and Malla stated; 'It is never going to be the same without Keith.'

'Yes, it will, he is still part of our lives and he is here. It is important to remember that' added Geordie.

'Damn right,' said Stan.

'Listen, nothing changes, to have the same relentless stupidity as always, Keith will be listening,' suggested Norman.

'Alright, let's get the ball rolling, who has any news or scandal then?' asked Andy.

'You will be a father soon Harry, will you not?' asked Tom.

'I certainly will, within a week I reckon,' I replied.

'Well, what are you going to call this new addition to the family dynasty then?' asked Norman.

'If it is a boy, we are torn between Adolph or Bluto. If it is a girl, it will probably be Layla.'

'Why don't you name it after its father then, HMS *Sheffield*,' joked Malla.

'Cheeky bastard,' I replied, as I threw a beer mat his way.

'We will have to wet the baby's head after it's born,' said Andy.

'I am sure that can be arranged.'

'What about you Norman, you are still one of the great unwashed, a full-time student. Are you going to university next summer?' asked Stan.

'Thanks for that less than complimentary accolade Stan. Yes, I plan to complete a degree,' stated Norman.

John enlightened us on Andy's university experience; 'Andy was at Newcastle University from a very early age, did you know that boys?'

'Was he indeed?' I asked.

'Oh yes, he spent ten years in a pickle jar, in the science lab,' added John.

Andy's only response to this insult was the raising of two fingers in John's direction, as the rest of us chuckled with laughter.

'Didn't you spend time in a pickle jar Harry?' quipped Malla.

'This is better, Keith would be proud,' said Geordie.

Tom changed the subject and asked Malla about his love affair with Caroline; 'Now then Malla, how is the romance going?'

Malla was a little reticent to provide details on his relationship; 'It's fine thanks Tom, we spent time together last month. She met me at York and we had the weekend together.'

Norman joined the debate and asked; 'Where exactly did this weekend take place, you dirty, lucky swine?'

'At her aunt's house, but we were in separate rooms,' sighed Malla.

'Oh dear, so no hanky panky then,' asked Stan.

'I refuse to answer that question on the grounds of insanity,' joked Malla.

Now it's your turn Norman, what's the script with Laura?' asked John.

Norman was a little more forthcoming with information; 'Not good I am afraid; she lost her mother three weeks ago.'

'I am sorry to hear that, I didn't know she had died,' I said; 'Oh no, she is not dead, Laura lost her in the Grainger Market in Newcastle. The police tracked her down to a brothel in Hamburg. She was serving coffee and sweetmeats to the customers,' joked Norman.

'Now that was funny Norman, which is very rare for you,' added Geordie.

'I would be happy with the coffee, but I don't fancy the bull's bollocks,' added Andy.

'Andy, you are a real moron, sweetbreads are bull's bollocks and sweetmeats are chocolates or sweet delicacies,' stated Tom.

Norman offered an explanation as to Andy's lack of intelligence; 'Andy, you remind me of someone in a cataleptic fit, who cannot speak, cannot move, and suffers no pain. Yet, you are perfectly conscious of all that goes on, but play no part.'

'That is a perfect description of Andy,' added Stan.

Andy's response was predictable if not a little unusual; 'Norman, I hope your balls turn into drumsticks and beat your brains out.'

'Now that is original,' added Tom.

Andy had noticed that a fair maiden had appeared behind the bar; 'She's a bit of alright.'

Norman offered words of encouragement; 'Can I suggest that you grasp the nettle my friend and seize the opportunity. I happen to know that young lady. She is a student at the Marine & Technical College here in South Shields. I think she is studying sociology and psychology. You will provide her with mountains of research material Andy.'

That last point was lost on Andy, but he seemed keen on the prospect of trying his luck; 'What's her name then?'

'Samantha,' replied Norman, with just a touch of mischief in his voice.

'Go on fill your boots,' added John.

'It's my round anyway, what you having Harry and Stan?'

'Same again.'

'Bloody hell, this is one way of getting the tight swine to the bar,' shouted Tom.

Andy raised his index finger, in Tom's direction and made his way to the bar. He stood at the bar and waited while the fair damsel served another customer; 'Three pints of Lorimers Best Scotch please.' It's Samantha, is it not?'

'No, it's not,' she replied

'Oh sorry, but don't you study at the Marine and Technical College?'

'No, I don't, I work at the STD clinic at Harton Hospital.'

What a bastard that Norman is, Andy thought to himself. But he was undaunted and carried on; 'Sounds like an interesting job.'

The barmaid gave Andy a look of surprise; 'Well, I suppose it is, if you like looking at pox-ridden dicks.'

Andy collected the beers, expressed his thanks and trudged back to his pals, with his tail between his legs. On his return to the table, he cursed Norman; 'I should punch you in the gob, you bastard.'

'Now Andy, you are not going to give up that easy, are you? Think of the benefits,' suggested Norman.

'You knew where she worked you pig,' said Andy.

'Yes, she lives next door and her name is Janet,' added Norman.

'I hope that beer is off and you shit the bed tonight,' was Andy's rebuke.

John suggested that Andy should not be put off, she was indeed very attractive with all the right physical proportions. 'God loves a trier, but the search for love continues,' added Stan.

Geordie revealed that he had met a girl last week and they had arranged a date on Sunday night. 'You are a cool customer Geordie, let's have the details,' asked Malla.

'In good time,' replied Geordie.

'It's not that boiler with the wooden leg, is it?' asked John.

'No, it's not her, this girl works in Binns in King Street and that's all you lot need to know,' stated Geordie.

'What is her name then and where does she live?' I asked.

'No, that information is being withheld Harry, because I don't want you lot raining on my parade.'

'Well, who does that leave without a chick then?' asked Malla.

'That would be Tom, Stan, Andy and John,' I replied.

'I reckon Andy will start to have romantic liaisons with farmyard animals,' suggested Stan.

'We will see, that bird at the bar is still on my radar anyway,' added Andy.

Tom suggested it was time for more beer and Andy informed all those interested that he was going outside for a spliff. John and Geordie nodded in agreement and joined him on a short walk in Cauldwell Avenue. It would not be prudent to enhance the pub environment with the aroma of marijuana. The rest of us discussed the news of the past week and Norman commented upon last Sunday's *Weekend World* on ITV. The Vietnam War was the lead story. Norman expressed his reservations on the USA's continued carpet bombing over huge swathes of North Vietnam saying; 'It defies logic that they think they are going to garner support from the people of that country with this mass murder. It will all end with a total waste of life and the yanks will pull out, mark my words.'

I changed the subject; 'Did you know the theme tune for *Weekend World* is *Nantucket Sleighride* by Mountain.'

'What the hell is a *Nantucket Sleighride* Harry?' asked Malla.

'It's a term used to describe whaling on the east coast of the USA. It refers to the sperm whale, when it is harpooned and as a result it drags the boats for many miles before it becomes exhausted and finally succumbs to its death,' I replied.

Geordie, John and Andy returned suitably invigorated and a further round of beers were ordered. It was now 8.15 and the lounge had acquired an enhanced gathering of customers, both young and old. Stan returned to the subject of girlfriends; 'So, it seems that Geordie has joined the ranks of lovers, with this mysterious lady from Binns.'

Norman decided to offer his own slant on this romantic revelation; 'Geordie, you surely have come a long way in your quest for love. It's not that long ago that your mother was considering involving a psychiatrist, because of your somewhat weird nocturnal activities.'

'Is that true?' asked Malla.

'Oh yes, indeed,' added Norman.

'When did you discover this?' asked Tom.

Geordie had a look of resignation on his face, but sat and offered no protest.

'Well Tom, this information was relayed to me by Geordie's mother in the post office on Dean Road,' replied Norman.

'Please go on,' said Tom.

'It appears that Geordie was engaging in bizarre sexual activities involving a warm scarf, a jar of worms and his neighbours Welsh corgi,' added Norman.

Raucous laughter ensued that drew the attention of the landlord, who gave us a slightly troubled look. Geordie just smiled; 'Norman, I will be glad to see the back of you, when you go off to university, you bastard.'

Tom then informed us of his recent acquisition of a pair of new football boots saying; 'I bought some new boots at Sportspack at the Nook.'

'What make were they?' I asked.

'Puma, and John Pack did me a good deal.'

How many goals have you notched so far? Asked Andy.

'Nine so far and I hope to add to that this weekend, we are playing Consett. I scored two against them earlier in the season.'

'Well, let's hope the new boots make a difference,' added Norman.

The lounge was now well-populated and the evening was becoming a little lively. Then, in walked 'Angry John'.

'Shit, just look who has walked in,' whispered Stan.

'Bollocks, what the hell is he doing here?' asked Tom.

'He's barred from most of the pubs in town,' I answered.

'Someone should tell the landlord,' added Andy.

'Well, here is your chance to impress that girl behind the bar. Go and tell her you need to speak to the landlord,' said John.

'Brilliant idea that, I am on my way,' answered Andy.

Sadly, Angry John had already managed to buy a pint at the bar. Andy carefully manoeuvred to the end of the bar and caught the attention of the barmaid; 'Janet, can I have a word please?'

'Who is Janet, my name is Deborah,' she sighed.

I will cripple that bastard Norman. 'Sorry, Deborah but I need to speak to the landlord it is very important.'

'Oh well, if it is important, I will see if he is available then,' she replied.

The landlord appeared and Andy tried to be discreet and very quietly informed him that the man at the other end of the bar was

Angry John a well-known troublesome individual, he has been barred from many town centre pubs. This was a result of his violent nature and he was well-known to the police. The landlord looked at Angry John; 'He looks fine at the moment.'

'That's the calm before the storm,' stated Andy.

'Alright, if you don't mind, I will ring a friend of mine, he is the landlord of the West Park for his opinion,' replied the landlord.

As the landlord turned, he said; 'Sorry, I didn't get your name son.'

'Norman,' replied Andy, and then returned to his friends.

The landlord returned after his conversation with his chum at the West Park, a little more anxious than he was before and took up a position close to where Angry John was standing at the bar.

Angry John looked around at those gathered, trying to identify a familiar face. He spotted a young couple chatting at a table and moved across to indulge in conversation. It did not last long, he must have said something untoward, because the bloke rose to his feet and said; 'Piss off, or I will knock you out.'

Angry John seemed amused and wandered back to his place at the bar. His behaviour had not gone unnoticed by the landlord who said; 'I think you should drink up and leave.'

Angry John just grinned; 'How long have you been humping this barmaid then?'

Before the landlord could respond, Deborah threw a pint of Lorimers Best Scotch over Angry John.' This of course, did not please the recipient and Angry John began shouting and swearing. This created a mass exodus and most of the customers in the lounge sought refuge in the bar. Except for our little gathering.

The landlord did his best to placate Angry John, but the touch paper was now well lit and he was now in the mood to administer violence on anything or anybody.

Stan whispered; 'We are going to have to deal with this boys.'

'Shit, he is a big bastard,' added John.

Angry John was about 6 ft 3 in and weighed in at around 17 stone. He was now a bear that wanted to dismember any living thing. Tom shouted to the landlord to call the police. Angry John was not best pleased with this announcement; 'It's a bastard ambulance you will need when I have finished giving you a fucking kicking.'

'Stuff this, let's just give him a doing,' I suggested.

The big ugly swine moved closer to our table; 'Right, which one of you wankers is going to be first in the ambulance?'

Tom and Stan rose to their feet and moved to confront the big swine; 'Get him to swing a punch and I will kick him in the nuts,' I said to Tom.

Stan and Tom started bouncing up and down and throwing punches. I raced forward and slammed my right foot in to Angry John's nuts. He hardly flinched, but then he gave me a right hook to the side of my head that sent me flying across a table full of drinks. It was now a free for all, John and Malla joined the fray and they managed to subdue the big bastard. In order to keep our adversary subdued both Tom and Stan landed a few heavy blows to his head and body and he crumpled into a corner, semi-conscious. His eyes were starting to swell up and two of his teeth had come through his bottom lip.

He still managed to rise to his feet, and laid a few punches on John, Andy and Geordie, before he was finally put down. Within five minutes the police were on hand to take charge of the situation. This was not as easy as they hoped it would be. As they moved to put the handcuffs on, Angry John swung another punch which connected with one of the officers. Then the truncheons were drawn and the big swine was given a going over before he was dragged out to the waiting police van.

Once the big brute was safely locked up in the van, the two officers returned to the lounge. A statement would be needed in order to press charges. One officer asked if he assaulted any of us?

'Yes, he lamped me and my head is bloody sore,' I said.

'Do you need hospital treatment?' he asked.

'No, I will recover,' I replied.

The other copper then asked; 'He must have fallen over a few times, judging by his injuries then?'

'Oh yes, he just went berserk officer, we feared for our lives,' added Norman.

'Well, can you all call into the police station in Kepple Street sometime tomorrow and make a statement.' The coppers informed us that Angry John had just been bailed two days ago on another charge of assaulting his probation officer. Their preliminary indications were that the mad bastard would get at least six months in Durham jail. The time was now 9.30 pm and we helped the landlord return his lounge to the state it was in prior to the evening's entertainment. Andy ensured that he assisted Deborah with the cleaning up, despite constant ridicule from the rest of us. During the clean-up, Tom raised the issue of Norman's absence during the mayhem; 'Your comment about Angry John's behaviour was a bit rich. You weren't even in the room.'

'No, that is correct Tom, I was splashing my boots in the netty. When I came out, I saw Angry John being catapulted into the corner of the lounge. So, I am sorry I wasn't available to assist in the melee that took place. However, I think I would have taken a more pragmatic approach in quelling his taste for violence. You have to find out what makes him tick? You need to try and understand his behaviour, get under his skin, in other words,' offered Norman.

John had another view which we all tended to support; 'Norman, the man is a serial violent offender. He has put more people in hospital than TB. Do unto him, as he would do unto you. Here endeth the fucking lesson, so buy the beers.'

'Fair enough,' replied Norman.

Then he made his way to the bar accompanied by Andy who continued to woo the lovely Deborah. The landlord provided all the beers for our brave efforts in neutralising the mad monster. The customers that had evacuated the lounge when all hell broke loose, gradually trickled back into the lounge.

I had a nice big lump on the side of my head, that was colouring up nicely. As I was sent sprawling across the table, I suffered a cut to my left hand from a broken beer glass. The landlord's wife, who had missed all the fun, treated the wound and bandaged it up. Having noticed my wedding ring, she asked; 'What is your wife going to make of all this then?'

'Oh, I am sure she will understand,' I replied. She just gave me a wry smile; 'I am not sure I would.'

The rest of the evening was somewhat benign compared to the earlier shenanigans. Andy had managed to fix up a date with Deborah the barmaid. She agreed to an evening at the cinema to watch *The Godfather*. This was arranged for Tuesday night. Geordie suggested we all should attend, but Andy was less than enthusiastic; 'No fucking way, that's all I need. You seven idiots spoiling my night.'

We decided not to impinge on our good friend's special night and

Norman offered Andy some advice; 'Now remember Andy, you must wear jeans that are not too tight. Remember to let her choose where you sit and this is very very important, don't tell her about your recent penis enhancement operation, that comes later.' More laughter at Andy's expense.

'That was excellent Norman, you really should be on the stage, it leaves in ten minutes,' joked Tom.

'Anyway, what's this *Godfather* film about then?' asked Geordie.

'It's about the Mafia in New York in the 40s and 50s,' I said.

'Yes, it has had great reviews,' added Norman.

Malla chose that moment to announce that he was learning to play the bass guitar and suggested that we could form a musical combo. The idea did not generate much enthusiasm and Stan asked; 'Where is the gear coming from?'

John has got a harmonica; Harry has a guitar and Andy can't even fucking whistle. It's hardly the recipe for a chart-topping band, now is it?' added Tom.

Malla was determined; 'We could borrow the gear from Simonside youth club and practice there.'

'I can play chopsticks on the piano,' joked Norman.

Tom poured scorn on the proposed venture into the world of rock and roll; 'Listen, my life is far too important to me, to form a group of untrained, tone deaf and untalented misfits. In the hope that anything that resembles music, might just make us millionaires.'

'I reckon that has curtailed our rock star ambitions fellas,' I added.

As usual, Norman had to try and provide a positive slant on the idea; 'Gentlemen, we should consider the positive aspects of just such a venture. This is a multifarious group of young men, who can surprise the musical world with a symphony that encapsulates the sound of a generation.'

'Have you been smoking cordite again Norman, you really should stop it. It's just not healthy for you,' suggested Tom.

'Are we still getting free drinks at the bar?' asked Geordie.

'Don't know, it's your round anyway,' added Stan.

Geordie made haste to the bar, while there, he noticed that the couple who Angry John insulted had returned. He felt the need to find out what Angry John had said to them: 'So, what did Angry John say to you, when he came across to your table?'

The bloke shouted; 'He is a lunatic him, he said; 'I am surprised to see you here tonight. I thought you would be at home, humping your girlfriend's mother.'

Geordie failed to realise the gravity of the situation; 'Oh, does Angry John know your girlfriend's mother then?'

The bloke just gave Geordie a look of disgust and turned away. Geordie then asked the landlord if drinks were still on the house and received a pleasing response; 'The next round is free, but after that you boys will have to cough up for last orders.'

'That's fair enough, it was my round anyway,' replied Geordie.

After his rebuke regarding a possible venture into the rock world, Malla suggested a night at the dogs. 'We could do a block booking and get discount. Plus, you get a pie and peas supper thrown in.'

'Yummy,' replied John.

Geordie was informed of the plan on his return to the table; 'Sounds like a good idea, I know a couple of lads in the club who race greyhounds.'

'Christ, they must be quick, racing fucking greyhounds,' joked Tom.

'That was quick Tom, you're so sharp you will cut yourself,' stated Andy.

Malla would not be put off; 'I will get a few tips; I will put the wheels in motion boys.'

'I thought we were going to the dogs?' laughed John.

When last orders were called, a unanimous decision to buy a whisky and salute our absent friend was made. Tom suggested our next gathering should be a celebration of my impending child; 'Let us all know when your ankle biter makes an appearance Harry and we will meet for a few beers.'

'Will do,' I replied. As our band of buddies left the pub, Stan could not resist a statement on Andy's latest medical condition. He ensured that Deborah was well within earshot; 'So, Andy, when do you get those genital warts removed?'

Andy just grinned at Deborah as he left the lounge and when we were outside, Andy said; 'You know what, I think you bastards are jealous of my new love affair.'

'Well, one thing is certain Andy, you will never be short of penicillin,' added Malla.

GONE TO THE DOGS

An evening at the local greyhound stadium was arranged for our band of idiots. Malla arranged the night for a Saturday, starting at 7 pm at the Boldon track. We decided to meet in The Grey Horse at 6 pm for an early drink to get us in the mood. Greyhounds have been racing at Boldon for thirty years and it was a popular night out, as it also had a discotheque on site.

John, Geordie, Malla and Tom were all present when Stan, Andy and I arrived, just before 7 pm.

'Now where is Norman?' asked Tom.

Before anyone could respond, in walked Norman with his girlfriend Laura. There were a few wary looks around the table as she sat down. She put our minds at ease; 'Don't worry boys; I won't be joining you at the dogs. I have just brought Norman here in my dad's car.'

Norman had gone to the bar and Andy asked; 'Would you like a drink, Laura?'

Laura answered; 'It's alright, Norman is getting me a coke.'

Tom could not resist a dig at Andy; 'Nothing changes does it Andy, there you are trying to be the perfect gentleman, knowing full well that Norman was getting Laura a drink. You must still have your first penny.'

'Oh, it's fine, don't be too hard on him, you won't have had much fishing in this week, have you Andy?' Laura asked.

Andy sighed, 'Thank you Laura, yes you are correct, it has been a poor week. We only had the boat out once and it was a poor catch. Mostly crabs, a few lobsters and a couple of boxes of ling.'

'I didn't know you were knowledgeable about deep-sea fishing Laura?' added Tom.

Laura just smiled; 'There is a lot about me that you don't know Tom.'

'Well, are we having a kitty then?' asked John.

'Yes, a fiver each to start, let's have your money out you morons,' I said.

The cash was handed over to Tom, our resident beer banker, Norman returned with his and Laura's drinks.

'Andy said he would pay for them,' stated Malla.

Andy gave Malla a filthy look and resisted the temptation to voice any obscenities in his direction.

'They are just being horrible to Andy,' added Laura.

After acquiring our beers and settled in our seats, Laura raised the issue of Keith, saying; 'It was just terrible what happened to Keith.'

She had just uttered those words, when Geordie said; 'Shit, where is his chair?'

We all looked at each other with a sense of guilt and Tom rose, collected another chair and placed it next to Laura. She looked surprised and then Norman explained the reason for the empty chair.

'He will always be with us,' added Stan.

The conversation centred on Keith, and then Laura suggested; 'Well boys, we must raise a toast to Harry's baby. How is she doing Harry?'

'She is fine thanks Laura,' I replied.

'What did you call her in the end?' she asked.

'Layla,' I replied.

'That's a lovely name and a great song,' she added.

'A toast to Layla and health and happiness to all the family,' said Norman.

And we all raised our glasses. She then bid us all goodnight and added; 'Have a good night and don't lose too much money.'

She gave Norman a kiss, which resulted in cheers and whistles from his pals, much to his embarrassment.

When Laura left, Geordie could not hide his enthusiasm; 'Laura looks great Norman, what the hell she sees in you beats the shit out of me.'

Norman as ever was prepared for that insult and responded with; 'I feel the need to remind all those present that Laura has revealed extraordinary taste in her choice of men. She has sensed a quiet intelligence that sadly very few men possess. She has identified an alacrity of spirit in me, that many women could only dream of. In addition, she has enjoyed my wit and conversation, which all too often is wasted within the confines of this gathering. But fear not my friends, I will not abandon you and allow you to succumb to the despair of mediocrity. Laura has a man who is destined for fame and fortune and she will journey with me as I fulfil my ambitions.'

'I think we have just been insulted again, but I am not sure,' I joked.

'She is still too good for the likes of you,' added John.

'Cheers John, it's heartening to know you appreciate my predicament,' replied Norman.

'Never mind all that shite, anyone have any hot tips for the dogs tonight?' asked Stan.

Malla suggested a couple of possible winners called Donna's Wind and Gold Phoenix. He worked with a bloke that trained greyhounds and also did a lot of hare coursing, who gave him these tips.

'The dogs are as bent as horse racing, just stick to a trap number all night and you will break even,' added Tom.

'Now there is logic for you, what number would you suggest Tom?' asked Andy.

Tom answered; 'Number seven.'

Andy's knowledge of greyhound racing was limited and nobody felt inclined to inform him that only six dogs were allowed to take to the track for any given race.

Tom gave us all a resumé of his thoughts on the skulduggery that is associated with greyhound racing; 'It's rife and they do all sorts to nobble their rivals, feed them with dodgy food. They give them sleep potions, put food in the traps. If you win anything it will be down to luck and nothing else.'

'Now that is very cynical Tom, I am sure there are many honest people within the dog racing fraternity,' added Norman.

'What the hell, a grand time will be had by all, regardless, and there is a disco after the racing. So, we might pick up some birds,' added Geordie.

John laughed and said; 'More likely to get distemper or rabies than cop off with a bird.'

Norman alluded to a little history with regard to the Boldon stadium; 'Did you know that it first opened in 1940 and the first meeting had eight races and the first race was won by a dog called Percheron from trap 2 at 5/2? What is now a disco, used to be a ballroom for dancing.'

'Where do you gleam all this meaningless information Norman?' asked Geordie.

'It can be found in a place where you obviously don't normally visit Geordie, the town library. It is amazing what you can find out if you make the effort,' suggested Norman.

'Thanks for the history lesson Norman, now it's time for a joke. Did you hear about the burglar who fell in the cement mixer? Now he is a hardened criminal,' joked John.

Stan then informed us about problematic neighbours; 'Apparently, arguments about fences are the major cause of feuds between neighbours. So, I went and took our neighbours fence down, just to be on the safe side.'

The happy banter continued and Malla offered another comic quote; 'What do you call a man with an elephant on his head? An ambulance.'

I suggested we should drink up and make our way down Sunderland Road to the greyhound stadium. Within five minutes we were on our way, it was now 7.15 pm. The weather was unseasonably good for January, a clear night sky and not too cold. As we entered the car park Malla gave us all our tickets and as our group entered through the ticket office, Andy asked the receptionist if there were any discounts for people with a mental handicap. On receiving a negative response, he turned to Geordie and said; 'Sorry mate, not this time.'

Geordie's reply, was fairly predictable; 'Go forth and multiply Andy.'

We all trooped in and made our way to the bar. A round of drinks were ordered and a table was selected that would accommodate the eight of us, it had a decent view of the track. We were in time for the first race at 7.30 pm, but only just. No time for scrutinising the form, selections were chosen and bets were placed. Most of us went for the favourite called Dark Knight at 7/2. Andy chose trap 3 with Sister Sue at 10/1 and Tom picked out Bonny Boy at 5/1. Much to our disgust and Andy's joy he had the winner, gaining £5 as his reward for a 50p bet.

Tom suggested that any winnings should be shared out between us and Andy's response to that was; 'You can all piss off, you are on your own, I am a fiver up already and I am not sharing with nobody.'

'You may well regret that statement Andy, are the rest of us sharing then boys?' I asked.

The overwhelming reply was in the affirmative and Norman informed us of a number of tips he had procured from an uncle of his, who was a regular punter. He was keen to only confide in those of us that were happy to join the syndicate we had established; 'Oh dear Andy, it is a pity you have decided to go it alone, you may have been a little hasty in that regard. I have a few winning tips from my uncle Jack, he is generally pretty accurate in his selections, so I am regularly informed.'

'We will see, I feel lucky tonight. I feel it in my water,' replied Andy.

'You need a doctor then,' joked John.

The place had filled up by now and all the tables were populated. A party of ladies on a hen night had a table just behind us and a mixed party on a works night out were just to our left. Stan was sitting next to me, and he whispered in my ear; 'Harry, have you seen that girl in the hen party with the green dress on, she has the face of an angel.'

'Yes, she is certainly a looker alright,' I said.

'What are you two on about then?' asked Malla.

'Hen party green dress, but don't make it obvious,' whispered Stan.

Malla turned around pretending to look for someone and glanced across at the hen party. Having spotted the vision of loveliness, he answered; 'Dear me, she is a darling.'

We all placed our bets for the next race and the outcome was favourable for our little syndicate, with Stan and Tom winning £10 each for their selection in trap 3 called Makam Flyer, our pot was now £12 in the black. Andy's dog came in last and Geordie suggested his luck had deserted him saying; 'Well then Andy, who's sorry now?'

'It's early days, we will see who is laughing at the end of the night.'

The hen party was in full swing, the bride-to-be was adorned in all manner of appendages including badges, notes, condoms and L-plates. They were getting pretty loud and they were asked to refrain from using suggestive language by a member of staff. Having spotted Andy, one of the hen party moved across to our table; 'Hello Andy, haven't seen you in a long time.'

She then sat next to Andy, in Stan's seat, he was at the toilet. She was dressed in a figure-hugging red dress that left nothing to the imagination. Her breasts were somehow defying the laws of gravity and were very close to spilling out of what appeared to be very inadequate scaffolding. It was very apparent that Andy was not too pleased to see her and said very little in response to her greeting.

Tom took the opportunity to relieve the pressure on Andy; 'Hello, my name's Tom and I look after Andy now. He has had a torrid time of late. Since the operation he has to be careful, he could just lose control and you never know what he is going to do.'

Andy looked at Tom; 'Tom you talk bollocks, take no notice of him Karen.'

'Ah it's Karen is it, pleased to meet you, Karen. You look lovely tonight. Will you be going to the disco later on?'

'I might, depends who else is going and how much alcohol the bride-to-be has consumed, I guess.'

The rest of us were concentrating on Karen's fulsome cleavage and hoping that her top bollocks were about to make an appearance. Unfortunately, they remained under cover, much to the disappointment of all concerned.

Karen bid us farewell and returned to her hen party.

Norman was the first to put Andy on the spot; 'Alright Andy, what's the story about Karen?'

'She is my cousin you idiot; she is my uncle Jim's daughter,' stated Andy.

'You don't get many of them to the pound,' joked John. Referring to her well-endowed chest.

Norman suggested that Tom was keen on the heavily laden Karen and gave him some advice; 'I would tread carefully in your pursuit of this damsel Tom. She has been well-provided for in terms of suckling babies, but you need to be very wary of her intentions my son. What you cannot get in your mouth is just wasted remember. If you manage to manoeuvre yourself in between those splendid examples of breasts, you will need to breathe through your ears; a difficult exercise at the best of times.'

'He will have to climb over me first,' joked John.

The beer was flowing and the banter was good as we considered our dogs for the next race. Andy spent time weighing up his selection. This was not lost on Malla who observed; 'Are you waiting to see what dogs are selected, courtesy of Norman's uncle?'

'Kiss my arse Malla, I have the winner of the next race,' replied Andy.

We were then served with our pie and peas supper. Ours was the first table to be served, much to the annoyance of the hen party. We gleefully exchanged banter with this flock of demented geese and John suggested that any surplus pies should be directed to our table. The supper was consumed with gusto, but sadly no extra pies were forthcoming. So, John announced our next action; 'Come on now, place your bets gentlemen. Time is of the essence; the next race starts in five minutes.'

I decided to go for a £1 accumulator of the first two past the post, which I procured at 20/1. The rest of the syndicate opted for a tip from Norman's uncle. Andy kept his selection to himself. In the final straight both my dogs hit the front and finished first and second. The dog out of trap 1 finished last and collided with the fence, and Andy shouted; 'Bastard, that mutt should be put to sleep, I can run faster than that.'

'I take it you have not won then Andy?' asked Stan.

'Shite off,' was Andy's terse reply.

Our winnings had now grown to a healthy £32 and John suggested we imbibe in a whisky to celebrate our good fortune saying; 'How about a Jameson all round my fine chums?'

I smiled; 'A splendid idea Johnny.'

'Oh, dear how disappointing for you Andy, you do enjoy a Jameson don't you?' added Norman.

'Go on, get him one; he is not having much luck. Bless his cotton socks,' suggested Tom.

Having savoured the Jameson, we sat contemplating the next race, Geordie enlightened us on a recent visit to a relative's house the previous Sunday. 'I went to visit my aunt and uncle in Low Fell last Sunday, with my mam and dad. They have this massive, terraced house with about 200 bedrooms. Anyway, I had been there about twenty minutes when I realised, I needed a shite. I climbed the stairs to the bathroom, which was bigger than our back garden and it had two toilets, so I placed my casing on the smaller pot. It was a real heavy evacuation and I was straining like the anchor-man in a tug of war competition. Having removed the barnacles, I tried to flush the toilet. But the two large yule logs would not budge. I waited and flushed again, but again they would not swim to safety and boy did it stink.

I looked around the bathroom for something to break them up with, without success. I then walked into the nearest bedroom and looked in a wardrobe and eureka! I found a wire coat hanger. I returned to the bathroom and finally managed to slice up the turds, enough to flush them away.'

'What did you do with the coat hanger?' asked John.

'I cleaned it as best I could and put it back in the wardrobe. When I walked into the living room, my old man said; 'You have been a long time, any problems?'

'No, but the small toilet has no seat.'

'That's the bidet, replied my aunt.'

The laughter went on for ages, Stan was helpless, he could not stop laughing at the thought of Geordie sitting on that bidet.

It was now 9.15 and there were two races left. Norman felt obliged to include Andy in our good fortune and revealed the last two tips that his uncle provided. The penultimate race was a disaster, nothing was gained and Andy was full of ridicule as to the quality of Norman's so-called tips; 'So much for the expert, that tip in trap 1 was last out and the dog ran like it had a banjo up its arse.'

'Never mind it's only money, we have enough to get into the disco and a couple of rounds of drinks. And, the last race is yet to come, who knows it might be another winner. Why don't we all stick a fiver on a dog,' added Malla.

Andy uttered, 'I would rather stick one on you, I have spent enough tonight,'

Stan informed our gathering that the disco opened at 10 pm and it cost £1 for admission. The hen party was now in full flow, with lots of singing and impromptu dancing. They had stopped betting an hour ago and seemed content just to drink themselves into oblivion.

John and I had struck up a conversation with two fellows on the adjacent table to us. They worked in the offices at Reyrolle in Hebburn. They were both well-dressed in suits and ties. One of them called Mike had a very loud kipper tie on that would have choked a Cape buffalo. His mate Bob had a more conservative tie, a slim red leather affair. Mike's kipper tie was not lost on John and he asked; 'Who got you that tie mate?'

'My wife bought it as a birthday present.'

'She must fucking hate you, I bet she plays away.'

The guy was stunned at this rather personal slur and I thought he would take exception to that remark and lamp John. But on the contrary, he just answered; 'You don't know her, do you? She is a right boiler and she is going the journey soon, I have had enough.'

I felt the need to intervene in this somewhat delicate matter; 'It seems my friend has touched a nerve, Mike; can I apologise for any embarrassment that has been caused.'

'It's fine lads, she is a right brass nail. I don't know why I married her. At least we don't have kids.

John and I nodded in agreement and I suggested he should go into the disco with us, but lose the tie.

He laughed; 'Sounds like a good idea, we might just do that.'

John and I returned to the bosom of our pals and bets were placed on our chosen mutts.

The well-endowed Karen rejoined us at the table. She was tipsy but not as bad as some of the others within the hen party, a number of whom were struggling to stand upright. Of course, she had a plethora of admirers within our conclave with Tom and Geordie vying for her attention.

The last race was beneficial for both Stan and John who had the winner, coming in at 6/1.

The hen party were again reminded to control their boisterous behaviour, it was now 9.50 pm and we were counting the cost of our gambling in terms of profit. With John and Stan's winnings, a sum total of £38, had accumulated. It was £8 for our entry into the disco, leaving £3.75p each for alcoholic refreshment.

Norman was in a reflective mood and he had been surprisingly quiet, however he did not let us down. When a member of the bar staff chose to admonish Geordie for his agricultural language, Norman took the opportunity to enhance his outlook on life and the consequences of intolerance saying; 'Sometimes, our individual personality manifests itself in an extraordinary way. The thrill of the chase, the fear of the unknown or the realisation that things are not what they seem. We live in an ever-changing world that puts men on the moon and weapons are created that can destroy humanity. I say this to you little fellow, that the time for recriminations is over. Let us be bold in this time of adversity. If I can provide you with a sobering thought, it is this:

> *Learn from yesterday, live for today, hope for tomorrow. The important thing is to not stop questioning.*

By doing this you will greatly enhance your aspirations and honestly reflect upon your misadventures in life.'

We all stood and listened to this tirade of rhetoric that Norman enjoyed and when he finished, the barman just stood with his brain working overtime trying to digest what he had just heard. There was no response needed, again Norman had entertained us with a monologue that perfectly matched the occasion.

As we entered the disco, I asked him who the quote was from?

'Elementary Harry, Albert Einstein of course,' he replied.

Mike and Bob joined us in the disco, which was well-populated, much to our surprise. The hen party arrived and quickly advanced to the dance floor to the sound of *Honky Tonk Woman* by the Rolling Stones.

Andy and Tom were in deep conversation at the bar; 'What's appertaining lads?' I asked.

'Just scanning the birds Harry and considering which if any, we should put the bite on,' joked Tom.

'Well, I think you're spoilt for choice gentlemen,' I added.

Andy's cousin Karen, was sitting at a table close to the dance floor and Tom asked; 'I think I should ask Karen for a dance, what do you think fellas?'

'Go on, fill your boots son,' I replied.

Tom made his way to her table and sat next to her. She smiled and began chatting. After a few minutes they rose to their feet and hit the dance floor to the sound of *Sunshine of Your Love* by Cream. John, Stan and Geordie were enjoying a smoke at the end of the bar. Andy and Norman were conspicuous by their absence.

'Where is the poet laureate and his monkey?' asked Malla.

Andy then appeared walking from the toilet and joined us at the bar; 'Norman's in the bog, he has just been lamped by that barman who told Geordie to pipe down half an hour ago.'

'Is he alright then,' I asked.

'Yes, he has a fat lip, that's all,' answered Andy.

'Did Norman not give him a dig,' said Malla.

'No, it's Norman remember, I have never known him to smack anybody, have you?' asked Andy.

We encouraged Stan, John and Geordie to join us and told them about Norman's little episode.

'Where is he now?' asked Stan.

'He is cleaning himself up in the toilet,' replied Andy.

Stan and John walked to the toilet, and after five minutes they returned with Norman, he was suffering from a cut to his top lip, which was swelling up rapidly.

'That will put a stop to your necking with Laura,' I suggested.

'He smiled and then grimaced,' and uttered; 'Don't make me laugh it hurts like hell.'

'It seems that not everyone enjoys your monologues Norman, you will have to be particular who you subject them to,' added Stan.

Tom seemed to be getting on well with Karen and he brought her to the bar for a drink. This was a brave decision by Tom, bearing in mind he would be open to a deluge of derogatory comments. Stan was the first to speak; 'Well then it didn't take you long Tom, I do hope this lovely lady has expensive tastes. Will it be champagne, Campari or a cocktail I wonder?'

Karen answered; 'Oh no, just half of Carling will be fine.'

John joined in the conversation; 'So, Tom how is the wife, she must do long hours as a policewoman, is she on nightshift tonight?'

Karen shot Tom a worried look; 'You're married, are you?'

'No, he is just taking the piss. There will be a few more insults about my health and sanity as well as my criminal activities, am I correct you arseholes?'

Karen noticed Norman's enhanced top lip and asked how it came about?

'Well, it appears that my intelligence is lost on certain individuals and they seem to be bereft of any common decency. Thankfully, I have a good group of friends who are always supportive of my aims,' replied Norman.

'He hasn't answered the question, has he?' asked a confused Karen.

'Ah well, this is what he does so well. He has a knack of evading the question and talking bollocks, which he does with great skill,' I added.

We continued to enjoy the evening without any further incident. Tom ended up taking Karen home via a taxi. Andy and Geordie left to walk home just after midnight. The rest of us sank a few more beers and ordered two taxis to take us all home. Me and Stan booked a car for Simonside and Norman, John and Malla booked a car for the town centre.

When outside waiting for our transport, we noticed the barman who had inflicted the injury on Norman's 'boat race', was sitting on the curb nursing one hell of a black eye.

'Well, what do we have here? Looks like retribution for an earlier error of judgement. The moral of the story being, violence is not the answer you idiot. I wonder who carried out this vengeful act?' I asked.

The barman looked up; 'One of you bastards, as you well know,' he said.

John had a final word on the subject; 'A lesson learned mate, anyway, here is a joke for you. A lorry load of tortoises crashed into a trainload of terrapins. It was a turtle disaster.'

The barman looked up; 'You lot are round the twist.'

As we climbed into the taxi, Stan asked; 'Well, was it you who belted the barman, Harry?'

'No, I thought it was you.'

'Not guilty I am sorry to say.'

'Well, we will find out at our next soirée in two weeks time. At the Buffs Club at 7 pm, in the back room.'

'Time to *Garn Yem* driver and do not spare the horses.'

THE FUTURE BECKONS

As we had agreed on our last gathering, the venue for our next soiree was the Buffs Club in Laygate. Norman, Andy and Malla were the last to appear at just after 7 pm arriving in a downpour of rain. They trudged into the club like drowned rats and John suggested; 'Take your wet clothes off boys, you will get cold and mammy will have to rub the Vic on your chests before you go to bed.'

'Very funny, I gather you lot managed to avoid the rain then?' asked Norman.

'That is because those present were on time, in fact I was here at 6.45 pm,' replied Geordie.

The late arrivals bought their beers and joined their comrades and Stan asked; 'Who is up for a game of darts then?'

'I will throw a few arrows with you,' replied Tom.

While they were at the dartboard the rest of us discussed the events of the last fortnight. The effect of Keith's funeral was still a source of sadness and Malla suggested that his absence would be hard to overcome. He pulled a chair alongside; 'Well Keith, here is your chair mate and how about we all raise our glasses to our departed friend.'

Tom and Stan halted their game of darts to join us in remembrance of Keith and Malla added; 'To a great friend, who sacrificed his life for freedom and liberty, to Keith Harper.'

Our conversation drifted onto our night at the dogs a few weeks earlier and Andy quizzed Tom on his date with his cousin Karen; 'Hey Tom how did it go with Karen then?'

Tom ignored Andy's remark and threw his third dart straight into the scoreboard at the side of the dartboard, much to Stan's delight. Tom turned to look at Andy; 'She never arrived; she stood me up. I waited half an hour but she didn't show, so I had a few beers in The Pier.'

Tom was now subjected to a crescendo of ridicule from his peers and Geordie put his slant on the unfortunate Tom; 'Oh dear Tom, love has turned its back on you, my son. Just as well really, messing with Andy's bloodline was always going to be a problem. Any offspring would have certain deficiencies, such as not getting the beers in.'

'Go on have a laugh, enjoy it while you still have teeth Geordie,' countered Tom as another dart failed to reach its target and bounced off a wire and landed on the floor.

It took Andy a short time before the insult registered but eventually, he added; 'Hang on you swine, that's my family you are degrading Geordie.'

John lightened the ethos somewhat when he added a touch of humour; 'I think my neighbour fancies me. She knocked on my door and said; 'I've noticed you looking at me.'

'I was so surprised that I dropped my binoculars.'

As we sat and conversed Malla noticed a guy at the bar and looked at me and said; 'Hey Harry, that's 'Scratcher' Thompson at the bar, remember him.'

I looked over to the bar and recognised him; 'Yes, that's Scratcher; haven't seen that bugger in years,' I replied.

'Alright then, why Scratcher?' asked Norman.

'Go on Malla, you tell him.'

'Well, Scratcher had problems with head lice in junior school. I mean they were big; you could see them moving in his hair, they were that big. He was one of eleven kids and personal hygiene was not high on the agenda in their hovel. The council moved them to a bigger house in Brockley Whins. Their old man had died from a heart attack, having fathered five of the kids and various blokes took it upon themselves to partake in sexual proclivities with the mother and therefore increase the brood.'

'Nobody would sit next to Scratcher in class, so he had to sit alone,' I added.

Much to the surprise of all of us, Malla shouted over to the bar; 'Hey Scratcher Thompson, come and join us.'

Scratcher, turned and realised it was Malla, and smiled; 'Malla is that you? Well, I will eat hay with a donkey.'

He walked over to our table and noticed me and added; 'Harry Wainwright as well, where the hell have you two been hiding all these years?'

As soon as he made his mind up to sit, the distance between chairs began to increase and just as he was going to plonk his arse down on Keith's chair Tom said; 'That chair is spoken for mate.'

Scratcher looked puzzled and when Norman explained he understood; 'Oh sorry fellas, I'll grab another one from the corner.'

As he went to retrieve a chair, we all moved our chairs again. This left an obvious space for Scratcher to position himself.

'So, Scratcher how are things with you then? asked Malla.

'I am married and I have two kids, little swine's they are mind. Me wife works at Westoe Pit, but I am on the dole,' he replied.

'She doesn't go down the pit, does she?' asked a bemused Geordie.

'No, she works in the canteen,' he answered.

Scratcher still had a full head of hair and John couldn't help but observe his swede for signs of life, as he was sitting next to him and close to the action. He informed us the he lived in Alice Street and he often drank in the Buffs Club. Tom and Stan rejoined us after Stan had won their game of darts. Judging by the odour now permeating from Scratcher, the family trait of not spending money or time on personal hygiene was being maintained. He added that he was still known as Scratcher by his mates and even his wife called him Scratcher, as she preferred that to Septimus, his birth name. On hearing this John nearly choked as he took a mouthful of his beer.

Thankfully, Scratcher had to leave us as his missus would have his tea ready and Tom could not resist a parting shot; 'So, Scratcher what you having for tea then?'

'Well, I am having beans on toast; but the kids are having a boiled egg each. It's Friday you see and the wife has been paid.'

He rose to his feet having supped his pint; 'I will no doubt see you fellas around,' and as he made his way to the door Stan shouted; 'Enjoy your beans on toast.'

He turned and waved; 'I will, I just hope she hasn't 'bont' the toast.'

His departure meant we could now start to laugh and some of us were helpless. Tom took the opportunity to put the chair that Scratcher was sitting on, back in the corner of the room.

Geordie spoke of the various odours that were in evidence; 'He stunk of piss and God knows what else, the smell was making me feel sick.'

Tom accentuated the scenario when he added; 'I bet when he goes for a shite, he whistles while he is on the pot.'

'Why is that then Tom?' asked Andy.

'It will help him to remember which end to wipe,' replied Tom.

Malla stood up and announced; 'I am off to the long cabin to syphon the python.'

'More like a cocktail sausage,' joked Stan.

The subject of romance was raised and Norman said; 'Well, my friends how goes it with the fairer sex. Have any of you entered into affaire d'amour recently?'

Geordie could not help himself; 'I would never pay for sex anyway.'

Norman was quick to correct Geordie; 'There you go, if you are not sure Geordie keep your clagger shut. I was asking if any of you cretins had met a nice young lady or had entered into a relationship. If I had asked about prostitution I would say; *fille de joie* Geordie.'

'Well, it's all Dutch to me,' joked Geordie.

Then Andy told us of his latest flirtation with the opposite sex saying; 'I was in the Cleadon Club with my uncle Sid last Thursday and I caught sight of the new barmaid serving in the lounge. I bought a round of drinks and made sure she served me, so I could chat her up. I asked her how long she had been working at the club and she said; only two days. She lives up on the Lawe Top, in Vespasian Street. She is a student at the Marine and Tech.'

'Come on then; name, looks, age, figure etc.' interrupted Geordie.

'She is a blonde aged eighteen and her name is Julia; her measurements well, I would say she is 36, 26, 32, and she has piercing blue eyes.'

'Well, have you fixed up a date then?' asked Norman.

'Surprisingly, she asked me for a date boys,' declared Andy with a wide grin on his face.

'I am not having that; did she have a white stick?' joked Malla.

'That's not a hint of jealousy creeping in is it, Malla?' added Andy.

'Look, she has seen a reasonably handsome guy, with all the charm of a bucket of shit and she is smitten. It happens all the time fellas, but wait until she is on the lash with Andy and realises that she has to pay. Then all his sweet-talking and aspirations of romance will be scuppered,' added Norman.

Andy just raised his middle finger; 'You surprise me Norman, I thought you were my mate.'

Tom decided to regale us with a joke; 'A drunk bloke appears in front of the judge. The judge says; You've been brought here for drinking. The drunk says; Right let's get fucking started.'

'Well, good pals it's that time again; we must make our way home and return to the bosom of our loved ones. Thank you for a pleasant evening gentleman and a safe journey home to one and all. Can I just add a word of warning to you Andy; Don't forget to put your boxing gloves on before you climb into bed, you will sleep much better.'

Andy joined in the hilarity; 'Norman, there is only one thing in the world worse than being talked about, and that is not being talked about.'

'Very good Andy, Oscar Wilde; from *The Picture of Dorian Gray*, I do believe.'

'Correct Norman.'

THE LETTER

It was a cold February in 1973 and our band of brothers were meeting for another conclave. This time our chosen hostelry was The County Hotel. John and I arrived after the allotted time to find Geordie and Tom at the bar ordering drinks.

'Splendid I will have a pint of Lorimers,' said John.

'I will have the same thanks,' I added.

Geordie groaned, 'That was bad timing Tom, I thought it was going to be a cheap round.'

'Well, we will stay in rounds with these two tossers I suppose. They are generally good at getting their round in Geordie,' quipped Tom.

'Charmed I'm sure,' replied John.

We found a couple of tables in the back room and set a chair aside for Keith. Within five minutes; Malla, Norman, Andy and Stan joined us.

'This is not good enough gentlemen, punctuality is of great importance,' I suggested.

Stan was not happy, 'Well, so is money and Malla and me, have been doing a half-shift up to 6 pm. So, stick that in your pipe Harry.'

'What's your excuse then Norman? asked Tom.

'Both Andy and I have enjoyed a cheeky pint in The Chichester Arms,' replied Norman.

Andy then enlightened us about an accident in Chichester Road the previous night. 'A guy was killed last night when his motorbike hit the wall on that bend before Westoe Bridges. He must have lost control; it was reported in the *Shields Gazette* tonight.'

'What was his name Andy? asked Stan.

Andy answered; 'He was from Simonside I think, a lad called Trevor Harrison.'

'Christ no, we were mates at school,' I whispered.

'He just lived around the corner from me, he loved biking. I was only talking to him on Wednesday in the paper shop,' added Stan.

We all sat and contemplated what his family must be going through, and I spoke; 'Rest in peace Trevor, you will be sadly missed my son.'

Norman offered some words of solace; 'A life lost that will never be replaced. A young man in the prime of his life gone, but I am sure never forgotten by his family and friends. It puts into context how fragile we all are and it should ensure that we all live our lives to the full. We should raise our glasses to both our friend Keith and sadly now to Trevor who has friends among us.'

We all stood, raised our glasses and said together; 'To Keith and Trevor.'

The mood was now a little sombre, but John livened up the proceedings with his latest escapade; 'I was out last Friday with Bob Ramsey and Fred Armstrong. We got a flyer from work and we were in The Scotia at 11.10. We supped about four pints and then had some grub at Carrick's café in King Street. We then had more drink in The Garrick's Head, The Criterion and The North Eastern. By 6 pm I was well-cattled and I told Bob and Fred that I must *Garn Yem*, I think I am going blind. Five minutes later, Fred was asleep and Bob was just staring into space. Time to go I thought.

Well, I staggered out of The North Eastern and bang, the fresh air hit me. I managed to reach the Lawe Top and somehow arrived on my street. However, the council had the entire pavement up, doing some pipe laying. This meant that you only had one slab of paving outside your own front door. The rest of the street was a series of ditches about five feet deep.

Yes, you can guess what happened next. I slipped and fell into one of the bastards. I was so inebriated I must have fallen asleep. The next thing I know is that I am being stretchered into a bastard ambulance. One of my neighbours had seen me fall into the ditch and dialled 999, thinking I had succumbed to a heart attack. When I got to the Ingham Infirmary, I rolled off the stretcher as they carried me into A&E. One of the ambulance crew spoke to the nurse; 'I think he is just pissed, but you better just check him out.

The doctor arrived and quickly realised what the script was; Have we had a drink then sir? Oh yes, I certainly have my good fellow and would you have that blonde nurse shower me and sent to my tent. I was quickly removed to a side room where I slept it off and left about 11 pm in a taxi.'

'I am surprised the police were not called,' added Norman.

'What for, he was only pissed and not causing any bother,' I added.

The laughter quickly enhanced the somewhat subdued atmosphere that had been evident earlier. 'You must have been thick of clarts, after falling into that ditch John,' exclaimed Tom.

'It didn't matter I only had my work togs on anyway,' he replied.

'The moral of this story should not be lost on us my dear friends' added Norman.

'So that would be what then Norman?' asked Malla.

'Well, if the council are digging up your street, then don't get hammered,' suggested Norman.

Stan then revisited our night at the dogs; 'Come on then, who lamped the barman after the disco that night? He was smarting a black eye when me and Harry spotted him as we went for our taxi.'

'That was me, he deserved it anyway,' answered John.

'Well, he certainly did, how dare he inflict pain on our distinguished team member,' Malla retorted, and then he made an announcement; 'Right then, I have some news that you may or may not want to hear, but I must tell you anyway. I received a letter from Keith's parents yesterday. It was about Keith's death in Belfast.'

'I think you mean murder, don't you,' suggested Andy.

'Yes well, you're right I guess, but it was in a sealed envelope. The envelope was addressed to the *Shieldsmen*,' and Malla produced the envelope from his jacket pocket.

'I haven't opened it, I felt it was only fair to do it when we are all together.'

'A thoughtful decision Malla,' added Norman.

'Who wants to read it then?' asked Malla.

'I think it should be Norman, don't you fellas?' I asked.

We all agreed and Norman opened the envelope; 'This is from Lt. Colonel Perkins and it is addressed to the *Friends of Corporal Keith Harper*. It is from the Ministry of Defence and some of the content of the letter has been concealed. Norman then revealed the letter to all of us, showing some of the lines and words that were blacked out. This is because the information is restricted and therefore subject to censorship.' He continued and read what he could of the letter.

> *I would like to inform you all as to the progress that has been made in relation to finding the perpetrators of Keith's death. There are extracts of this communication that have been deemed sensitive by the MOD and I apologise for this concealment. However, after recent investigations that led to the whereabouts of certain _____ I can inform you that we sought and eliminated those responsible for both Corporal Harper and Private Humble's murder. This action was taken _____ ago in the border region of ____*

where three combatants were engaged and successfully neutralised. While I realise that both Keith's parents and your good selves, may want further information as to the identity of those responsible for Keith's demise, I am at this time unable to furnish you with that sensitive knowledge. The reason being that we are still engaged in an active exercise that requires sensitive intelligence. I can assure you, that those responsible for Keith's murder will no longer be a danger to the British Army, the RUC and the general public of Northern Ireland.

As I said at Keith's funeral, it will be the people of Northern Ireland who will ultimately decide on a means of peace in the province and put an end to violence. Once the MOD are satisfied that it is deemed safe to reveal the names of the perpetrators, that information will be passed on to the media. Again, can I pass on my deepest sympathies and I do hope this letter affords you some degree of closure, while holding your dear friend Keith in the highest regard. We will remember him.

Yours's sincerely, Lt. Colonel Perkins

The mood fell into one of quiet reflection and then Tom spoke; 'Revenge is not the outcome, but it is some kind of retribution for the loss of someone close. But I don't think Keith's parents will feel any better for knowing that those who killed him have also left this mortal coil.'

'Really, I am fucking over the moon that the bastards are dead,' added Geordie.

It was now 8.30 pm and Andy was at the bar when a couple walked in. The guy was tall and well-built. The girl on his arm was something else and John whispered; 'Don't look yet but I have just seen a vision of horror, just out of a Hammer film. He is at the bar with a good-looking girl.'

Tom could not help himself; 'Christ, it would be a sad day for humanity if all men looked like that. She must have a white stick surely.'

Discreet laughter ensued as the couple got their drinks and sat at a table opposite us. Andy returned with drinks for him and Tom. He hadn't noticed the monster when he came in and as he sat down, he asked; 'Well, where are all the good-looking wenches then?'

On hearing this, the monster turned and looked in our direction. On seeing him, Andy nearly sent a cascade of beer hurtling across the table, but managed to limit the amount lost as he gagged to redeem control of the ale in his gob. The unknown visitor gave us all a look of contempt, but his girlfriend/lion tamer seemed unperturbed by the situation.

It was difficult to analyse what he actually looked like. A trained and experienced zoologist may have been able to shed some light on what sat opposite, but we were all somewhat perplexed as to what it was. He knocked the term ugly into another dimension. It was difficult to ascertain his height, due to the fact that his knuckles scraped the floor as he walked. His face resembled scrap iron sinking into quicksand. His hair sprang from many different locations including his ears, nose, chin and his top lip. It was difficult to ascertain if he had hair on his head as he was wearing a cloth cap. His companion seemed oblivious to the spectacle sitting opposite her and began to talk to him and exchanged genial comment. Norman took the opportunity to regal us with his thoughts on this apparition and went on; 'Now young men of Shields, this is what love is all about. As you all know beauty is in the eye of the beholder. Who are we to ridicule such a relationship, that young couple have cemented a powerful bond and provided they are both sterilised, a great future lies in wait!'

'I am going to the bar, who wants a beer? asked Stan.

John joined Stan at the bar and between them they provided us with further refreshment. Malla went to the toilet, closely followed by the monster's female companion. The companion then made her exit from the toilet and as she passed our table, she had a knowing smile on her face. We all looked at Tom and Malla, then Geordie asked; 'Come on then, what's the script with her?'

Tom then enlightened us; 'Well it seems that the burglar's dog over there has got more money than *Soft Mick*.

'It's that *Soft Mick* again,' queried Andy.

'Never mind bastard *Soft Mick'* get on with it Tom,' added John.

'It appears that he is the only son of the MD of The Port of Tyne Authority,' stated Tom.

'Looks like he has just been pulled out of the fucking Tyne,' joked Geordie.

'So, his old man is a doctor then,' added Andy.

We all looked in despair at Andy and Norman said; 'He is the managing director you imbecile.'

Tom continued to divulge the information he ascertained when he was talking to the girlfriend outside the toilet. 'She, told me she met him in the Cottage in Cleadon Village a month ago and she plans to marry him. She is a clerk and she works for Gateshead Council.'

'Well, it seems she is marrying the money then gentlemen, she is destined for a life of relative luxury compared to our poor selves,' added Norman.

'Just imagine waking up next to that every morning and it gets up and starts cavorting around the bedroom like a demented gorilla,' said Malla.

'What's his name? I asked.

'Charlie,' replied Tom.

'That says it all,' quipped Stan.

The conversation reverted to our night at the dogs the previous month and Andy asked; 'So Tom what happened with my cousin Karen or should I not ask?'

Tom considered the question and was a little reticent with his reply, saying; 'Well, she had a good excuse for standing me up, saying that her grandma was unwell. I am taking her to the flicks on Monday night.'

'What you going to see?' asked Malla.

'*Love Story,*' replied Tom.

This resulted in an extended bout of ridicule from those present and Stan offered some advice; 'The writing is on the wall now Tom. It's just a matter of time before she will get her claws in and before you know it, you will be skint, with five kids, no teeth, no hair and haemorrhoids.'

More laughter and John added; 'Tom, the worst part of it all, is that you will have bonded with Andy's bloodline and God only knows what the outcome of that will be.'

Andy was not too impressed and suggested that John should go and play with the traffic on Sunderland Road.

Malla suggested another night out the following Friday; 'What about starting at the Buffs Club next Friday, the Little Waster is on at 8 pm.'

'Who's that then?' asked Andy.

'Are you for real, it's Bobby Thompson you nutter. He is hilarious,' added Tom.

We all agreed, despite Andy's protestations to meet at 7 pm in the bar and have a game of darts before ascending the stairs to the concert room.

Norman stood, raised a glass; 'A toast to Harry's nipper Layla and to Andy, who has managed to maintain a relationship with the lovely Deborah. The bonus of that love affair is that Andy can get regular inspections of his genitalia.'

Andy responded; 'Very funny Norman,' as the rest of us chuckled at Norman's discourse.

LAUGHTER IS THE BEST MEDICINE

A cold day in March brought our band of brothers together in the RAOB Club in Laygate. The Buffs Club as it was more commonly known had booked the well-known comedian Bobbie Thompson. I arrived with Stan at 7 pm to find John, Malla and Norman in the bar. Stan got two bottles of Brown Ale and we joined our pals at a table.

'What's the script?' asked John.

'The plan I have in mind gentlemen, is to enjoy the humour of the Little Waster and then move onto another hostelry for further refreshment. I would suggest the Lord Clyde, which is a ten-minute walk from here.'

'Where are Andy, Tom and Geordie?' asked Stan.

'They are on their way; they are having a pint in the Eureka,' added Malla.

'How the hell do you know that, Malla?' I asked.

'Well Harry, I took a call at the bar here about five minutes ago from the Eureka. It was Andy and he told me they would be here in about twenty minutes.'

'That's strange, he would normally send a carrier pigeon,' I replied.

'The humour has already begun; this all bodes well for the evening dear friends. Can I offer you a funny story?' asked Norman

'Do you have to?' added John.

Norman smiled at John; 'Yes, I do. This is for those of you that have a particular interest in astronomy. During the night of the next equinox, head outside and face south. Bend over at an angle of 45 degrees, slightly relax your knees and lower your head so you can look back between your legs. Finally, hold a small mirror in your left hand and adjust the angle so it's parallel with your face. Congratulations, you can now see Uranus.'

'That was very good Norman, even for you,' quipped Stan.

John joined in; 'I am reading a great book on anti-gravity; I can't put it down.'

The mood was now jovial and after a few more jokes, our three missing companions arrived to a chorus of ridicule and Stan asked; 'Oh, it's nice of you to make the effort, is the atmosphere in the Eureka; not to your liking then boys?'

'No, it was Geordie he decided to do his 'bloke with a nervous tick' routine while at the bar.'

'You will get a good hiding one of these days Geordie,' added Malla.

Geordie's little bit of acting was funny, but he had to choose the right environment for it to have the best result. John suggested that he should give it another go in the Buffs as the bar was starting to fill up.

'Let me get a pint first,' said Andy.

'I suggest we wait until Geordie has to get a round in, it will have a much greater effect, giving him more time to perfect the performance.'

We all managed to sit at two tables along with Keith's empty chair. General banter about work, football and the news of the day was remarked upon and the bar was well-populated with punters lined up at the bar counter. Geordie felt the time was right for his act of entertainment to be performed and he rose from his seat and asked; 'Who is ready for another pint?' then jerked his head to the right and left.'

'Oh no, here it comes,' Norman declared.

The round consisted of four pints and Geordie made his way to the bar, he found a decent space that would enable a good vantage point for his comrades to witness. The barman asked him what he wanted. This bit of madcap humour always starts with the use of the eyes. Geordie would not make eye to eye contact with the barman, instead, he would focus his eyes on the top of the barman's head. This confused the barman; he thinks that Geordie has a sight impediment. Geordie then asks for the drinks and then closes his eyes and reopens them as if he is cross-eyed. As the barman puts the pints on the bar Geordie makes a sudden movement by lifting his left arm as if he is going to scratch his head and makes a noise of a duck quacking. The barmen then is undecided whether Geordie is extracting the urine or if it is a genuine involuntary motion. Then Geordie does it again, the barman has now laid four pints on the bar. His main concern now is that if Geordie picks up two glasses of beer, one or both may well have their contents cascading over the customers in close proximity. The barman looks over to our table and says; 'Do some of you guys want to help this guy with your drinks?'

'No, he will be fine,' said John.

The barman is now in a quandary and as he is considering his next move, Geordie goes to put his money on the table, he again lifts his left arm. This time with the money in his hand and he does a very good impression of a chicken, moving his head back and forth without sound. Geordie then places the money on the bar and goes to lift a pint, but again his left arm is raised. The punters at the bar are now keeping a safe distance. The barman has had enough now and says; 'Look son, I will get the barmaid to bring your pints to the table, alright.'

Then Geordie completes the performance with a verbal response which sounds like he is taking in air and ends with a quack and long raspberry.

In order to give the episode an air of realism, Norman says; 'Geordie, have you taken your medication today?'

Geordie nods and jerks his head to the left and smiles. The barman is not sure how to read the situation and keeps a watchful eye on Geordie.

We decide to take our beers to the concert room, in readiness for Little Bobby. He starts his first set in his oversized army uniform and regales the audience with his heroics during the war. His one liners are legendary and his presence on the stage is great. After that first set, we made the decision to depart and head for the Lord Clyde.

It was now 9 pm and the Lord Clyde had a decent crowd in. We managed to grab a table after spending around twenty minutes at the bar. The theme of comedy was sustained when Andy told a joke; 'At the last England game Alf Ramsey said to Rodney Marsh; If you don't work hard, I am going to pull you off at half-time. Marsh turned to Nobby Stiles and stated; At Man City all we get is a cup of tea and an orange.'

'I can better that one, listen up you brainless plonkers,' shouted Tom.

'Frank was out hunting when he tripped over. His gun discharged, shooting him in his genitals. Later at the hospital, his doctor said; I have some good news and some bad news. The good news is that you are going to be okay. The damage was only in your groin area and we were able to remove all of the shot. What's the bad news? asked Frank. The bad news is that the shot left a lot of small holes in your member. I'll have to refer you to my sister. Frank asked; Why, is your sister a plastic surgeon? 'No, answered the doctor, she's a flute player in the London Symphony Orchestra. She is going to teach you where to put your fingers, so you don't piss in your eyes.'

Raucous laughter resounded around the table and Norman chose the opportunity to give us one of his mind-numbing monologues and went on; 'Good soulmates one and all, what say you to this. I have been thinking about this for ages.'

'Careful Norman, we have warned you about exposing yourself in public,' joked Stan.

Norman would not be distracted and continued; 'I have an idea that will enhance our appreciation of the great outdoors. Why don't we all go camping in the Lake District? Let us follow the trails of Wainwright and get back to nature. As Robert Browning wrote:

> *Oh, to be in England now that April is there,*
> *And whoever wakes in England sees, some morning unaware,*
> *That the lowest boughs and the brushwood sheaf.*
> *Round the elm – tree bole are in tiny leaf,*
> *While the chaffinch sings on the orchard bough.*
> *In England – now!*

We all looked at one another and then Andy said; 'You know what, that is a bloody good idea, Norman.'

Now attention was focussed on Andy and Malla laughed; 'Andy, the thought of untangling you after you have mounted a sheep halfway up The Old Man of Coniston, will not enhance my understanding of the great outdoors.'

More laughter at Andy's expense, then Geordie chipped in with, 'Who is the Old Man of Coniston then?'

'It's a bloody mountain you daft sod,' I shouted.

'Look, it will be great to get away for a few days, over a weekend maybe,' added Norman.

'There are a few teething problems Norman, for example, who has a tent? Unlike Andy, the rest of us are used to sleeping under cover,' added John.

'Shite off John,' was Andy's terse reply.

'Well, I think this idea has some mileage fellas. We could muster enough tents I'm sure, and we could use the trains and buses to get around,' said Tom.

After further discussion it was left to Norman to look into the logistics of the proposed undertaking, which he would feedback to this band of miscreants the next week. The conversation drifted onto the dialect of the North East and how we converse with one another when

Tom said; 'Have you ever wondered what people who live south of Darlington make of our dialect?'

'Now that is a good point young Tom, let us all consider that for a moment,' suggested Norman.

'Oh no, here we go again Norman is off on one,' added John.

'Come on then, let's get this show on the road,' said Stan.

'*Ah daint nar wot ya tarkin aboot,*' joked Malla.

'Now there is a prime example of sandancer gibberish my friends. That is as nonsensical as you can get,' replied Norman.

'Oh no it's not, listen to this,' joked Geordie. '*Divint, tark shite, had ya gobs. Noo, ah ye arl garn doon to the big hoose and garn on the hoy. I am clammin for a pint.*'

'Very good Geordie, *my old man carls me a nyep and a hoyte sometimes,*' I suggested.

'When I am at work, blokes will often ask me; *ay yee hord oot,*' added John.

'*Hadaway, ye a arl getting too porsnal noo, daint start tarkin tripe. We nar wot it's arl aboot. Daint tark like ye are cliver, ye will get tarked aboot arl over the toon,*' quipped Stan.

'Enough, this is ridiculous one should speak correctly and in an erudite manner my dear chums. If one is to woo the ladies, one should converse in the Queens English and not this colloquial claptrap,' replied Andy.

'*Wots garn urn, a divint nar much aboot owt. But a dee nar this, ye a arl roond the bastard twist, yee lot,*' added John.

Norman added; Here the lesson ends my friends, it's bad enough to have the accent. But to embellish it in this way, will not endear ourselves to the inhabitants of foreign fields.'

'Good point Norman, since we will be all sleeping in a field in the not-too-distant future,' joked Stan.

'I am going to bring a two-bar electric fire, it will be sodden freezing at night,' added Geordie.

We all looked at Geordie in disbelief, and it was left to Tom to educate our good friend on the prospects of him tapping into the national grid, in order to generate warmth in a tent in the barren landscape of the Lake District. Once the penny had dropped Geordie stated; 'I am still bringing a hot-water bottle.'

Tom brought the conversation into the realms of eating; 'Right then, what is your favourite biscuit. Come on who is going first?'

'Well, I am partial to a garibaldi myself,' said Norman.

'He plays for Inter Milan?' joked Geordie.

'No no, the best scoits are sports biscuits. I used to get a 3oz bag on a Friday morning, from Theobalds in Henderson Road, before I went to school,' I added.

'Why do you call them scoits Harry?' asked Malla

'It is short for biscuit birdbrain,' I replied.

'No, it's not, it's spelt with a u,' said John.

'Look, in my world it's scoits, that is the way I pronounce it,' I shouted.

'I like ginger snaps,' added Stan.

'Yes, but remember dear friends, don't forget the three second rule. If you are a dunker in your tea, that is,' added Norman.

'I am fond of a chocolate finger,' said Tom.

'There is no answer to that, what you do in your spare time is private Tom,' joked Andy.

John had another theory relating to dunking; 'Chocolate biscuits are no good for dunking, you lose the taste.'

'Who the hell dunks chocolate scoits in their tea? That is disgusting,' I replied.

Tom answered; 'I do, all the time it's lush.'

'Well Tom, I am severely brought down by that admission. I thought you were a man of good moral standing. But really, you are just a disgrace to society; aren't you?' I quipped.

'Harry, you are just a tuppence halfpenny snob, you were dragged up in Simonside.'

'I will have you know that I come from rare breeding stock Tom.'

'Yes, that is true I suppose; considering your mother was a Shetland pony and your father was in the Fifth Battalion of the Coldstream Guards,' joked John.

BIBLIOGRAPHY

North East Life in the 1970s by A. Clark & S. Taylor. Summerhill Books. Newcastle. 2017.
South Shields by J.& J Carlson. The Peoples History. Seaham. 1998.
South Shields Pubs by Eileen Burnett. Amberley Publishing. Stroud. 2014.
Hamlet by William Shakespeare. Edited by George Rylands. Clarendon Press. Oxford. 1969
The Holy Bible. King James Version. Collins. London. 1958.
Best Loved Poems by Neil Philip. Little, Brown & Company. London. 2001.
The Complete Works of William Shakespeare by Peter Alexander. Collins. London. 1951.
The Oxford Concise Dictionary of Quotations. Oxford University Press. Oxford. 1997.
Poems for Speaking by Richard Church. J. M. Dent & Sons Ltd. London. 1950.
Twice Told Tales by Nathanial Hawthorne. *The Readers Digest*. London. 2000.
One Empty Chair by Haydn Watson.

QUOTATIONS AND SONG LYRICS

Various quotations are included within the narrative and are attributed to the following; Raymond Chandler, Oscar Wilde and Albert Einstein.

In addition, some of the lyrics of three songs are also recorded;
Ticket To Ride by the Beatles.
Presence of The Lord by Blind Faith (Eric Clapton).
We're Going Wrong by Cream (Jack Bruce).
Let It Be by The Beatles (John Lennon & Paul McCartney).